Study Gui

Essentials of Business Law

SECOND EDITION

Jeffrey F. Beatty
Boston University

Susan S. Samuelson
Boston University

Prepared by

Ronald L. Taylor
Metropolitan State College of Denver

WEST

Australia · Canada · Mexico · Singapore · Spain · United Kingdom · United States

Study Guide for **Essentials of Business Law, 2e**

Jeffrey F. Beatty and Susan S. Samuelson

VP/Editorial Director:
Jack W. Calhoun

Publisher and Acquisitions Editor:
Rob Dewey

Developmental Editor:
Bob Sandman

Marketing Manager:
Steve Silverstein

Senior Production Editor:
Kara ZumBahlen

Technology Project Editor:
Amy Wilson

Media Editor:
Kelly Reid

Manufacturing Coordinator:
Doug Wilke

Printer:
Globus Printing, Minster, OH

Printed in the United States of America
1 2 3 4 5 07 06 05 04

ISBN: 0-324-20637-2

For more information
contact South-Western,
5191 Natorp Boulevard,
Mason, Ohio 45040.
Or you can visit our Internet site at:
http://www.swlearning.com

Contents

CHAPTER ONE
INTRODUCTION TO LAW

CHAPTER OUTLINE

I. Three Important Ideas about Law
   A. Power
   B. Importance
   C. Fascination

II. Origins of Our Law
   A. English Roots
   B. Law in the United States

III. Sources of Contemporary Law
   A. Constitutions
      1. United States Constitution
      2. State Constitutions
   B. Statues
   C. Common Law
   D. Equity
   E. Administrative Law
   F. Other Sources of Law
      1. Treaties
      2. Executive Orders

IV. Classifications of Law
   A. Criminal and Civil Law
   B. Substantive and Procedural Law
   C. Public and Private Law

V. Jurisprudence
   A. Law and Morality
   B. Legal Positivism
   C. Natural Law
   D. Legal Realism

VI. Working with the Book's Features

WHAT YOU SHOULD KNOW

After reading this chapter you should understand:

how the law involves power, and why most people find it fascinating and important;

what the English roots of American law are;

what a precedent is;

what the sources of contemporary American law are;

the difference between common and statutory law;

the difference between criminal and civil law;

the difference between substantive and procedural law;

the difference between private and public law;

the different schools of jurisprudence; and

how to analyze a judicial decision.

REVIEW OF TERMS AND PHRASES

MATCHING EXERCISE

Select the term or phrase that best matches a definition or statement stated below. Each term or phrase is the best match for only one statement or definition.

Terms and Phrases

a. Administrative law
b. Civil law
c. Criminal law
d. Equity
e. Executive orders
f. Precedent
g. Procedural law
h. *Stare decisis*
i. Statutory law
j. Substantive law

Statements and Definitions

____ 1. Classification of law that defines the steps required to enforce legal rights and obligations.

____ 2. Body of law that is created by federal and state administrative agencies.

____ 3. Classification of law that defines legal rights and obligations.

____ 4. Principles used by a court if a party seeks an injunction or specific performance.

____ 5. Body of law that is created by Congress and state legislatures.

____ 6. Rule of law (principle) adopted by a court for the first time.

____ 7. Classification of law that prohibits certain conduct that is threatening to society.

____ 8. Principle that generally requires precedents to be followed in future, similar cases.

____ 9. Classification of law that regulates the rights and duties between parties.

____10. Directives issued by the President of the United States or state governors.

REVIEW OF CONCEPTS

TRUE-FALSE QUESTIONS

Circle **T** for true or **F** for false

T F 1. One major problem with the law is that it rarely affects the average person.

T F 2. Every society of which we have historical records had some kind of legal system.

T F 3. The five Iroquois nations created a unitary system of government in which one superior nation governed all others.

T F 4. A major benefit of the American legal system is that lawyers and other people may look the law up in a single book.

T F 5. Most states permit television coverage of real trials.

T F 6. An English jurist who was influential in developing the concept of precedent was Henry de Bracton.

T F 7. The United States Constitution provides that all powers remain with the national government.

T F 8. Civil law concerns behavior so threatening that society outlaws it altogether.

T F 9. Legal positivists believe that law is composed of those actions in which people customarily engage.

T F 10. A basic concept of natural law is that evil law is to be avoided.

MULTIPLE CHOICE QUESTIONS

1. ____ Carol stole inventory from Acme, Corp., her employer, violations of both civil and criminal law. Eventually, Carol was apprehended. Under these facts:
   a. Acme may sue Carol for money damages in criminal court.
   b. The state may prosecute Carol for theft in civil court.
   c. Acme may sue Carol for money damages in civil court, and the state may prosecute Carol for theft in criminal court.
   d. Acme may sue Carol for money damages in criminal court, and the state may prosecute Carol for theft in civil court.

2. ____ Trenton Antiques contracted to sell a painting to Janis for $500. The painting is a rare antique portrait that cannot be replaced. Subsequently, Trenton Antiques refused to perform this contract and Janis sued. In this lawsuit, the relief that Janis requested is an order of specific performance that would require Trenton Antiques to perform the contract. Under these facts:
   a. Principles of common law will determine whether Janis will be awarded the relief that she has requested.
   b. Principles of equity will determine whether Janis will be awarded the relief that she has requested.
   c. Janis will be entitled to a jury trial in this case.
   d. b and c.

3. ____ Roger and Kim owned competing grocery stores. Roger told a group of Kim's customers that she had been convicted of selling spoiled meat. Kim claimed this statement was false, and she sued Roger for $50,000 for defamation (i.e., the wrongful injury to the reputation of another). Roger raised two defenses: (a) he did not commit this wrong because what he said was true; and (b) the court did not have jurisdiction to hear this case because Kim had violated certain laws that set forth the steps she had to take in order to sue him. Under these facts:
   a. Defense (a) is based on procedural law.
   b. Defense (b) is based on procedural law.
   c. Defense (b) is based on substantive law.
   d. a and c.

4. ____ Which of the following is an example of common law?
   a. The legislature passes a statute requiring businesses with more than 10 employees to offer a maternity leave program for the employees.
   b. In resolving a legal controversy between two parties, the state supreme court adopts a rule of law that an agreement is not enforceable unless there is both a valid offer and acceptance.
   c. The President issues an executive order restricting exports to a hostile nation.
   d. The Department of Motor Vehicles changes the fee for renewing a driver's license.

5. ____ Raymond Inc. was sued by a government agency for violating federal antidiscrimination law. At its trial in a lower federal trial court, Raymond asserted that the law in question was unconstitutional. However, in a previous case involving other parties, the U.S. Supreme Court held, for the first time, that this law was constitutional. Under these facts:
   a. The prior decision of the Supreme Court is a precedent.
   b. Under the principle of *stare decisis*, the trial court in Raymond's case is generally bound to follow the Supreme Court's prior decision and to hold that the law is constitutional.
   c. Under the principle of *stare decisis*, the trial court in Raymond's case is not bound to follow the Supreme Court's prior decision and it may find that the law is unconstitutional.
   d. a and b.

6. ____ A state supreme court adopted a principle of law which holds that a skier can sue a ski area for negligence even if the skier is skiing out of bounds (constitutional rights are not involved). Under these facts:
   a. The principle of law adopted by the state supreme court is constitutional law.
   b. The principle of law adopted by the state supreme court is statutory law.
   c. The principle of law adopted by the state supreme court is administrative law.
   d. The principle of law adopted by the state supreme court is common law.

7. ____ Thomas Television Network (TTN) aired a show entitled "Do It Yourself." This program instructed the audience on how to make certain illegal drugs and where to buy the necessary ingredients. TTN was notified that it was being charged with violation of a regulation of the Federal Communications Commission, a federal agency. What type of law was TTN charged with violating?
   a. Constitutional law.
   b. Statutory law.
   c. Administrative law.
   d. Common law.

8. ____ Assume that you are Mildred de Fleury and you live in Lewes, England in the year 1345. You entered into an agreement with your neighbor Estelle to pay her a sum of money for ten pounds of butter. You intended to use the butter to make shortbread cookies, which you were going to sell at the next Lewes fair. Unfortunately, Estelle failed to live up to her end of the bargain. You would like to sue Estelle for the value of your lost profits (you can't make and sell the cookies without her butter), but the judge will not hear your case. Your other option for getting this case heard by a royal official is:

a. Take the case to the Admiralty court.
b. Take the case to the Court of Chancery.
c. Take the case to rota.
d. Take the case to the Court of Permanent Justice.

9. ____ Federalism is a system of government that involves at least two levels of sovereign power, and each level has certain specified powers that the other level or levels do not have. An early example of a federalist system of government was created by:

a. Abraham Lincoln.
b. St. Thomas Aquinas.
c. The Iroquois Nations.
d. Confucius.

10.____ Confucius believed that society would operate best if:

a. All law was written.
b. Family ties were weak.
c. The peasant classes ran society.
d. Causes of litigation were eliminated.

11.____ Which of the following statements most accurately summarizes legal realism?

a. Who enforces the law and by what process the is enforced are more important that what the written law actually states.
b. Law is what the ruler of the government says it is.
c. An unjust law is no law at all.
d. There really is no such thing as law in modern societies.

12.____ An English jurist who helped to establish the legal doctrine of precedent was:

a. Sir Thomas Moore.
b. Henry de Bracton.
c. Thomas a Becket.
d. Henry II.

13.____ In order for plaintiffs in royal English courts in the fifteenth century (1400s) to bring a case against a defendant, the plaintiff first had to:

a. Overcome the defendant in battle.
b. Present four oath helpers.
c. Request a series of grand jury hearings.
d. Obtain a writ from the central government.

14.____ The United States Constitution does which of the following?

a. Establishes local governments.
b. Prohibits the exercise of many basic rights.
c. Provides that powers not given to the national government are retained by the states.
d. Creates five main branches of government.

15.____ One afternoon over a steaming hot cup of coffee, you and several of your friends are discussing the question "what is law?" You take the position that the law is what the President of the United States and Congress say that it is, and anything that falls outside this definition is simply not law. Under these facts, you would best be described as:

a. An anarchist.
b. A legal realist.
c. A legal positivist.
d. A believer in natural law.

SHORT ESSAYS

1. Discuss the different forms of jurisprudence. What are the basic strengths and weaknesses of each system? Explain whether a particular system of jurisprudence is superior to other systems.

2. Identify the major sources of American law and discuss how these sources of law relate to one another. Identify and explain which source of the law in the United States is the most important?

CASE PROBLEM

Society generally embraces the belief that wealthy persons have a moral obligation to help those who are in need. Nonetheless, Madeline, a wealthy heiress, refuses to contribute to any charities or to otherwise help the poor.

One day a charity worker asked Madeline for a $10 donation that would be used to help find shelter for an unfortunate family, including two young babies, who were stranded on the street in cold, harsh weather. Madeline replied: "No, I won't help that family. Maybe a little more suffering will teach them a lesson." No legal action can be brought against Madeline by the state or by the needy family due to her refusal to donate the requested money. Under these facts:

1. Analyze whether Madeline violated the civil and/or criminal law.
2. Analyze whether Madeline may have acted immorally.
3. Discuss whether a person can act immorally without acting illegally.

CHAPTER TWO
BUSINESS ETHICS AND SOCIAL RESPONSIBILITY

CHAPTER OUTLINE

I. Why Bother With Ethics?

   A. Society as a Whole Benefits from Ethical Behavior

   B. People Feel Better When They Behave Ethically

   C. Unethical Behavior Can be Very Costly

II. What is Ethical Behavior?

   A. Analyzing the Ethics Checklist

      1. What are the Facts?

      2. What are the Critical Issues?

      3. Who are the Stakeholders?

      4. What are the Alternatives?

      5. What are the Ethical Implications of Each Alternative?

      6. Is More than One Alternative Right?

III. Applying the Ethics Checklist: Making Decisions

   A. Organization's Responsibility to Society

   B. Organization's Responsibility to Its Customers

   C. Organization's Responsibility to Its Employees

   D. Organization's Responsibility to Its Shareholders

   E. Organization's Responsibility Overseas

   F. Employees/ Responsibility to Their Organization

WHAT YOU SHOULD KNOW

After reading this chapter you should understand:

why it is important for business people to think about ethics;

why people feel better when they behave ethically;

why unethical behavior can cost companies lots of money;

some guidelines for making ethical decisions in actual cases;

the kinds of ethical obligations an organization may have to society;

the kinds of ethical obligations an organization may have to its customers;

the kinds of ethical obligations an organization may have to its employees;

the kinds of ethical obligations an organization may have to its shareholders;

the kinds of ethical obligations an organization may have overseas; and

the kinds of ethical obligations employees may have to their organizations.

REVIEW OF TERMS AND PHRASES

MATCHING EXERCISE

Select the term or phrase that best matches a statement or definition stated below. Each term or phrase is the best match for only one statement or definition.

Terms and Phrases

a. Categorical imperative

b. Ethics

c. Stakeholders

d. Utilitarianism

e. Utility

f. Values

Statements and Definitions

____ 1. Branch of philosophy that focuses on values relating to how people should act and the moral goodness of human motives and actions.

____ 2. Interests that one seeks to produce as a result of his or her actions.

____3. Different constituencies of a business, often holding conflicting goals for the business.

____ 4. Theory of ethics suggesting that one should act so as to produce the greatest good for the members of one's group.

____ 5. Usefulness of an activity.

____ 6. Concept that you should not do something unless you may reasonably wish that everyone will act in the same manner.

COMPLETION EXERCISE

Fill in the blanks with the words that most accurately complete each statement. Answers may or may not include terms used in the matching exercise. A term cannot be used to complete more than one statement.

1. ______________ ______________ and ______________ ______________ ______________ were two English philosophers who helped develop the theory of utilitarianism as a method for determining what is ethical to do in a given situation.

2. ______________ ______________ is the individual who developed the concept of the categorical imperative as a method for determining what is ethical to do in a given situation.

3. ______________, ______________, ______________, and ______________-______________ are four fundamental values that have been revered in most societies.

REVIEW OF CONCEPTS

TRUE-FALSE QUESTIONS

Circle **T** (true) or **F** (false)

T F 1. Ethical decision-making by U.S. companies should consider their responsibility to persons overseas who may be impacted by their operations.

T F 2. There is strong evidence to support the claim that corporations that behave ethically in the short run are more profitable than unethical corporations.

T F 3. Unethical companies never perform well financially.

T F 4. One reason why managers behave ethically is because such behavior makes the manager feel better personally.

T F 5. Some of the costs of unethical behavior may include reduced productivity of workers.

T F 6. One problem with ethical decision making is that the interests of stakeholders often conflict.

T F 7. Stakeholders are all those people who might potentially be affected by a manager's ethical decisions.

T F 8. When considering whether a certain action is ethical, managers should consider how they would feel if their actions were made known to the public.

T F 9. Ethical decision making oftentimes involves making a choice between two different actions that are both right.

T F 10. Although there is fairly general support for the proposition that employers owe employees ethical obligations, there is no support for the proposition that employees owe employers ethical obligations.

MULTIPLE CHOICE QUESTIONS

1. ____ Martin Luther King, Jr. was guilty of breaking the law in Birmingham, Alabama in 1963. Reverend King was the leader of illegal sit-ins and illegal marches. When asked about his illegal behavior King said:
   a. The laws of the United States did not apply to him or to the protesters.
   b. He was not interested in the law, only in his cause.
   c. He believed that unjust laws are not valid laws.
   d. He believed that St. Augustine was wrong, and people are compelled to follow the law.

2. ____ Two Forks Village is considering adopting a law that prohibits selling pornographic books within the city. This law is intended to protect the public morals. Ken, who sells this type of book, objects to this law, maintaining that it will impair his freedom of personal action. Under these facts:
   a. Protecting public morals is not a value that should be considered.
   b. Protecting personal rights is not a value that should be considered.
   c. If the town enacts this law, then it is preferring the value of protection of public morals over the value of protection of personal rights.
   d. If the town enacts this law, then it is preferring the value of protection of personal rights over the protection of public morals.

3. ____ If you were to study the profitability of companies that supply people with some of their vices, such as tobacco, alcohol, and gambling, you would find that:
   a. Because these companies engage in unethical behavior they are unproductive.
   b. Because these companies engage in unethical behavior they are unprofitable.
   c. Because these companies engage in unethical behavior they have been generally shunned.
   d. Just because these companies engage in behavior that some people label unethical does not mean that they are unproductive.

4. ____ A young man canceled his plans for a wedding reception after his bride-to-be died. The young man contacted the owner of the restaurant where the reception was to be held and asked to have his deposit returned. The owner refused to return the money. As a result of this action:
   a. The public found out about his behavior, refused to patronize the restaurant, and the owner was forced into bankruptcy.
   b. The owner faced no ill consequences.
   c. The owner was forced to go to jail for his unethical behavior.
   d. The owner declared that he had no moral obligation to return the money.

5. ____ A first step in deciding whether or not an action is unethical would be to determine whether:
   a. The action would make the company a lot of money.
   b. The manager would benefit financially in a personal way.
   c. The manager could easily hide the action from his or her superiors.
   d. The action was illegal or not.

6. ____ When deciding whether or not an alternative is an ethical alternative, a manager might want to consider:
   a. Fundamental values.
   b. The ease with which the manager can avoid responsibility for the action.
   c. The ease with which the manager can shift blame to coworkers.
   d. How much personal benefit in monetary terms the manager will get from the action.

7. ____ When advertisers create ads, they might want to consider:
   a. How to avoid promoting their product.
   b. How to ignore the underlying messages they convey.
   c. Always running insensitive ads.
   d. Attempting, in a general way, to avoid exploitative or demeaning ads.

8. ____ The textbook discusses a case about Sheldon Baskin and his partners who owned an apartment house that was primarily rented to poor and elderly tenants who paid a low, governmentally-subsidized rent. Which of the following statements is most correct regarding Sheldon Baskin's duties when considering what to do with the apartment house?
   a. Sheldon Baskin owed no legal or moral duty to consider his partners' welfare.
   b. Sheldon Baskin owed both a legal and moral duty to consider his partners' welfare.
   c. Sheldon Baskin owed a moral duty to consider the tenants' welfare.
   d. b and c.

9. ____ In the case of Enron, one of the important areas of ethical concern was:
   a. Whether Enron should provide a pension plan for its rank-and-file employees.
   b. Whether Enron should provide a pension plan for its executive employees.
   c. The differences between the pension plans provided to its rank-and-file employees and the pension plan provided to its executive employees.
   d. a and b.

10. ____ One area of ethical concern for a corporation in its dealings with shareholders is:
   a. The salary levels of corporate CEOs.
   b. The high level of corporate care for elderly citizens.
   c. The excellent corporate image of boards of directors.
   d. The loyalty of private companies.

11. ____ In most states, adultery is neither a civil wrong nor a crime. However, society views adultery as being morally wrong. If Gina engages in an adulterous relationship, then Gina is acting:
   a. Legally.
   b. Illegally.
   c. Immorally.
   d. a and c.

SHORT ESSAYS

1. There may be a number of good reasons for a company to promote ethical behavior. Discuss the reasons why a company might want to promote ethical behavior among all levels of employees. What are some of the benefits of such ethical behavior?

2. One of the leading health problems in the United States is obesity. Are companies that produce ice cream and other high-fat content food products under an ethical obligation not to produce these products? Are they under any ethical obligations towards their customers? If yes, explain what ethical obligations these companies might owe to their customers.

CASE PROBLEMS

Answer the following case problems, explaining your answers.

1. Gordon, president of Ace Cigarettes, believes that all people have the right to freedom of choice and action. Thus, he directs his marketing department to actively pursue sales to younger individuals, including minors. Society, on the other hand, has determined that it is both morally and legally wrong to sell cigarettes to minors.
   a. What legal obligations may Gordon have in this case.
   b. Evaluate whether Gordon acted morally in this case.

2. Margaret works for a law firm in New Jersey that specializes in environmental law. She discovers that a company, which the firm represents, has engaged in some illegal dumping of hazardous materials in another state.
   a. What legal obligations may Margaret have in this case.
   b. What ethical obligations may Margaret have in this situation?

3. Wally's Shoe Warehouse has had trouble collecting accounts receivables from certain customers. Wally tells his general manager to "do whatever is necessary to get paid." The general manager responds by hiring a collection agency that has a reputation for making threats and using physical force if necessary to convince customers to pay their debts.
   Evaluate the morality of the general manager's conduct.

4. Pal's Publishing is committed to taking care of its employees. Therefore, the company's general manager decides to make all of its employees undergo mandatory drug testing at least once a year. He undertook this action because drug use is illegal and a crime.
   Evaluate the morality of the general manager's conduct.

CHAPTER THREE
DISPUTE RESOLUTION

CHAPTER OUTLINE

I. Three Fundamental Areas of Law
   A. Dispute Prevention
   B. Litigation versus Alternative Dispute Resolution

II. Alternative Dispute Resolution
   A. Negotiation
   B. Mediation
   C. Arbitration
   D. Mandatory Arbitration
   E. Other Forms of ADR

III. Court Systems
   A. State Courts
      1. Trial Courts
         a. Trial Courts of Limited Jurisdiction
         b. Trial Courts of General Jurisdiction
      2. Appellate Courts
         a. Court of Appeals
         b. State Supreme Court
   B. Federal Courts
      1. Federal Question Cases
      2. Diversity Cases
      3. Trial Courts
         a. United States District Court
         b. Other Trial Courts
         c. Judges
      4. Appellate Courts
         a. United States Courts of Appeals
         b. United States Supreme Court

IV. Litigation
   A. Pleadings
      1. Complaint
      2. Service
      3. Answer
      4. Counter-Claim
      5. Class Actions
      6. Judgment on the Pleadings

B. Discovery
   1. Interrogatories
   2. Depositions
   3. Production of Documents/Things
   4. Physical and Mental Examination
   5. Requests for Admission
   6. Crucial Clue
   7. Other Discovery
   8. Plaintiff's Discovery
C. Summary Judgment
D. Final Preparation

V. Trial
   A. Adversary System
   B. Right to Jury Trial
   C. Voir Dire
   D. Opening Statements
   E. Burden of Proof
   F. Plaintiff's Case
   G. Rules of Evidence
   H. Motion for Directed Verdict
   I. Defendant's Case
   J. Closing Argument
   K. Jury Instructions
   L. Verdict
   M. Motions after the Verdict

VI. Appeals

WHAT YOU SHOULD KNOW

After reading this chapter you should understand:

what ADR and litigation are and how they differ;

the structure of the state and federal court systems;

how a court can exercise power over parties to a lawsuit;

how the federal and state court systems are structured;

the stages of a lawsuit; and

what happens when a case is appealed.

REVIEW OF TERMS AND PHRASES

MATCHING EXERCISE

Select the term or concept that best matches a definition or statement set forth below. Each term or concept is the best match for only one definition or statement.

Terms and Concepts

a. Alternative dispute resolution
b. Arbitration
c. Award
d. Diversity case
e. Federal question case
f. Jurisdiction
g. Litigation
h. Mediation
i. Mini-trial
j. Summary jury trial

Definitions and Statements

____ 1. Type of ADR whereby a third person renders a legally-binding decision regarding a dispute between two parties.
____ 2. Type of ADR whereby a third person tries to help parties reach a settlement of a dispute by meeting with the parties to help them resolve their dispute on mutually-agreed terms. The third person does not render a legally-binding decision.
____ 3. Federal case the jurisdiction for which is the fact that it involves residents of different states.
____ 4. Type of ADR initiated and supervised by a court that involves the parties' lawyers presenting to a mock jury a brief synopsis of what the witnesses at trial would say.
____ 5. Federal case's jurisdiction is based on the fact that the lawsuit involves the United States Constitution, a federal statute, or a federal treaty.
____ 6. Name for out-of-court procedures that help parties settle legal disputes without going to court.
____ 7. Decision of an arbitrator.
____ 8. Term that refers to lawsuits, the process of filing claims in court, and going to trial.
____ 9. Type of ADR that involves a staged trial before a panel of three "judges." This type of ADR may be particularly useful in commercial disputes.
____ 10. Term that refers to the power of any court to hear and decide a case.

COMPLETION EXERCISE

Fill in the blanks with the words that most accurately complete each statement. Answers may or may not include terms used in the matching exercise. A term cannot be used to complete more than one statement.

1. In a civil lawsuit, the plaintiff's burden of proof is to prove his or her case by a ________________ _____ _____ ________________.

2. In a criminal case, the prosecution's burden of proof is to prove its case ________________ _____ ________________ ________________.

3. A ________________ is a type of discovery procedure that allows a party to take the oral testimony of a witness outside of court.

4. A ________________ ___________ is a ruling by the court that the plaintiff has completely failed to prove his or her case and that the defendant is entitled to win as a matter of law.

REVIEW OF CONCEPTS

TRUE-FALSE QUESTIONS

Circle **T** (true) or **F** (false)

T F 1. If you suffer a legal harm you must file a lawsuit in order to resolve the controversy.

T F 2. Alternative dispute resolution is the process that involves filing a complaint with a court and ultimately going to trial.

T F 3. The major benefits of arbitration include quicker resolution of disputes and reduced costs.

T F 4. If a contract contains a mandatory arbitration clause, the contracting parties must arbitrate claims relating to the contract instead of filing a lawsuit based on such claims.

T F 5. A trial court focuses on determining the facts in the case pending before it and applying the law to those facts in order to resolve the legal controversy.

T F 6. The verdict is the jury's determination of who should win a lawsuit.

T F 7. In order for a federal court to hear a case based on the fact that it involves citizens of two different states, the case must involve at least $100,000.

T F 8. The first step in the trial process is the plaintiff's filing of a complaint with a court.

T F 9. Only the defendant can make a motion for summary judgment.

T F 10. The documents that commence a lawsuit are collectively called pleadings.

MULTIPLE CHOICE QUESTIONS

1. ____ Some courts, such as probate courts and small claims courts, may hear only cases involving certain kinds of legal harms. These courts are known as:
   a. Courts of general jurisdiction.
   b. Courts of limited jurisdiction.
   c. Courts of de novo jurisdiction.
   d. Appellate courts.

2. ____ Todd has a dispute with Carla and he wants to use a type of ADR that will produce a legally binding decision. Which of the following would meet Todd's needs?
   a. Arbitration
   b. Mediation.
   c. Mini-trial.
   d. a and c.

3. ____ James and Ellen have a dispute involving a contract. James contractually agreed to buy Ellen's car for $5,000. Ellen delivered the car to James but he refuses to pay. Ellen suggests that she and James sit down and that they attempt to resolve their dispute. Ellen is suggesting that she and James:
   a. Arbitrate their dispute.
   b. Conduct an informal mini-trial.
   c. Negotiate their dispute.
   d. Take part in a court-annexed mediation.

4. ____ Kevin intends to sue his employer in federal court for violation of federal antidiscrimination laws. Under these facts, the federal trial court that will first hear and decide this case is the:

a. District court.
b. Court of appeals.
c. Supreme Court of the United States.
d. Tax Court.

5.____ Tina plans to file a civil lawsuit against Julia based on the fact that Julia negligently applied a harmful chemical to Tina's hair, which caused her hair to fall out. Under these facts:

a. Tina should start her lawsuit by filing a complaint with the court.
b. Tina should start her lawsuit by filing a summary judgment with the court.
c. Tina should start her lawsuit by filing an answer with the court.
d. Tina should start her lawsuit by filing a counter-claim with the court.

6.____ Joanne worked for the Metropolis city government. One day at work a co-worker approached her and asked whom she planned to vote for as mayor in the next election. Joanne told her colleague that she didn't think much of either candidate, and she didn't plan on voting for either one. The next day Joanne's boss fired her because he felt that Joanne should not have expressed any negative views about elected officials.

Joanne plans to file a lawsuit against the city based on its violation of her federal constitutional freedom of speech. If Joanne files her lawsuit in federal district court:

a. The court may hear her case based on federal-question jurisdiction.
b. The court may hear her case based on diversity jurisdiction.
c. The court cannot hear her case because it does not have jurisdiction of this matter.
d. a and b.

7.____ Phyllis and Daryl were involved in an automobile accident. Phyllis properly commenced a lawsuit against Daryl. Daryl does not believe that he is liable to Phyllis. Also, Daryl believes that Phyllis is liable to him due to this accident. In this case, Daryl should:

a. File an answer denying the incorrect allegations stated in Phyllis' complaint.
b. File a counter-claim asserting his claim against Phyllis and requesting appropriate relief.
c. Do nothing.
d. a and b.

8.____ Bob filed a civil lawsuit against Acme Corp. Bob is suing Acme for physical injuries that he suffered due to Acme's negligence. All pleadings have been filed. Select the correct answer regarding Acme's right to discover information from Bob.

a. Acme cannot discover any information from Bob.
b. Acme can request Bob to submit to a physical examination by a doctor.
c. Acme can take Bob's deposition regarding the accident.
d. b and c.

9.____ Fernando sued Larry claiming that Larry recklessly drove his car into Fernando's truck, which was parked on the street. Judgment was rendered by the trial court against Fernando. Fernando then filed an appeal claiming that the trial court made a number of errors during the trial. In general, what type of error will the appellate review?

a. Errors of law.
b. Errors of fact.
c. Errors of both law and fact.
d. The appellate court will not hear the appeal since it is only a civil lawsuit.

10. ____ Kim sued Tyler for breach of contract and the trial court entered judgment against Kim. Kim appealed her case, and the appellate court determined that Kim should have prevailed. The appellate court issued its opinion stating that Kim and not Tyler won the lawsuit. Under these facts, the appellate court has:

a. Remanded the trial court's decision.
b. Affirmed the trial court's decision.
c. Reversed the trial court's decision.
d. Modified the trial court's decision.

11. ____ Rosa sued T&S Co. for breach of contract. Based on substantial factual evidence, the jury returned a verdict for $5,000 in favor of Rosa, and the judge entered judgment in favor of Rosa for this amount. If T&S Co. appeals this judgment to the court of appeals, the court of appeals:

a. May set aside or modify the judgment if the lower court committed serious errors of law.
b. Will have the witnesses testify again.
c. Will conduct a new trial.
d. b and c.

SHORT ESSAYS

1. Discuss the types of alternative dispute resolution. Discuss the strengths and weaknesses of alternative dispute resolution compared to the litigation process.

2. Identify and describe three discovery procedures.

CASE PROBLEM

Answer the following case problem, explaining your answer.

Carson Trucking bought a forklift from Dependable Equipment Sales. The forklift's engine went out one week later. Carson demanded its money back, but Dependable refused. The sales contract for the forklift states, "All disputes arising out of this agreement shall be submitted to binding arbitration."

1. Must the parties arbitrate this dispute?
2. If the dispute is arbitrated, is the arbitrator's award legally binding?
3. Discuss Carson's right to join other parties as plaintiffs in a class action lawsuit against Dependable and its right to a jury trial in this matter.

CHAPTER FOUR
COMMON LAW, STATUTORY LAW, AND ADMINISTRATIVE LAW

CHAPTER OUTLINE

I. Common Law
   - A. Stare Decisis
   - B. Bystander Cases

II. Statutory Law
   - A. Bills
     1. Committee Work
   - B. Discrimination: Congress and the Courts
     1. Debate
     2. Conference Committee
     3. Statutory Interpretation
        a. Changing Times
     4. Voter's Role
     5. Congressional Override
     6. The Other Player: Money

III. Administrative Law
   - A. Background
     1. Classification of Agencies
        a. Executive - Independent
        b. Enabling Legislation
        c. The Administrative Procedure Act
     2. Power of Agencies
        a. Rulemaking
        b. Investigation
        c. Adjudication

IV. Limits on Agency Power
   - A. Statutory Control
   - B. Political Control
   - C. Judicial Review
   - D. Informational Control and the Public
     1. Freedom of Information Act
     2. Privacy Act

WHAT YOU SHOULD KNOW

After reading this chapter you should understand:

what is meant by the "common law;"

how the common law rule of bystander liability has changed;

how statutes are created;

how courts interpret statutes;

how administrative agencies are created and how they operate; and

how administrative agencies are controlled.

REVIEW OF TERMS AND PHRASES

MATCHING EXERCISE

Select the term or phrase that best matches a statement or definition below. Each term or phrase is the best match for only one statement or definition.

Terms and Phrases

a. Administrative agency
b. Administrative Procedure Act (APA)
c. Congressional override
d. Executive agencies
e. Freedom of Information Act
f. Independent agencies
g. Plain meaning rule
h. Subpoena

Statements and Definitions

____ 1. Vote by both houses of Congress to enact legislation despite a presidential veto.

____ 2. Federal law that generally permits public inspection of federal agency records.

____ 3. Governmental body that may be created by the legislative or executive branch to implement legislation and to regulate a particular segment of the economy or society.

____ 4. Statutory interpretation rule that interprets ordinary words according to their everyday meaning.

____ 5. Court order for a person to appear at a stated time and'place to give evidence.

____ 6. Administrative agencies that are part of the executive branch.

____ 7. Administrative agencies that are not part of the executive branch.

____ 8. Federal law that establishes procedures for federal administrative agencies.

COMPLETION EXERCISE

Fill in the blanks with the words that most accurately complete each statement. Answers may or may not include terms used in the matching exercise. A term cannot be used to complete more than one statement.

1. Congress creates an administrative agency by passing ____________ ______________.

2. Administrative hearings of certain agencies may be conducted by independent hearing officers called ______________ ______________ ______________.

3. Proposed legislation is called a ______________.

4. Major administrative agencies may ______________ new rules, i.e. they may create new rules.

5. The common law is ______________-______________ law.

6. A ______________ is a rule of law adopted for the first time by an appellate court.

7. ______________ ______________ are an agency's interpretation of existing laws.

8. ______________ ______________ are new laws created by an administrative agency.

REVIEW OF CONCEPTS

TRUE-FALSE QUESTIONS

Circle **T** for (true) or **F** for (false)

T F 1. The common law is comprised of laws that are written in the United States Code.

T F 2. In Latin, stare decisis means "let the superior party accept responsibility."

T F 3. Under old common law rules, a bystander did not have a duty to help an injured party unless the bystander created the danger.

T F 4. The Fifth Amendment protection against self-incrimination does not apply in administrative hearings.

T F 5. The majority of the work in Congress takes place not on the floor of each house, but rather in committee meetings.

T F 6. Courts sometimes interpret statutes by examining the legislative history to determine the legislature's intent in enacting such statutes.

T F 7. Only when the legislative intent of a statute is clear will courts interpreting the statute evaluate public policy concerns.

T F 8. Perhaps the most noteworthy "other player" that affects the federal legislative process is the impact that grass root campaigns have on Congress.

T F 9. The executive branch cannot create agencies.

T F 10. An agency that is engaging in formal rulemaking must hold a public hearing.

MULTIPLE CHOICE QUESTIONS

1. ____ Suppose you are standing by the edge of Lake Wanateega. You and some friends have just finished a delicious picnic and are admiring the view across the lake. Suddenly, you see a small sailboat overturn. The passengers cling desperately to the edge of the overturned boat, yelling for help. You and your friends look on in horror, but no one swims out to help the people. Both passengers on the sailboat drown.

   If the families of the deceased passengers sue you when they find out that you didn't attempt to rescue the passengers, the most likely outcome of this case would be:

   a. You would be held not liable for the passengers' deaths based on bystander cases.
   b. You would be held not liable responsible for the passengers' deaths based on the informational control rule.
   c. You would be held not responsible for the passengers' deaths based on the hearsay rule.
   d. You would be held responsible for the deaths based on the Tarasoff case.

2. ____ Assume that Congress is considering adopting new regulations for leveraged buy-outs and mergers of American companies. Also assume that Congress is debating whether it can create a new federal administrative agency to administer these laws and what powers this agency may exercise. Under these facts:

   a. Congress cannot create an agency; only the President can create agencies.
   b. Congress can create an agency, but it can only authorize the agency to enforce federal statutes.
   c. Congress cannot authorize the agency to exercise legislative or judicial powers.
   d. Congress can create an agency, and Congress can generally authorize the agency to exercise legislative, executive, and judicial powers.

3. ____ Assume that North Dakota is considering the formation of a bureau to oversee the rental of homes and apartments. The proposed agency would have executive, legislative, and judicial functions carried out by appointed officials. Under these facts:

   a. North Dakota cannot create an agency; only the federal government can create agencies.
   b. A state can create an agency and appoint officials to carry out legislative, executive, and judicial functions.
   c. North Dakota can create an agency but the agency's officials must be elected, not appointed.
   d. North Dakota can create an agency. However, the agency cannot combine executive, legislative, and judicial functions because the agency could not be impartial.

4. ____ Suppose the Federal Trade Commission (FTC) conducted an investigation and public hearing regarding the safety of razors made by various manufacturers. Cutting Edge, a razor manufacturer, was investigated and it filed a request under the Freedom of Information Act (FOIA) to inspect certain records relating to this matter. Pursuant to its FOIA request:

   a. Cutting Edge is generally entitled to inspect FTC records of the public hearing.
   b. Cutting Edge may require other razor manufacturers to disclose their trade secrets regarding the design of their razors.
   c. Cutting Edge is generally entitled to compel other razor manufacturers to allow Cutting Edge to inspect their financial records relating to the manufacturing cost of their razors.
   d. a and b.

5.____ Assume that you are the director of the EPA. You propose that the EPA pass a new rule that limits the number of coyote that people may kill because you feel that coyote should be protected. The rule that you are proposing is best described as:

a. An interpretive rule.
b. A judicial rule.
c. An executive rule.
d. A legislative rule.

6.____ Suppose an EPA inspector notices a suspicious pool of oil on your property and the inspector decides that it should be investigated. If the EPA wants to check out this condition on your land, it may:

a. Forcibly remove you from your property.
b. Order you to remove the pool of oil before determining what it is.
c. Conduct a search of your land.
d. All of the above.

7.____ Jones Co. was accused of violating certain worker protection laws. An administrative agency having jurisdiction of this matter conducted a hearing, followed proper procedures, and the administrative law judge entered a decision against Jones Co. Under these facts:

a. Jones Co. may appeal this decision directly to an appellate court.
b. Jones Co. may appeal this decision within the administrative agency.
c. Jones Co. can appeal this decision to the legislature.
d. Jones has no right to appeal this decision.

8.____ If you wanted to determine what the common law of Ohio was, you would:

a. Consult the Ohio Civil Code.
b. Consult the Restatement of Common Law.
c. Consult the rules of each Ohio agency.
d. Consult the appellate cases issued by Ohio judges.

9.____ Important goals of the common law are:

a. Inscrutability and firmness.
b. Predictability and flexibility.
c. Resolving broad social problems through legislation.
d. Resolving discrete, technical problems through rulemaking.

10.____ In order for a piece of legislation to become a statute it must pass through a series of steps. For example, the legislation has been voted upon and received the approval of both houses of Congress, it will typically:

a. Go the Supreme Court for Constitutional approval.
b. Go to a House-Senate Conference Committee for further consideration.
c. Go to all affected federal administrative agencies.
d. Go to all affected states for state approval.

11.____ The law that generally forbids federal agencies from secretly giving information about a person to other agencies or organizations without the individual's written consent is the:

a. Freedom of Information Act.
b. Administrative Procedure Act.
c. Privacy Act.
d. U.S. Constitution.

SHORT ESSAYS

1. Over the past sixty years a substantial amount of the law in the United States has come in the form of statutes. Briefly explain the process by which statutes are enacted.

2. Federal agencies control a vast number of activities in the United States. However, employees of federal agencies are not elected officials and, therefore, they are not directly accountable to the voters of the United States. Thus, if the head of the Federal Drug Administration does something that most Americans disagree with, voters cannot vote him or her out of office.

   Despite the lack of direct voter control over the activities of administrative agencies, there are other controls over the conduct of federal administrative agencies. In what way can the general public indirectly control the activities of federal administrative agencies? Discuss other ways by which federal agencies are controlled, explaining the strengths and weaknesses of each form of control.

CASE PROBLEMS

Answer the following problems, briefly explaining your answers.

1. The Federal Aviation Administration (FAA) is given broad authority by Congress to regulate all matters necessary to protect the safety of interstate air transportation. Assume that the FAA proposes to adopt a new rule that regulates the procedures for emergency landings by commercial airlines. Under these facts:
   a. Does the FAA have the power to enact this regulation?
   b. Would the FAA have the power to investigate suspected violations of this rule?

2. Medco manufactures and sells a certain type of vitamin. A number of individuals and state health agencies allege that the vitamin violates regulations of the Food and Drug Administration (FDA), a federal agency. The FDA is given broad power to enforce its regulations. Under these facts:
   a. Can the FDA conduct a hearing to determine whether Medco has violated its regulations?
   b. Is Medco entitled to have a jury determine the case?

CHAPTER FIVE
CONSTITUTIONAL LAW

CHAPTER OUTLINE

I. Government Power
   - A. One in a Million

II. Overview
   - A. Separation of Powers
   - B. Federalism
   - C. Individual Rights

III. Powers Granted
   - A. Congressional Power
     1. Interstate Commerce
     2. Substantial Effect Rule
     3. State Legislative Power
     4. The Supremacy Clause
   - B. Executive Power
     1. Appointment
     2. Legislation
     3. Foreign Policy
   - C. Judicial Power
     1. Adjudicating Cases
     2. Judicial Review

IV. Protected Rights
   - A. Incorporation
   - B. First Amendment: Free Speech
   - C. Fifth Amendment: Due Process and The Takings Clause
   - D. Fourteenth Amendment: Equal Protection Clause
   - E. Individual Rights and State Action

WHAT YOU SHOULD KNOW

After reading this chapter you should understand:

how the separation of political power in the United States works;

how the Commerce Clause operates;

what the Supremacy Clause requires;

what guarantees are provided by the First Amendment;

what guarantees are provided by the Fifth Amendment; and,

what the Equal Protection Clause involves and how courts monitor government action involving equal protection.

REVIEW OF TERMS AND PHRASES

MATCHING

Select the term or phrase that best matches a statement or definition stated below. Each term or phrase is the best match for only one statement or definition.

Terms and Phrases

a. Commerce Clause
b. Commercial speech
c. Constitution
d. Due Process Clause
e. Equal Protection Clause
f. Incorporation
g. Judicial activism
h. Judicial restraint
i. Judicial review
j. Preemption

Statements and Definitions

____ 1. Process that extends most individual protections to all levels of government.

____ 2. Written document that generally sets forth the structure and powers of a government.

____ 3. Communications that primarily communicate a business-related message.

____ 4. Constitutional provision that guarantees all persons and classes the same protection of the law.

____ 5. Doctrine that grants the federal courts the power to declare other laws or governmental actions unconstitutional.

____ 6. Provision of the Constitution that authorizes the federal government to regulate many business activities.

____ 7. Judicial approach that encourages courts to be adopt rules of law relating to important issues.

____ 8. Doctrine that allows Congress to exercise the exclusive power to regulate an activity.

____ 9. Judicial approach that encourages courts to leave lawmaking to the legislature and to refrain from declaring other laws unconstitutional if possible.

____10. Constitutional provision that generally prohibits unreasonable government actions.

REVIEW OF CONCEPTS

TRUE-FALSE QUESTIONS

Circle **T** for true or **F** for false.

T F 1. The substantial effect rule holds that Congress can regulate any activity that has a substantial effect on interstate commerce.

T F 2. One way to view a constitution is to consider it as a series of compromises about political power.

T F 3. The executive branch is given exclusive power to control international commerce, including exports.

T F 4. The Supremacy Clause holds that state law controls when state and federal law conflict.

T F 5. Although the Supreme Court was created by the Constitution, Congress creates the lower federal courts.

T F 6. Speech related to religion is protected by the First Amendment, however, political speech is not protected by this Amendment.

T F 7. Obscenity is never protected by the First Amendment of the United States Constitution.

T F 8. In general, the Due Process Clause of the Fifth Amendment is concerned with ensuring that citizens receive fair treatment by the government.

T F 9. The Takings Clause of the Fifth Amendment requires that the government pay just compensation to a private person when the government takes that person's property for a public use.

T F 10. Courts that review laws or regulations involving economic and social relations will apply a strict scrutiny test to determine whether or not the laws are constitutional.

MULTIPLE CHOICE QUESTIONS

1.____ Assume Congress enacted a law prohibiting open-pit uranium mines. State X then passed a law allowing mining companies to operate open-pit uranium mines within the state. Under these facts:

a. The state law is unconstitutional because it violates federal supremacy.
b. The state law is unconstitutional because it seeks to regulate interstate commerce.
c. The state law is constitutional because the state has the police power to regulate this activity.
d. The state law is constitutional because the federal government cannot regulate intrastate commerce.

2. ____ Wood Inc. manufactures and sells furniture in interstate commerce. Wood's manufacturing plant is located in Chicago, Illinois. Under these facts:

a. The federal government has the power to regulate Wood's business.
b. Subject to certain limits, Illinois has the power to regulate Wood's business conducted in Illinois.
c. Illinois does not have the power to regulate any aspect of Wood's business; states do not have the power to regulate any matters that the federal government regulates.
d. a and b.

3. ____ Federal law generally requires that private employers pay their employees time and a half for hours worked in excess of 40 hours per week. Assume that a state law directly conflicts with this federal law by requiring payment of time and a half for only those hours worked in excess of 50 hours per week. Under these facts:

a. Federal law controls.
b. State law controls.
c. Neither federal nor state law controls; conflicting federal and state laws cancel each other.
d. Neither federal nor state law controls; government cannot regulate private businesses.

4. ____ One of the major problems with the Articles of Confederation was that:

a. It created an overly elaborate federal court system.
b. It allowed the Secretary of State to automatically override Presidential vetoes.
c. It gave the central government excessive powers to raise money.
d. It gave the central government little ability to regulate commerce.

5. ____ Roscoe owns three restaurants in one southern state. The restaurants primarily cater to local customers, but occasionally travelers from other states stop in to have a meal. Roscoe refuses to pay the minimum wage required by federal law, arguing that he is not engaged in interstate commerce and, therefore, he is exempt from federal law. Is Roscoe engaged in interstate commerce?

a. No. Roscoe does not sell goods across state lines.
b. No. Roscoe does not have businesses in more than one state.
c. No. Roscoe's business does not substantially affect interstate commerce.
d. Yes. Roscoe's business activities fall within the broad meaning given to "interstate commerce."

6. ____ One of the primary cash crops grown in State X are apples. In order to protect its in-state apple producers, the legislature of State X enacted a law forbidding the sale of any apples grown outside the state. Without this law, many smaller in-state apple producers may be driven out of business. Under these facts:

a. This law is constitutional. State X is properly exercising its police power.
b. This law is unconstitutional. State X cannot regulate any aspect of interstate commerce.
c. This law is unconstitutional. State X is discriminating against interstate commerce.
d. b and c.

7.____ Which of the following actions may violate the U.S. Constitution's guarantee of due process?

a. Amy is fired by her private employer without being given a hearing prior to her termination.
b. The EPA (a federal agency) imposed a fine on Dill Corp. for violating federal law. Dill Corp. was not given a hearing to determine whether it actually violated the law.
c. Congress adopted a law. Elroy Co., which is subject to this law, asserts that the law violates due process because it objects to this law.
d. All of the above.

8.____ State X adopted a law that forbids the sale of products in plastic containers, but it does not forbid the sale of products in glass containers. This law and the distinction it makes between plastic and glass containers is rationally and reasonably related to protecting the environment because plastic containers pose a greater danger to the environment than glass containers. Assume that the class of firms that sell products in plastic containers asserts that this law violates equal protection. Does it?

a. No, because equal protection only prohibits laws that discriminate on the basis of race or religion.
b. No, because equal protection does not prohibit laws that distinguish between certain classes of businesses if the classification is reasonable and has a rational basis.
c. No, because equal protection does not apply to laws adopted by state governments.
d. Yes, because equal protection prohibits the government from adopting any law that may treat any class of persons or businesses differently from other classes.

9.____ Some people have suggested that the federal government needs to more closely regulate the Internet. If the federal government decided to do this, then:

a. The executive branch would adopt and carry out needed laws, and the judicial branch would enforce the laws against violators.
b. The legislative branch would adopt and carry out needed laws, and the judicial branch would enforce the laws against violators.
c. The legislative branch would adopt needed laws, the executive branch would carry out the laws, and the judicial branch would enforce the laws against violators.
d. The judicial branch would adopt, carry out, and enforce needed laws.

10.____During the late 1780s, a series of debates took place about the political power the national government should have. Those people who thought that the federal government should be kept fairly weak and that states should retain maximum authority were known as:

a. Confrontationalists.
b. Federalists.
c. Anti-federalists.
d. Anti-establishmentarians.

11.____ The portion of the United States Constitution that sets forth the basic liberties of individual citizens of the United States is known as:

a. The Commerce Clause.
b. The Supremacy Clause.
c. The Establishment Clause.
d. The Bill of Rights.

12.____ Among the powers granted to Congress in the Commerce Clause is:

a. The power to regulate international commerce.
b. The power to prevent eminent domain actions.
c. The power to raise an army.
d. The power to mint money.

13.____ The federal government relies on a division, or separation, of powers to keep each branch of government from gaining excessive powers over the others. One important way that the judiciary helps to maintain the balance of power in our political system is by:

a. Passing the federal budget.
b. Negotiating treaties with foreign countries.
c. Reviewing the constitutionality of government actions or statutes.
d. Creating federal agencies as needed.

SHORT ESSAY

As interpreted, the U.S. Constitution allows the government to treat members of groups differently depending on the nature of the classification that is used to distinguish between various groups and the government's justification for the dissimilar treatment. Discuss briefly the basic types of classifications that the government uses to distinguish between groups and the justification that is required to treat groups differently based on each of these classifications.

CASE PROBLEM

Answer the following problem, briefly explaining your answer.

Amex Corp.'s manufacturing plant is located in Missouri. Amex Corp. sells its goods in several states, and it conducts a significant portion of its business in Colorado. Under these facts:

1. Is Amex Corp. engaging in interstate commerce?
2. Does the federal government have the right to regulate Amex Corp.'s business?
3. In general, does Colorado have the constitutional power to regulate business conducted by Amex Corp. in Colorado?
4. What restrictions will apply if Colorado regulates Amex Corp.'s business activities?

CHAPTER SIX
TORTS

CHAPTER OUTLINE

I. Intentional Torts
   - A. Defamation
   - B. False Imprisonment
   - C. Intentional Infliction of Emotional Distress
   - D. Additional Intentional Torts

II. Damages
   - A. Compensatory Damages
   - B. Punitive Damages

III. Business Torts
   - A. Tortious Interference with Business Relations
   - B. Privacy and Publicity

IV. Negligence
   - A. Duty of Due Care
   - B. Breach of Duty
   - C. Factual Cause and Foreseeable Harm
   - D. Injury
   - E. Damages

V. Strict Liability
   - A. Ultrahazardous Activity

WHAT YOU SHOULD KNOW

After reading this chapter you should understand:

what a plaintiff must prove to succeed on a claim of defamation;

what the tort of false imprisonment involves;

the elements that must be proven in order to establish the tort of intentional infliction of emotional distress;

the difference between assault and battery;

the types of damages a plaintiff may seek in a tort case;

the kinds of business torts that a defendant may commit;

what the elements of negligence are;

what it means to have a duty of due care;

how a person can breach a duty of care;

what is meant by the "factual cause" of harm;

what is meant by the "foreseeable cause" of harm;

the difference between contributory and comparative negligence; and

what kinds of torts are considered strict liability torts.

REVIEW OF TERMS AND PHRASES

MATCHING EXERCISE

Select the term or phrase that best matches a statement or definition stated below. Each term or phrase is the best match for only one statement or definition.

Terms and Phrases

a. Assault
b. Battery
c. Commercial exploitation
d. False imprisonment
e. Fraud
f. Intentional infliction of emotional distress
g. Intrusion
h. Libel
i. Negligence
j. Negligence per se
k. Res ipsa loquiter
l. Slander
m. Ultrahazardous activity

Statements and Definitions

____ 1. Intentional, wrongful touching of another's body.

____ 2. Defamation of another person that is communicated orally.

____ 3. Wrongful, intentional restraint of another person.

____ 4. Wrongful and offensive invasion of another's physical privacy.

____ 5. Defamation of another person that is communicated by written word or visual communication.

____ 6. Causing another to have apprehension of an imminent battery.

____ 7. Doctrine which holds that a person's negligence may be implied from the facts under certain circumstances.

____ 8. Extreme and outrageous conduct that causes another serious psychological harm.

____ 9. Intentional misrepresentation of facts that deceives another.

____ 10. Wrongful use of another's picture or voice for business purposes.

____ 11. Conduct by a party that exposes the public to an especially great risk of harm thereby justifying imposition of strict liability upon the party for any harm that is caused.

____ 12. Failure to act as a reasonably prudent person would act under similar circumstances.

____ 13. Violation of a statute that causes injury to a person who is intended to be protected by such law.

COMPLETION EXERCISE

Fill in the blanks with the words that most accurately complete each statement. Answers may or may not include terms used in the matching exercise. A term cannot be used to complete more than one statement.

1. In connection with the torts of slander and libel, an elected government official is classified as being a ______________ ______________.

2. ______________ ______________ is money that is awarded by a court to punish a wrongdoer.

3. Libel and slander are two types of ______________.

4. The standard of care that is used to determine whether a party is negligent is what a hypothetical ______________ ______________ would have done under similar circumstances.

5. A plaintiff's negligence that is partly responsible for the plaintiff's injuries is called ______________ ______________.

6. A defendant is not liable for negligence unless the defendant caused some type of ______________ harm to the plaintiff.

7. Under the theory of ______________ ______________, a plaintiff may recover a portion of his or her damages from a defendant even if the plaintiff also is negligent.

8. Economists sometimes examine legal issues by studying ______________, which are the costs and benefits that a person's conduct may cause to others.

REVIEW OF CONCEPTS

TRUE-FALSE QUESTIONS

Circle **T** (true) or **F** (false)

T F 1. A tort is best described as a violation of a duty that that prohibits public officials from violating certain provisions of the criminal law.

T F 2. In a tort case, the plaintiff (either a private party or the government) typically seeks compensation from the defendant (either a private party or the government).

T F 3. In general, intentional torts are based on defendants' acting in a careless manner towards others.

T F 4. In a defamation action, the plaintiff must prove that the defendant communicated a false statement to a third party.

T F 5. A public figure who sues for defamation needs to prove only that the defendant was careless regarding the truth of its statement.

T F 6. In a case of false imprisonment, one person unreasonably keeps another person restrained.

T F 7. Typically, rude behavior is sufficient to establish a claim of intentional infliction of emotional distress.

T F 8. Negligence may best be described as an intentional tort.

T F 9. The purpose of awarding plaintiffs compensatory damages is to compensate the plaintiffs for the harms they have suffered.

T F 10. In order to bring a case for tortious interference with a prospective advantage the plaintiff must prove that he or she had a valid contract with a third party with which the defendant wrongfully interfered.

T F 11. If the defendant's breach of duty physically led to the plaintiff's ultimate harm then the breach is the factual cause of the plaintiff's harm.

T F 12. One way to determine whether a defendant owed a plaintiff a duty of care is to ask whether the defendant could foresee the harm that the defendant caused to the plaintiff.

T F 13. In order to recover damages in a case of negligence, the plaintiff need to prove only potential harm.

T F 14. Defendants who engage in ultrahazardous activities are almost always strictly liable for any harm they cause.

T F 15. The U.S. Supreme Court has held that a trial court may use a defendant's wealth as justification for awarding any amount of punitive damages that the trial determines.

T F 16. The U.S. Supreme Court has held that a trial court generally should not allow punitive damages to be more than nine times higher than the compensatory damages awarded.

MULTIPLE CHOICE QUESTIONS

1. ____ Maria and Barb were competing for head cheerleader. With the intent to cause emotional harm to Maria, Barb repeatedly made terrible, harassing, and obscene phone calls to Maria. Maria was so frightened by the calls that she suffered a nervous breakdown requiring her to be hospitalized. Under these facts:
   a. Maria can sue Barb for the tort of battery.
   b. Maria can sue Barb for the tort of intentional infliction of emotional distress.
   c. Maria can sue Barb for the tort of slander.
   d. Maria can sue Barb for assault.

2. ____ Ken is a famous politician who is running for public office. In which situation can Ken sue for the tort of invasion of privacy?
   a. The *Evening Star*, a magazine, hid a camera in the ceiling of Ken's bedroom in order to get some exclusive photos of Ken's personal life.
   b. The *Daily News* published a story about Ken's recent behavior at a local, public nightclub.
   c. Without Ken's permission, Armco Inc. used Ken's picture to advertise its deodorant products.
   d. a and c.

3. ____ Joe was angry with a clerk and, standing a foot away from the clerk, Joe drew his arm back with a clenched fist and stated, "I am going to punch your lights out." What tort did Joe commit?
   a. Libel.
   b. False imprisonment.
   c. Battery.
   d. Assault.

4. ____ Which of the following is fraud?
   a. Nigel offered to sell his car to Jawan, explaining that the clutch was worn out.
   b. When negotiating to sell his old, used car to Maureen, Jack stated that the car was "a beauty." Actually, the car was a worn-out junk heap.
   c. Sally offered to sell her car to Mark. She stated to Mark that all of the car lights worked, not knowing that one rear tail light had just burned out.
   d. Guillermo sold Kim a car that he stated had two years left on the warranty even though he knew that the warranty had run out six months before.

5. ____ In front of a large crowd of people, Lester announces that Sam has AIDS. If this is in fact a false statement, Sam could sue Lester for:
   a. False injury.
   b. Libel.
   c. Slander.
   d. Battery.

6. ____ Rene owns a word processing company. One day, Rene intentionally planted a virus in software of a competitive firm with the intent to destroy the information stored in the competitor's computer system. The virus soon destroyed all of the information that had been stored in the competitor's computer system. Under these facts:
   a. The competitor can sue Rene for only actual damages.
   b. The competitor can sue Rene for only punitive damages.
   c. The competitor can sue Rene for actual and punitive damages.
   d. The competitor cannot sue Rene for damages. Rene's conduct is a crime, not a tort.

7. ____ Assume that the Worldly Journal, a nationally syndicated magazine, printed an article about a U.S. Senator, stating that the Senator had cheated on her exams while in law school. If the Senator sues the Worldly Journal for defamation, then the Senator must prove that:
   a. The statement stated the truth.
   b. The statement was false and it was made carelessly.
   c. The statement was false and it was made with reckless disregard of its truth.
   d. b or c.

8. ____ Carlos Agriculture Inc. had a two-year contract to supply vegetables to S&S Groceries. Acme Inc., a competitor of Carlos, wanted this contract and, with the intent to cause S&S Groceries to breach this contract, Acme convinced S&S Groceries to breach its contract with Carlos and to instead buy its vegetables from Acme. Under these facts, Acme committed the tort of:
   a. Fraud.
   b. Tortious interference with a contract.
   c. Tortious interference with a prospective advantage.
   d. Commercial exploitation.

9. ____ Assume that Cindy developed a wonderful gadget that increases the muscle bulk of upper arms. When designing packaging for this product, Cindy used a picture of a famous actor on its front. Cindy did not first obtain the actor's permission to use his picture. If the actor sues Cindy, he would sue for what tort?
   a. Intentional infliction of emotional distress.
   b. Tortious interference with a prospective advantage.
   c. False light.
   d. Commercial exploitation.

10.____ Compensatory damages are designed to restore a plaintiff to the condition that he or she was in before the defendant caused an injury. In order to restore the plaintiff to this pre-injury condition, a court may award compensatory damages for which of the following losses or purposes?
   a. For hospital bills that the plaintiff has incurred.
   b. For an amount of money to punish the defendant for his or her conduct.
   c. For lost wages incurred by the plaintiff.
   d. a and c.

11.____ In order for a plaintiff to prove a claim of tortious interference with a prospective advantage, the plaintiff must prove that:

a. The defendant had entered into a valid contract.
b. The defendant acted with reckless disregard for the truth of its statements.
c. The defendant intended to restrain the plaintiff.
d. The defendant maliciously interfered with the formation of a business relationship.

12.____ E&E Explosives was testing some new explosive compounds at its testing facility outside of town. During testing, some new experimental explosives were set off. The reaction caused by these explosives triggered an earthquake that damaged several buildings in the town. E&E exercised due care in testing these explosives, but this type of activity poses an inherent risk of harm to others no matter how careful E&E acts. Under these facts:

a. E&E is liable for the damage to the buildings only if it intentionally tried to cause this harm.
b. E&E is liable for the damage to the buildings only if it acted negligently when testing these explosives.
c. E&E is liable for the damage to the buildings even if it did not intentionally or negligently cause this harm
d. a and b.

13.____ Kyle was driving on a freeway and he passed under an overhead roadway that was being repaired by LSO Construction. As Kyle emerged from under the overpass, a steel truss dropped from the roadway above, smashing into Kyle's car and injuring Kyle. At the time of the accident, LSO was working alone on the overhead roadway and had exclusive control over the steel trusses being installed. Kyle sued LSO for negligence. Under these facts:

a. The court would infer negligence by LSO under the doctrine of res ipsa loquitur.
b. The court would not infer negligence by LSO under the doctrine of res ipsa loquitur.
c. If the court infers negligence, then LSO will be held liable and will not be allowed to prove that it did not cause the harm.
d. a and c.

14.____ One afternoon, Carrie slipped on grapes that had fallen on the floor in the produce department of Acme Groceries, injuring herself. Acme inspected the floor once in the morning and once at closing for spilled produce, even though it knew that produce was dropped on the floor more often. Is Acme liable for negligence?

a. No, Acme owed no duty to Carrie.
b. No, Acme did not breach its duty to Carrie.
c. No, Acme's conduct was not the cause of Carrie's injuries.
d. Yes, Acme was negligent and is liable to Carrie.

15.____ You are a pedestrian and are struck by a motorist. It is proven at trial that the motorist's negligence was fifty-five percent responsible for the accident and that your negligence was forty-five percent responsible for the accident. If you prove you suffered $10,000 in damages, then under the *rule of contributory negligence* you can recover:

a. $0.
b. $4,500.
c. $5,500.
d. $10,000.

16.____ You are a pedestrian and are struck by a motorist. It is proven at trial that the motorist's negligence was fifty-five percent responsible for the accident and that your negligence was forty-five percent responsible for the accident. If you prove you suffered $10,000 in damages, then under the *rule of comparative negligence* you can recover:

a. $0.
b. $4,500.
c. $5,500.
d. $10,000.

17.____ A state statute forbids manufacturing toxic chemicals within one mile of any residential properties. This statute is intended to protect residents from toxic poisoning. In violation of this law, Acme Corp. manufactured Killer Pesticide, a toxic substance, within one mile of Jesse's home. Some pesticide escaped during the Acme's plant, poisoning Jesse. Under these facts:

a. Acme may be held liable for negligence per se and Jesse does not have to prove that Acme breached a duty owing to him.
b. Acme may be held liable for negligence per se only if Jesse proves that Acme breached a duty owing to him.
c. Acme may be held liable for negligence per se only if Jesse proves that Acme's activity was ultrahazardous.
d. Acme cannot be held liable for negligence per se under any circumstance because it merely violated a statute.

18.____ Natalie exceeded the speed limit while driving on a busy freeway. Due to her speed, Natalie lost control of her car, which collided with Sebastian's car, setting off an accident involving ten cars. Under these facts:

a. Natalie's speeding was the cause in fact for the chain-reaction accident.
b. Natalie is liable for the damage to only Sebastian's car, and not for the damage to the other cars involved in the accident.
c. Natalie is liable for the damage to both Sebastian's car and the other cars because this damage was a reasonably foreseeable consequence of Natalie's speeding.
d. a and c.

19.____ A negligence tort may be described as:

a. One in which the degree of care taken never matters.
b. One in which the plaintiff must prove the defendant intended to harm her.
c. Unintentional or accidental.
d. Premeditated and malicious.

SHORT ESSAYS

1. Plaintiffs in tort cases want the court to award them damages.

   a. What kinds of items may be claimed as damages?
   b. What does the "single recovery principle" require of a court when it awards damages?

2. List the elements that a plaintiff must prove in order to recover based on the theory of negligence. Explain each element of the tort of negligence.

3. Explain the difference between the theories of contributory and comparative negligence. Analyze the strengths and weaknesses of each theory of negligence.

CASE PROBLEMS

1. Todd was an overzealous vacuum cleaner salesman. One day Todd went to the home of Mabel Jones, an elderly widow. Mabel invited Todd in but told Todd she was not interested after he gave his initial sales pitch. In response, Todd threatened to hit Mabel and pushed her aside. Todd then forced Mabel to sit down and would not let her leave while he gave his sales pitch again.

   What torts did Todd commit in this case?

2. One rainy day, Lily was driving to work. The speed limit was 45 m.p.h. and Lily was driving this speed as were some other drivers. A reasonable person, however, would have been driving only 30 m.p.h. Paul negligently rode his bike onto the road. Due to the speed Lily was driving, she could not stop and her car struck Paul. Paul suffered $5,000 damages, which were caused 80 percent by Lily's conduct and 20 percent by Paul's conduct.

   a. What duty did Lily owe to Paul?
   b. Was Lily negligent?
   c. If Lily was negligent, how much could Paul recover under the rule of contributory negligence?
   d. If Lily was negligent, how much could Paul recover under the rule of comparative negligence ?

CHAPTER SEVEN
CRIME

CHAPTER OUTLINE

I. Crime, Society, and Law
   A. Civil Law/Criminal Law
   B. Punishment
   C. The Prosecution's Case
   D. Defenses

II. Crimes that Harm Business
   A. Larceny
   B. Fraud
   C. Arson
   D. Embezzlement
   E. Computer Crime

III. Crimes Committed by Business
   A. Punishing a Corporation
   B. Selected Crimes Committed by Business
      1. RICO
      2. Money Laundering
      3. Other Crimes

IV. Constitutional Protections
   A. The Criminal Process
   B. The Fourth Amendment
   C. The Fifth Amendment
   D. The Sixth Amendment
   E. The Eighth Amendment

WHAT YOU SHOULD KNOW

After reading this chapter you should understand:

why societies choose to subject some conduct to criminal sanctions;

what a prosecutor has to prove in a case against a criminal defendant;

defenses that defendants may use in criminal cases;

the kinds of crimes that hurt businesses;

the kinds of crimes that may be committed by businesses;

how a business may be punished; and

how the U.S. Constitution protects defendants.

REVIEW OF TERMS AND PHRASES

MATCHING EXERCISE

Select the term or phrase that best matches a statement or definition stated below. Each term or phrase is the best match for only one statement or definition.

Terms and Phrases

a. Affidavit
b. Embezzlement
c. Felonies
d. Fraud
e. Grand jury
f. Indictment
g. Larceny
h. Misdemeanors
i. Money laundering
j. Plea bargain
k. RICO
l. Treble damages

Statements and Definitions

____ 1. Crime of taking profits from criminal acts and either using the money to promote crime or to disguise the source of the money.
____ 2. Judgment for three times the loss actually incurred.
____ 3. Agreement between the government and a defendant that the defendant will plead guilty to a lesser crime and that the government will recommend a more lenient sentence.
____ 4. A variety of crimes that all involve the deception of another for the purpose of obtaining their money or property.
____ 5. Crime of intentionally obtaining money or property by fraud or deception.
____ 6. Group of citizens who are selected to determine whether there is probable cause to believe that a party has committed a crime.
____ 7. Written statement signed under oath.
____ 8. Classification of less serious crimes that are typically punishable by a year or less in jail.
____ 9. Federal law for prosecuting racketeering that permits victims to sue for treble damages.
____ 10. Classification of serious crimes that are punishable by imprisonment for more than one year or by death.
____ 11. Government's formal charge that a defendant has committed a crime and must stand trial.
____ 12. Crime involving fraudulent taking of money or property by a party to whom it was entrusted.

COMPLETION EXERCISE

Fill in the blanks with the words that most accurately complete each statement. Answers may or may not include terms used in the matching exercise. A term cannot be used to complete more than one statement.

1. ______________ ______________ means that a defendant consciously disregarded a substantial risk of injury to others.

2. Two elements that the prosecution must prove in order to establish that a defendant committed a crime are ______________ ______________ and ______________ ______________.

3. _______________ is an acronym for federal and state laws that are intended to prevent and punish patterns of racketeering and criminal activities by organized crime.

4. In general, a person cannot be arrested unless there is _______________ _______________ to believe that the accused committed a crime.

5. Identify three defenses to criminal liability:

   a. ________________________________.

   b. ________________________________.

   c. ________________________________.

6. _______________ _______________ laws generally require mandatory long-term sentences for persons who are convicted of a third serious crime.

REVIEW OF CONCEPTS

TRUE-FALSE QUESTIONS

Circle **T** (true) or **F** (false)

T F 1. Businesses that are convicted of crimes often must pay fines and, in addition, they often suffer reputational penalties as well.

T F 2. Criminal defendants have a right to a jury trial only in federal cases.

T F 3. Someone convicted of a felony will typically be sentenced to three to six months in jail.

T F 4. The burden of proof in criminal cases is proof beyond a reasonable doubt.

T F 5. In most criminal cases, the prosecution must prove that the defendant intended to do whatever action the law prohibits.

T F 6. According to the M'Naghten Rule, a criminal defendant must be able to prove that the defendant understood what he or she was doing when the criminal act was committed, but that the defendant was unable to control his or her actions.

T F 7. The Supreme Court has forbidden all forfeitures as being cruel and unusual punishment under the Eighth Amendment.

T F 8. The Sixth Amendment guarantees a defendant's right to a lawyer at all important stages of the criminal process.

T F 9. The Patriot Act of 2001 gives governmental officials greater powers to investigate and prevent various types of terrorist activities.

T F 10. When a company engages in money laundering it is attempting to monopolize an industry and corner a particular market.

MULTIPLE CHOICE QUESTIONS

1. ____ Michawne is accused of shoplifting an expensive watch from a department store. The prosecution in the case against Michawne must prove that:
   a. Michawne accidentally left the store with the watch.
   b. Michawne passes the M'Naghten Rule.
   c. Michawne had no mens rea.
   d. Michawne committed the actus reus.

2. ____ Jesse is accused of killing his sister Flo. Jesse claims that he dearly loved Flo and would never willingly have hurt her. In fact, he claims that the only reason he killed his sister is because he was insane at the time of the act. Assume that Jesse lives in a state that uses the M'Naghten Rule. In this case, he must prove that:
   a. He had had minor episodes of depression in his childhood.
   b. He was able, at the moment of the killing, to control his behavior.
   c. He committed the actus reus.
   d. He suffered from a serious, identifiable mental disease.

3. ____ It is a federal crime to:
   a. Convert your own property.
   b. Require co-signing of out-of-state checks.
   c. Use independent auditors to recheck company accounts.
   d. Bribe a doctor to make false statement on Medicare forms.

4. ____ Assume that the FBI has a serious problem with the illegal sale of animals listed on the endangered species list. The FBI suspects that there is a smuggling ring, which sells rare animals to foreign buyers. Charlene, an FBI agent, poses as someone interested in buying red-cockaded woodpeckers (an endangered species that cannot be legally sold). Charlene knows that Jeff has some of these protected birds on his land. She approaches Jeff and offers $5,000 per bird if he traps them. Jeff refuses. Charlene repeatedly comes back, each time increasing the offer, but Jeff continues to refuse. Finally, Charlene offers $50,000 per bird and Jeff succumbs and traps two woodpeckers. Charlene arrests him as he attempts to deliver the birds. Under these facts, Jeff's best defense would be:
   a. Insanity under the M'Naghten Rule.
   b. Entrapment by the government.
   c. Duress.
   d. Insanity under the irresistible impulse rule.

5. ____ Over a period of four years, Allen knowingly and willfully engaged in numerous transactions that entailed the fraudulent sale of worthless swampland to elderly persons who lived in various parts of the United States. Mrs. Hinton unsuspectingly bought some of this worthless land from Allen, and she paid him $10,000 for the property. Under these facts:
   a. Allen can only be criminally prosecuted for violation of RICO.
   b. Allen can only be civilly sued by the government for violation of RICO.
   c. Allen can be criminally prosecuted for violation of RICO and he can be civilly sued by Mrs. Hinton for $10,000 for violation of RICO.
   d. Allen can be criminally prosecuted for violation of RICO and he can be civilly sued by Mrs. Hinton for $30,000 for violation of RICO.

6. ____ Employees of Jackson Electrical, Inc. were repairing power lines when one of its "cherry pickers" came into contact with a power line, electrocuting a worker. Prior to this accident, the employees had complained to Jackson supervisors that operation of this equipment so near to the power lines was unsafe and exposed them a significant risk of injury. The supervisors talked this over with Jackson and they all agreed: "We can always replace one of these employees if necessary, but we can't replace the client for whom we are doing this work." The supervisors then ordered the employees to continue to work (the crime of criminal negligence). Who can be prosecuted for this crime?

a. Only the supervisors.
b. Only the supervisors and Jackson.
c. Only Jackson Electrical, Inc.
d. The supervisors, Jackson, and Jackson Electrical, Inc.

7. ____ Roger, an employee, systematically took tools from his employer whenever he was left to lock up his employer's store. Roger was arrested one night while taking more tools. What crime has Roger committed?

a. Larceny.
b. Burglary.
c. Embezzlement.
d. Swindle.

8. ____ Jeanne worked as a computer programmer. One day, Jeanne was angry with her employer, and she intentionally planted a "virus" in her employer's software with the intent to destroy the information stored in the employer's computer system. Within a week, the virus had destroyed all of the information that had been stored in the employer's computer system. In most states:

a. Jeanne's conduct is unethical.
b. Jeanne's conduct is a tort.
c. Jeanne's conduct is a crime.
d. All of the above.

9. ____ When a person is charged with a violation of the criminal law:

a. They are never entitled to a jury trial.
b. They are always entitled to a jury trial.
c. They may request a jury trial only if they face six months or more in jail if they are convicted.
d. They may request a jury trial only if they face two or more years in jail if they are convicted.

10. ____ There are a number of possible reasons why a society would create criminal rules, instead of simply using civil rules, to restrain the behavior of its members. These reasons do not include:

a. Retribution.
b. Providing positive incentives for such behavior.
c. Attempting to generally deter such behavior.
d. Punishing wrongdoers.

11. ____ Under the Federal Sentencing Guidelines, if a corporation commits a criminal act, it may face reduced fines or other punishments, if:
   a. The corporation failed to comply with OSHA.
   b. The corporation had a compliance program in place at the time of the criminal activity.
   c. The corporation attempted to conceal money from the IRS.
   d. The corporation maintained its business through some criminal activity.

12. ____ The Fourth Amendment of the U.S. Constitution:
   a. Prohibits unreasonable searches and seizures.
   b. Requires the government to pay just compensation.
   c. Provides for equal protection under the law.
   d. Provides for due process under the law.

SHORT ESSAYS

1. In order to bring a successful case against a criminal defendant, a prosecutor must be able to prove a number of things.
   a. Describe what the prosecutor must prove in an criminal case.
   b. What is the standard of proof that the prosecutor must be able to meet to win his or her case?

2. Identify the major protections that are afforded to criminal defendants by the Fourth and Fifth Amendments of the U.S. Constitution. Why are these protections important for a free society?

CASE PROBLEMS

Answer the following problems, briefly explaining your answers.

1. Over a period of five years, Drake knowingly and willfully engaged in a pattern of criminal activity that entailed repeated fraudulent sales of worthless swampland to elderly persons. Drake advertised this land by mailing fraudulent brochures to persons in many states. Drake also paid money to government officials in order to obtain their approval of these land sales
   a. What federal crimes did Drake commit?
   b. What criminal penalties may be imposed against Drake?

2. Samuel offered to sell a plot of land to Roland. In order to induce Roland to buy, Samuel stated that there was an underground spring on the property with an attached irrigation system. Samuel knew that his statement was false. Since Roland was planning to grow corn on the land, the existence of adequate water and irrigation was important. Relying on Samuel's statement, Roland purchased the land for three times its actual value.
   a. What crime did Samuel commit?
   b. What must be established to prove Samuel's guilt?

CHAPTER EIGHT
INTERNATIONAL LAW

CHAPTER OUTLINE

I. MNEs and Power

II. Trade Regulation

- A. Export Controls
- B. Import Controls
- C. General Agreement on Tariffs and Trade (GATT)
- D. Regional Agreements

III. International Sales Agreements

- A. Direct Sales
- B. Indirect Sales through a Distributor
- C. Licensing a Foreign Manufacturer

IV. Investing Abroad

- A. Repatriation of Profits
- B. Expropriation
- C. Sovereign Immunity
- D. Foreign Corrupt Practices Act

WHAT YOU SHOULD KNOW

After reading this chapter you should understand:

what kinds of goods are subject to export restrictions and why;

what a tariff is and what the U.S. Tariff Schedule is;

what is meant by dumping and non-tariff barriers;

what the GATT and the World Trade Organization are;

the different ways you can purchase and sell products overseas;

typical ways that foreign sales agreements are financed;

ways in which people can invest abroad;

ways that sovereign immunity and the act of state doctrine may affect U.S. businesses; and

what the Foreign Corrupt Practices Act prohibits.

REVIEW OF TERMS AND PHRASES

MATCHING EXERCISE

Select the term or phrase that best matches a statement or definition stated below. Each term or phrase is the best match for only one statement or definition.

Terms and Phrases

a. CISG
b. Controlled Commodities List
c. Court of International Trade
d. Dumping
e. EU
f. Expropriation
g. GATT
h. IMF-World Bank
i. Letter of credit
j. Most favored nation clause
k. Multi-national enterprises
l. NAFTA
m. Quota
n. Subsidized goods
o. World Trade Organization

Statements and Definitions

____ 1. Companies doing business in several countries at the same time.

____ 2. Provision of GATT that forbids trade discrimination against member countries.

____ 3. Institution created after World War II to aid redevelopment and to help stabilize currencies.

____ 4. Tribunal that hears appeals of U.S. Customs' rulings.

____ 5. Nationalization of assets of a U.S. company by a foreign country.

____ 6. Agreement that establishes uniform rules for international sales contracts.

____ 7. Organization comprised of the major European trading partners.

____ 8. Sale of foreign goods in the U.S. at less than fair value.

____ 9. Agreement between U.S., Mexico, and Canada to eventually eliminate tariffs.

____10. Limit on the quantity of a particular good that a country will allow to be imported.

____11. Organization created by GATT to resolve trade disputes between member countries.

____12. Trading treaty among 125 countries that promotes nondiscriminatory trade among its members.

____13. Enumeration of items for which a license must be obtained in order to export them from the United States.

____14. Promise by a bank or other financial institution to pay a customer's debt if correct documents are first presented to the bank.

____15. Goods that may be priced lower because their manufacturer is provided financial assistance by the country where they are made.

COMPLETION EXERCISE

Fill in the blanks with the words that most accurately complete each statement.

1. Under the _______________ _______________ _______________ _______________, a U.S. company cannot give "anything of value" to foreign officials with the intent to corrupt.

2. _______________ is a regional trade agreement between nine Southeast Asian countries.

3. ____________________ is shipping goods or services out of a country.

4. ____________________ is shipping goods or services into a country.

5. Two important legal limitations on what can be exported from the United States are the _____________ _________________ _________________ ____ _____ and the _______________ _______________ _________________ _________________.

6. A _______________ is a duty or tax that is imposed on goods when they are imported into a country.

7. In the event of a conflict between the laws of two countries in connection with a lawsuit involving companies from different countries, the concept of ________________ ________________ requires that one court respect the legal system of the other country and decline jurisdiction if the case is more logically related to the foreign country.

8. The doctrine of ____________________ ________________ holds that courts do not generally have jurisdiction to hear lawsuits against foreign governments.

9. The ___________ ____ _______________ doctrine requires American courts to refrain from interfering with the ability of the President or Congress in conducting foreign affairs.

10. An ______________ ______________ tax is a tax that is assessed goods according to their value.

11. An ______________ ______________ is a regulation that absolutely prohibits the importation of certain products.

12. Identify three methods that a U.S. company can use in order to conduct international business.

    a. ____.

    b. ____.

    c. ____.

REVIEW OF CONCEPTS

TRUE-FALSE QUESTIONS

Circle **T** (true) or **F** (false)

T F 1. Because the virtues of free trade have been embraced by the United States, the country places no restrictions on exports.

T F 2. In the United States, certain goods may not leave the country if they threaten to harm U.S. foreign policy goals.

T F 3. Tariffs are taxes placed on goods that are imported into a country.

T F 4. The U.S. Tariff Schedule is a list of goods, a description of the goods, and the tariff rate attached to each.

T F 5. Nontariff barriers to trade include such things as countervailing duties.

T F 6. The GATT is a multilateral treaty designed to promote trade around the world by lowering tariff rates and eliminating non-tariff barriers.

T F 7. If an American company sells a good (product) in France, the transaction is governed by French commercial law.

T F 8. Although the United States has strong antitrust laws (the Sherman Antitrust Act, for example), Europe has no such protection.

T F 9. If Microworld, Inc. (a U.S. corporation) repatriates profits from its Senegal (Africa) manufacturing plant, this means that the company compensates the West African nation for use of its resources.

T F 10. The Foreign Corrupt Practices Act permits American companies to make payments to foreign officials if they are merely intended to help speed up performance of routine functions or such payments are expressly permitted by law in the foreign country.

T F 11. The members of the EU have failed to adopt the Euro as their common currency.

T F 12. Companies from CISG signatory countries who are selling goods to one another should include in their sales contract a term stating in what country litigation must be brought in relation to any contractual disputes.

T F 13. Letters of credit are valuable letters of introduction that American companies often use when trying to establish business relations with foreign companies.

T F 14. One of the realties of international business is that MNEs have the financial resources to often exercise significant power to affect the economies, workers and environment in many countries.

MULTIPLE CHOICE QUESTIONS

1.____ Carsman Co. wants to establish a mining business in a third world country. However, Carsman Co. fears that its business may be expropriated by this country in the future. What action can Carsman Co. take to reduce the risk of expropriation?

a. Purchase life insurance on the lives of its key employees.
b. Purchase insurance from the Overseas Private Investment Corporation.
c. Purchase insurance directly from the foreign government in which Carsman will be doing business.
d. Bribe the foreign leaders.

2.____ Kristen Jones is vice president of sales for Arnold Appliance Corporation. She wishes to expedite a sale of household appliances to a customer in a foreign country. Which of the following actions may Kristen take without violating the Foreign Corrupt Practices Act?

a. Kristen may bribe a high government official in order to gain the official's approval.
b. Kristen may make valuable gifts to high government officials in order to gain their approval.
c. Kristen may pay low-level government officials to expedite routine paperwork.\
d. Kristen may not make any kind of payment to any government official.

3.____ Micro-Tech, a U.S. corporation, entered into a contract to purchase transistors from a British company. Both the United States and Britain are signatories to the CISG. Under these facts, select the correct answer:

a. The CISG automatically applies to the sales contract unless the contract specifically states otherwise.
b. The contract must be written to be enforceable under the CISG.
c. The purchase price must be paid in the currency of the buyer, i.e., American dollars in this case.
d. All of the above.

4.____ The World Trade Organization administers the objectives of which of the following:

a. GATT.
b. The CISG.
c. UNCTAD.
d. NAFTA.

5.____ There are several reasons why the United States government might limit the number or kind of domestically produced goods that leave the country. These reasons include:

a. A desire to lessen international comity.
b. A concern over draining scarce resources.
c. A desire to promote the interests of foreign producers.
d. A concern over the Foreign Corrupt Practices Act.

6. ____ Some goods may not legally be exported from the United States unless an export license is issued by the government. These goods include:
   a. Any item listed on the Chicago Commodities Exchange.
   b. Items that threaten foreign producers.
   c. Goods listed on the Controlled Commodities List.
   d. Goods listed in the U.S. Tariff Schedule.

7. ____ One effect of U.S. tariffs is to:
   a. Raise revenue for foreign countries.
   b. Impose health and safety standards on foreign goods.
   c. Increase the domestic consumer choice.
   d. Reduce foreign competition in the United States.

8. ____ Sno and Go manufacturers snowboards. Sno and Go would like to sell its snowboards in Europe, where the sport is popular. However, Sno and Go faces tough competition from an Italian manufacturer of snowboards -- Paretti Ltd. In order to gain more of the European market Sno and Go decides to sell its snowboards for $150 each. It costs Sno and Go $175 to make each board. Sno and Go's selling of its snowboards for $150 each in Europe:
   a. Is lawful competition that is protected by U.S. antitrust law.
   b. Is lawful competition that is protected by EU antitrust laws.
   c. Is unlawful dumping.
   d. a and b.

9. ____ Select the statements that are correct under the CISG.
   a. Contracts do not have to be written to be enforceable.
   b. Acceptances can form a contract even if they change the terms of the offer.
   c. The CISG automatically applies to contracts between companies that are both from CISG signatory countries, unless the parties specifically agree otherwise.
   d. a and c.

SHORT ESSAY

A key issue in the international sale of goods is often the manner of paying for large purchases from an unfamiliar foreign company. Briefly describe a relatively safe way to make such purchases which serves to protect both the buyer and seller.

CASE PROBLEM

You are the owner Whisper Ride, a revolutionary new wheelchair. You currently sell your product in the United States and you want to start marketing and selling your product in foreign countries. Describe three approaches that you can use to establish an international distribution network. Identify one positive and one negative effect for each such approach.

CHAPTER NINE
INTRODUCTION TO CONTRACTS

CHAPTER OUTLINE

I. Introduction to Contracts

  A. The Purpose of a Contract

  B. Judicial Activism and Judicial Restraint

  C. Definition of Contracts

II. Development of Contract Law

III. Types of Contracts

  A. Bilateral and Unilateral Contracts

  B. Express and Implied Contracts

  C. Executed and Executory Contracts

  D. Valid, Unenforceable, Voidable and Void Agreements

IV. Remedies Created by Judicial Activism

  A. Promissory Estoppel

  B. Quasi-Contract

V. Sources of Contract Law

  A. The Common Law

  B. The Uniform Commercial Code

  C. The Restatement (Second) of Contracts

WHAT YOU SHOULD KNOW

After reading this chapter you should understand:

why we have contracts and what purposes they serve;

the difference between judicial restraint and judicial activism;

the definition of a contract;

how American contract law grew out of the English common law of contract;

what the different types of contracts are;

what promissory estoppel and quasi-contract are; and

what the sources of contract are.

REVIEW OF TERMS AND PHRASES

MATCHING EXERCISE

Select the term or phrase that best matches a statement or definition stated below. Each term or phrase is the best match for only one statement or definition.

Terms and Phrases

a. Bilateral contract

b. Executory contract

c. Express contract

d. Implied contract

e. Quantum meruit

f. Quasi contract

g. Unilateral contract

h. Valid contract

i. Voidable contract

j. Void agreement

Statements and Definitions

____ 1. Contract that is formed by an offeree's accepting an offer by promising to do a requested act.

____ 2. Contract that is created by the conduct of the parties.

____ 3. Contract that may be avoided by a party because it was not properly formed.

____ 4. Contract implied in law in order to avoid unjust enrichment.

____ 5. Contract that has not been fully performed by the contracting parties.

____ 6. Remedy allowing a party to recover for the reasonable value of services or goods.

____ 7. Agreement that has no legal effect.

____ 8. Contract that is created by a written or oral agreement.

____ 9. Legally binding contract that cannot be set aside by a party.

____ 10. Contract that is formed by an offeree's accepting an offer by doing a requested act.

COMPLETION EXERCISE

Fill in the blanks with the words that most accurately complete each statement. Answers may or may not include terms used in the matching exercise. A term cannot be used to complete more than one statement.

1. One of the primary purposes of a contract is to make business matters more _______________.

2. A ___________ _______________ is a type of contract whereby one party agrees to not compete against the other party.

3. A _______________ _______________ is a contract in which one of the parties is obligated to both sell goods and perform some other type of obligation.

4. The subject matter of a contract must be _______________ or else it is a void agreement.

REVIEW OF CONCEPTS

TRUE/FALSE QUESTIONS

Circle **T** (true) or **F** (false)

T F 1. One of the main purposes of contract law is to inject certainty into future dealings.

T F 2. Judicial restraint refers to judges who take a passive role in interpreting the law.

T F 3. When judges display judicial activism they make the law less flexible and more predictable.

T F 4. Contracts have a number of legally essential elements, among which are an agreement and consideration.

T F 5. The law enforces all promises, therefore, all promises are contracts.

T F 6. In the nineteenth century most American courts rejected the freedom-of-contract philosophy when interpreting contracts.

T F 7. In an implied contract, the conduct and also sometimes words of the parties indicate that they mean to enter into an agreement with each other.

T F 8. A contract is executed when one of the contracting parties has fulfilled his or her obligations.

T F 9. One of the key issues in a promissory estoppel case is whether the defendant made a promise to the plaintiff that the plaintiff detrimentally relied upon.

T F 10. Quantum meruit damages are awarded for the purpose of punishing the wrongdoer and deterring others from engaging in similar behavior in the future.

MULTIPLE CHOICE QUESTIONS

1. ____ An implied contract is created in which of the following situations?
   a. John voluntarily fixed his sister's car.
   b. Kami and Tom entered into a complete, written contract to sell Kami's condominium to Tom.
   c. Luci and Mary orally agreed that Luci would make a suit for Mary for $100.
   d. Mark requested that Clay's Roofing repair his roof and Clay's did so. The parties did not expressly agree upon all of the terms of the transaction, but Clay's expected to be paid for its work and Mark knew this.

2. ____ Eddie agreed to sell stolen bicycles to Foster for $500 and Foster agreed to buy them. Which statement accurately describes their agreement?
   a. The agreement is a voidable contract, which the parties may later affirm.
   b. The agreement is void and unenforceable.
   c. The agreement is enforceable if it is stated in writing.
   d. The agreement is a valid contract.

3. ____ In which of the following situations would a court recognize a quasi-contractual obligation to pay?
   a. Unknown to Grace, Todd's lawn service mistakenly mowed her lawn while she was at the store.
   b. Linda voluntarily cared for Sally's children for a week.
   c. Franklin and Lamar orally agreed that Franklin would paint Lamar's boat for $300.
   d. None of the above.

4. ____ Roger promised to sell his car to Reggie and Reggie promised to pay Roger $3,000 for the car. The parties have not yet performed their respective promises. This contract may be classified as:
a. An executed, bilateral contract.
b. An executory, bilateral contract.
c. An executed, unilateral contract.
d. An executory, unilateral contract.

5. ____ Tom shows up at Wynonna's home one afternoon and begins painting the house a beautiful shade of gray. Wynonna is inside baking brownies and sees Tom painting and thinks, "Gee, what a wonderful thing - this man is painting my house without my asking him to do so." Tom paints all day, and returns the next three days, completing the job after 4 days. The next day Tom presents a large bill to Wynonna. Shocked, Wynonna takes the bill and says, "What! I never agreed that you should paint my house! I won't pay! Under these facts, Tom's best legal argument in support of his claim for payment is:
a. Fraud.
b. Quasi-contract.
c. Promissory estoppel.
d. Moral guilt.

6. ____ Chris agreed to sell stolen goods to Gray, and Gray agreed to buy the goods. Under these facts:
a. This agreement is a void agreement.
b. This agreement is a voidable contract.
c. This agreement is a valid contract.
d. This agreement is legally enforceable if Chris and Gray don't often buy and sell stolen goods.

7. ____ Jackie offered to pay Glen $500 in consideration for Glen's complete trimming of all trees located on Jackie's property. This offer is an offer for a unilateral contract. Under these facts:
a. Glen can accept the offer by promising to trim the trees.
b. Glen can accept the offer by completely trimming the trees.
c. Glen can accept the offer by promising to trim the trees or by completely trimming the trees.
d. Glen cannot accept the offer; offers for unilateral contracts are illegal.

8. ____ Suppose that I promise to wash your car every Saturday for the next year, in return for which you promise to walk my precious West Highland terrier every afternoon for six months. Under these facts, we have entered into:
a. An implied contract.
b. A delegatory contract.
c. An olfactory contract.
d. A bilateral contract.

9. ____ A contract is an express contract when:
a. One party makes a promise that the other party does not accept.
b. Both parties state only some of their rights and obligations.
c. Both contracting parties state all of the important terms of their agreement.
d. Neither party states any of their intentions.

10. ____ When judges act with judicial activism:
   a. They are unwilling to create contracts where none really exist.
   b. They are less flexible than other judges.
   c. They are less predictable than other judges.
   d. They are more willing to enforce what they believe are unfair deals.

11. ____ If you want to find out what law governs the sales of goods in the various states in the United States you should consult:
   a. The statute of frauds.
   b. The Nolo Contendere Code.
   c. The Code of Civil Procedure.
   d. The Uniform Commercial Code.

SHORT ESSAYS

1. Societies that prosper have some form of contracting rules. Why is it important for a society to have rules of contract law? What are the benefits of such rules? Are there any disadvantages of having rules of contract law?

2. There are many different kinds of contracts, and a single contract may be classified in more than one category. Identify and explain the different kinds of contracts.

CASE PROBLEMS

Answer the following case problems, explaining your answers.

1. Betima has wanted to be a beautician for years. Betima's friend Julene is a wonderful beautician with a large clientele. Julene promises to teach Betima all the tricks of the trade, and to arrange for Betima to be licensed as a beautician. With Julene's encouragement, Betima sells her home so she will have enough money to live on while being trained by Julene and to then to go into business with Julene. A little later, Julene tells Betima that she is too busy to keep her promise and will not train her.
   a. Did the parties form a contract?
   b. What is Betima's best legal argument for recovering her losses from Julene?

2. Ken took his car to Acme to get an estimate for painting one fender. Unknown to Ken, the Acme manager mistakenly told the staff to completely paint Ken's car. When Ken returned to get the estimate, he found that his entire car had been painted.
   a. Discuss whether the parties entered into a contract.
   b. Does Ken have any legal obligation under quasi-contract to pay for Acme's services?

CHAPTER TEN
AGREEMENT

CHAPTER OUTLINE

I. Agreement
   A. The Issue
   B. Meeting of the Mind and The Objective Theory

II. Offer
   A. Problems with Intent
   B. Problems with Definiteness
   C. The UCC and Open Terms
   D. Termination of Offers

III. Acceptance
   A. Mirror Image Rule
   B. The UCC and The Battle of Forms
   C. Communication of Acceptance

IV. Promissory Estoppel

WHAT YOU SHOULD KNOW

After reading this chapter you should understand:

what is required under the common law for a valid offer;

what kinds of statements do not constitute a valid offer;

what kinds of offers are valid under the UCC;

how offers are legally terminated;

what is required under the common law for a valid acceptance;

what the mirror-image rule requires;

what kinds of acceptances are valid under the UCC;

what the mailbox rule means; and

how promissory estoppel relates to the common law of contract.

REVIEW OF TERMS AND PHRASES

MATCHING EXERCISE

Select the term or phrase that best matches a statement or definition stated below. Each term or phrase is the best match for only one statement or definition.

Terms and Phrases

a. Acceptance
b. Counteroffer
c. Firm offer
d. Offer
e. Option contract
f. Output contract
g. Rejection
h. Requirements contract
i. Revocation

Statements and Definitions

____ 1. Merchant's signed, written offer to buy or sell goods, which promises that the offer will not be revoked for a period of time, not to exceed three months.

____ 2. Offeree's expression that both rejects an offer and constitutes an offer by the offeree to contract upon different terms.

____ 3. Contract by which one party promises not to revoke an offer to enter into another contract for a stated period of time. Consideration must be given for the promise not to revoke.

____ 4. Offeree's manifestation that an offer is not acceptable.

____ 5. Contract to sell the entire production of a seller to a buyer.

____ 6. Termination of an offer by an offeror.

____ 7. Offeror's proposal to enter into a contract regarding a specific subject matter.

____ 8. Offeree's agreement to the terms of an offer.

____ 9. Contract by a buyer to purchase goods necessary to meet the good faith needs of the buyer.

COMPLETION EXERCISE

Fill in the blanks with the words that most accurately complete each statement. Answers may or may not include terms used in the matching exercise. A term cannot be used to complete more than one statement.

1. The ______________ ______________ generally provides that an acceptance that is properly mailed is effective when it is dispatched.

2. An auctioneer must sell a good that is being auctioned to the highest bidder if the auction is conducted ______________ ______________.

3. Ajax Coal Mines contracts to sell its entire 2006 production of coal to Newark Public Service Co. This contract is an example of an ______________ ______________.

4. Gee Whiz Car Manufacturer contracts to buy all of the tires that it needs for its 2007 Hurricane automobile from Generic Tire Co. This contract is an example of a _______________ _______________.

5. An agreement is comprised of a valid _______________ and a valid _______________.

6. In general, if an "acceptance" states terms that are different from the terms stated in the offer, then under the common law the acceptance is actually a _______________.

7. A _______________ is an offeror's termination of an offer.

8. Unless otherwise stated, an offer expires a _______________ _______________ after it was made.

9. _______________-_______________ _______________ are rules under the UCC for supplying missing contractual terms.

REVIEW OF CONCEPTS

TRUE/FALSE QUESTIONS

Circle **T** (true) or **F** (false)

T F 1. Courts have found that letters of intent are always contracts and enforceable.

T F 2. In order to have a meeting of the minds, contracting parties must both understand each other regarding the material terms of the contract.

T F 3. One key issue with regard to contracts is whether the offeree accepted the offer without change or addition.

T F 4. In order for an offer to be legally valid under the common law, it must have reasonably definite terms.

T F 5. Advertisements are typically considered valid offers.

T F 6. Under the UCC, open terms in a contract are not allowed.

T F 7. If a contract is governed by the UCC, all goods sold under the contract automatically have an implied warranty of merchantability.

T F 8. Rejection of an offer by the offeree does not terminate the offer.

T F 9. Under the common law, an offer must be accepted on exactly the same terms as those presented in order for the acceptance to be valid.

T F 10. Offers are binding as soon as they leave the offeror's control.

MULTIPLE CHOICE QUESTIONS

1.____ Which action manifests the necessary contractual intent to constitute a valid offer?
   a. Mandy calls Carlos and asks him the price for manure. He quotes her a price of $5 per bag.
   b. In response to Homeowner's request, Contractor submits a signed bid to Homeowner to do certain described remodeling work for $5,000.
   c. Central City posts a notice inviting contractors to submit bids to construct a new city hall.
   d. Henry distributes circulars stating that he will shampoo carpeting for $10 per room.

2.____ Which proposal is too indefinite to be a valid offer?
   a. Red proposes to sell a company to Melanie for a price to be mutually agreed upon in 30 days.
   b. Luis proposes to sell ten ounces of gold to Tony at a price equal to the closing bid price stated by the Bank of New York on January 1, 2005.
   c. Farmer proposes to sell his entire 2003 apple crop to Co-op for $5 per bushel.
   d. All of the above.

3.____ In which case was Alex legally entitled to revoke his offer?
   a. Alex offered to sell a business to Will. Alex promised not to revoke the offer for 24 hours in consideration for $100 paid by Will. One hour later and before Will had accepted, Alex revoked his offer, and he offered to return the $100 to Will.
   b. In a signed writing, Alex (a merchant) offered to sell Liz a car and promised not to revoke the offer for 48 hours. One hour later and before Liz accepted, Alex revoked his offer.
   c. Alex offered to sell his condo to Ben. Before Ben accepted, Alex revoked his offer.
   d. a and c.

4.____ Select the correct answer.
   a. Ike offered to sell a patent to Ken. Before Ken accepted the offer, Ike died. In this case, Ike's offer was not terminated, and Ken can still accept the offer.
   b. R&R Co. offered to sell some chemicals to Lex. Before Lex accepted the offer, Congress passed a law making the sale of the chemicals illegal. In this case, the offer was terminated.
   c. Tom offered to sell a business to Jack. The offer stated that the offer would expire on September 1. On September 2, Jack accepted the offer. In this case, a contract was formed.
   d. Vicky offered to sell a TV to Carl. Carl replied, "No, the price is too high." Then Carl reconsidered, and he accepted the offer. In this case, a contract was formed.

5.____ Seller offered to sell certain land to Joe for $90,000. Which of the following expressions by Joe would be a valid acceptance of the offer?
   a. In writing Joe stated: "I accept the offer provided that the price is reduced to $89,000."
   b. In writing Joe stated: "I accept the offer. Also, I would appreciate a tour of the property."
   c. In writing Joe stated: "I accept the offer. Also, I request that I be given a copy of the signed documents for my files."
   d. All of the above.

6.____ In which case does Tara effectively accept the offer in question?

a. Plantco offered to sell a box of exotic tulip bulbs to Tara. She replied, "They are lovely, and I'll really think about it very seriously."
b. Sam offered to sell a car to Tara. The offer stated that Tara's failure to expressly reject the offer within 24 hours would be an acceptance. Tara was silent, and she did not expressly reject the offer.
c. Bob mailed an offer to sell a motorcycle to Tara. Immediately upon receiving the offer, Tara mailed back a definite, unconditional acceptance of the offer.
d. b and c.

7.____ On April 1, Gina mailed Oscar an offer to buy his home. Oscar received the offer on April 5. On April 6, Oscar deposited a properly addressed, stamped acceptance in the mail. Gina received the acceptance on April 10. On April 8, Gina changed her mind, and she personally delivered a written revocation of the offer to Oscar. In most states:

a. A contract was formed on April 5.
b. A contract was formed on April 6.
c. A contract was formed on April 10.
d. A contract was not formed.

8.____ On August 1, Lori makes Kate the following verbal offer: "I will sell you my horse Killer for $4,000 and this offer will be held open until midnight, September 30." Under these facts:

a. Lori made an option contract.
b. Lori made a firm offer.
c. Lori cannot revoke her offer until October 1.
d. Lori can revoke her offer whenever she chooses.

9.____ Jessica says to Tymon, "I'm thinking of selling my 1969 Corvette. What do you think?" Tymon replies, "That's great! It's a top-quality car." Two weeks later Jessica shows up at Tymon's door with her car and a bill for several thousand dollars. She says, "Here's the car, I know you wanted it." When Tymon refuses to take the car, Jessica drives over to the local courthouse and files a breach of contract claim with the clerk. Under these facts, a court is most likely to decide:

a. There was a valid meeting of the minds.
b. The mailbox rule operates here.
c. There was no valid offer, only an invitation to bargain.
d. Because there were definite terms, this is a valid offer.

10.____ Larry runs an advertisement in the local paper: "Color television sets, 19 inches, $200." Ferdinand appears at Larry's store two days later and says, "I'll take one of those TVs." Larry tells Ferdinand that all the TVs he had at that price are gone. Ferdinand says that Larry made a valid offer, which he is now accepting. Under these facts:

a. There was probably no valid offer.
b. There was probably a valid offer because the terms were quite definite.
c. There were open terms and therefore, no valid offer.
d. There was a meeting of the minds, and therefore a valid contract.

11.____ Nagii manufactures bedroom furniture. He offers to sell beds to Sam, who owns a furniture store. The terms of the offer are: 100 oak, queen-size sleigh beds at $700 per bed, delivery on November 1. Sam wants the beds, but wants delivery on November 4 instead of November 1. He responds to Nagii, "Accept offer of 100 queen-size oak sleigh beds, for delivery on November 4." The change in the date of delivery is not important to Nagii. Under the UCC:

a. This acceptance is invalid because the terms are too indefinite.
b. This offer is invalid due to open terms.
c. This offer is invalid due to the change in terms.
d. This acceptance is valid.

12.____ Stash writes to Bernie offering to sell her two-dozen cases of an excellent French wine for $3,200. Bernie receives this offer on June 2. On June 3, Stash thinks again about his offer and hand delivers to Bernie a written revocation of his offer. Nonetheless, on June 4 Bernie sent an acceptance of the offer to Stash, which he received on June 6. Was a contract formed?

a. Yes, on June 2.
b. Yes, on June 4.
c. Yes, on June 6.
d. No.

SHORT ESSAY

There are many ways in which a valid offer may be terminated. What are the various ways in which an offer may be terminated? Provide examples to illustrate these methods of termination.

CASE PROBLEM

Answer the following problem, briefly explaining your answer.

Estelle is thinking of selling her champion Scottish terrier, McDoodle. Don has been an admirer of McDoodle's for several years now. Don finds out that Estelle is thinking of selling the exquisite hound and sends her a letter in which he says that he hopes she will contact him first if the rumors of the impending sale are true. Estelle writes back, saying: "I think you would be a fine owner for McDoodle. My lawyer and I are in the process of drafting a document for the sale of my little baby. You will be required to take McDoodle on August 1, after the big Greenville Dog Show (which, of course, I hope to win)." On August 1, Don arrives at Estelle's house to claim the champion pooch. Estelle refuses to turn her "little baby" over.

Have Don and Estelle formed a valid contract? Explain your answer.

CHAPTER ELEVEN
CONSIDERATION

CHAPTER OUTLINE

I. Consideration
   A. Bargain and Exchange
   B. Adequacy of Consideration

II. Mutuality of Obligations
   A. Illusory Promises
   B. Sales Law - Requirements and Output Contracts
   C. Past Consideration
   D. Promissory Estoppel
   E. Preexisting Duty

III. Settlement of Debts
   A. Liquidated Debt
   B. Unliquidated Debt
   C. Payment by Check

WHAT YOU SHOULD KNOW

After reading this chapter you should understand:

what consideration is;

what kinds of actions or things may be consideration;

how much consideration is needed in a given contractual situation;

what an illusory promise is;

what a requirements contract is;

what an output contract is;

how past consideration relates to consideration issues;

how the concept of promissory estoppel relates to consideration;

how a preexisting duty affects consideration issues;

what happens when an unforeseen circumstance arises in cases of preexisting duties;

what a modification is and how it occurs;

how debts may legally be settled;

what liquidated and unliquidated debts are;

what an accord and satisfaction is; and

how paying by check relates to accord and satisfaction and the settlement of debts.

REVIEW OF TERMS AND PHRASES

MATCHING EXERCISE

Select the term or phrase that best matches a statement or definition stated below. Each term or phrase is the best match for only one statement or definition.

Terms and Phrases

a. Accord
b. Consideration
c. Forbearance
d. Illusory promise
e. Liquidated debt
f. Past consideration
g. Promissory estoppel
h. Satisfaction
i. Unliquidated debt

Statements and Definitions

____ 1. A debt for an amount that is certain and undisputed.

____ 2. Benefit previously given as a voluntary gesture and not because the benefit was the price demanded for another's promise or act.

____ 3. Bargained exchange between contracting parties.

____ 4. Doctrine that permits enforcement of a promise if a promisor should reasonably expect that a promise will induce the promisee to substantially rely on the promise, and the promise does induce reliance in such a manner that injustice can only be avoided by enforcing the promise.

____ 5. Agreement between a creditor and debtor for the creditor to accept as payment something different than that which is owed.

____ 6. A debt that is for an uncertain amount or that is disputed.

____ 7. Promise that does not impose any legal duty.

____ 8. Refraining from doing (i.e., not doing) an act.

____ 9. Performance of an accord.

COMPLETION EXERCISE

Fill in the blanks with the words that most accurately complete each statement. Answers may or may not include terms used in the matching exercise. A term cannot be used to complete more than one statement.

1. In a _______________ contract, the considerations are the promises of the offeror and the offeree.

2. The considerations in a _______________ contract are the offeror's promise and the offeree's performance of a requested act or forbearance from doing an act.

3. A ____________________ ____________________ is a legal obligation that presently exists based on statutes, general rules of law, responsibilities of the promisor's office, or a current contract.

4. ____________________ ____________________ is an agreement by both contracting parties to cancel their contract.

REVIEW OF CONCEPTS

TRUE/FALSE QUESTIONS

Circle **T** (true) or **F** (false)

T F 1. Consideration involves bargaining that leads to an exchange between the contracting parties.

T F 2. In general, a promise will be enforced even if the other party does nothing in return for the promise and makes no return promise.

T F 3. Consideration can be anything of value, including another promise.

T F 4. Courts will enforce only agreements that require an exchange of things of equal value.

T F 5. Illusory promises are those promises that obligate both contracting parties to perform in a specific manner.

T F 6. In general, an agreement is not legally binding unless each party to the agreement gives consideration.

T F 7. When someone does extra work beyond what they have contracted to do, a promise to complete the extra work will be considered valid consideration.

T F 8. Under the UCC, a contract for the sale of goods may be modified without consideration.

T F 9. A promise not to trespass on someone's land (a tort) is consideration if the promisor does in fact refrain from trespassing.

T F 10. In many states, the UCC provides that an accord and satisfaction may be created if a party (other than an organization) signs and cashes a check that is endorsed "full settlement."

MULTIPLE CHOICE QUESTIONS

1. ____ Lyle promised to write a book for Minda in exchange for her promise to pay him $10,000. When Lyle finished the book, he requested an extra $2,000 for his work. Minda initially agreed, but later she changed her mind and refused to pay the extra $2,000. Under these facts, Minda is obligated to pay Lyle:
   a. $0.
   b. $2,000.
   c. $10,000.
   d. $12,000.

2. ____ Laura agreed to sell her ½ carat diamond ring to George for $150. The diamond is a good stone and is worth $800. Under these facts, the exchange of consideration:
   a. Is valid because the courts do not review the adequacy of the considerations exchanged.
   b. Is valid because it is an unliquidated debt.
   c. Is invalid due to the difference between the actual value of the ring and the amount that George agreed to pay.
   d. Is invalid based on the promissory estoppel doctrine.

3. ____ Violet promises to pay Dave $300 in exchange for his promise to walk Violet's dog every afternoon. Dave's promise is:
   a. A legal detriment to Violet.
   b. A legal detriment to Dave.
   c. Not consideration because a mere promise to do something cannot be consideration.
   d. Not consideration based on the preexisting duty rule.

4. ____ In October, Olivia promised to pay James, an employee, a $5,000 bonus at Christmas time if at that time she thinks that he deserves the bonus and she feels right paying it. Under these facts:
   a. Olivia's promise is consideration.
   b. Olivia's promise is consideration only if this promise is stated in writing.
   c. Olivia's promise is consideration only if she really meant to pay this bonus.
   d. Olivia's promise is an illusory promise and is not consideration.

5. ____ Assume that you own a fancy restaurant. You do not have a pastry chef, and instead buy all of your desserts fresh from local suppliers. Carla provides you with a wonderful chocolate-espresso cake. If Carla agrees to supply you with all the cakes you need, this is known as:
   a. An output contract.
   b. A requirements contract.
   c. A stand-by contract.
   d. A personam contract.

6. ____ Jane agreed to paint several rooms in Lisa's home. Jane did a beautiful job on the walls and Lisa paid her the agreed-upon sum of $4,000. Because Lisa was so pleased with Jane's work she also promised to pay her an extra $1,000 in two weeks. Two weeks came and went and Lisa failed to pay Jane. If Jane sues Lisa for the extra $1,000, the most likely outcome will be:
   a. The court will award Jane the money based on the theory of ordinary contract law.
   b. The court will award Jane the money based on the theory of promissory estoppel.
   c. The court will not award Jane the money based on the theory of past consideration.
   d. The court will not award Jane the money based on the theory of quasi-contract.

7. ____ Zelman is a fireman for the City of Poltis. One evening, he responds to an alarm at a residence. Outside the house, Bob grabs Zelman him by the shoulders and says: "My little daughter is in the house. Please save her! I'll pay you $20,000 if you get her out alive!" Zelman bravely rushes into the burning house and rescues the little girl. The next day, Zelman finds Bob and asks for his check. Bob refuses to pay. Under these facts:
   a. Zelman will lose based on the theory of preexisting duty.
   b. Zelman will lose based on the theory of past consideration.
   c. Zelman will be awarded the money based on the theory of ordinary contract law.
   d. Zelman will be awarded the money based on the theory of past consideration.

8. ____ Verna contracts to have Billy build a new house for her. The contract price for the house as designed is $130,000. Billy begins work on the house. Verna then decided that she wanted all stainless steel kitchen appliances instead of white as originally agreed. This meant that Billy had to return the white appliances and purchase stainless steel appliances at an additional cost of $3,000. When Billy finished the house, he gave Verna a bill for the additional $3,000. She refused to pay this additional sum because their contract was a home for $130,000. Under these facts:
   a. Verna does not have to pay the additional $3,000 because Billy agreed to build the house for $130,000.
   b. Verna does not have to pay the additional $3,000 based on the theory of past consideration.
   c. Verna does not have to pay the additional $3,000 based on the theory of preexisting duty.
   d. Verna must pay the additional $3,000 because Billy provided additional value.

9. ____ Candy signed a promissory note agreeing to pay $4,000 to you. Candy continually refuses to pay and, after more than a year, Candy agrees to pay $3,000 to you as payment in full. You take the $3,000 cash from Candy and then sue her for the remaining $1,000. Under these facts:
   a. You win because this debt is a liquidated debt.
   b. You win because this debt is an unliquidated debt.
   c. You lose win because this debt is a liquidated debt.
   d. You lose because this debt is an unliquidated debt.

10. ____ Wanda claims that Jack owes her $2,500. Jack argues that this amount is incorrect for several reasons and that he owes only $1,700. Jack then issues a check for $1,700 that is payable to Wanda and written on the back of the check are the words "full settlement of all claims by Wanda against Jack." Wanda then indorses and cashes the check. Under the UCC in a majority of states:
   a. These events constitute an accord and satisfaction.
   b. These events do not constitute and accord and satisfaction.
   c. Wanda is still entitled to sue to collect the disputed $800 from Jack.
   d. b and c.

11. ____ Which promise or agreement is generally binding?

a. Seller and Buyer agreed to modify a land sale contract by reducing the acreage that Seller was obligated to convey. However, the price was not reduced and Seller gave no consideration for this contract modification.
b. Hal agreed to pay $500 to Juan because Hal felt morally obligated to pay this sum because Juan had voluntarily tutored Hal the previous semester.
c. Seller and Buyer in good faith agreed to modify a contract for the sale of a car by reducing the price from $400 to $350. Buyer gave no consideration for this contract modification.
d. All of the above.

12. ____ In a case where a debt is unliquidated, the creditor agrees to accept less than the amount that the creditor claims is owed, and the debtor pays the agreed-upon amount, then the parties have entered into:

a. A unilateral contract.
b. A disclaimer contract.
c. An implied warranty contract.
d. An accord and satisfaction.

SHORT ESSAYS

1. Explain the difference between a liquidated and unliquidated debt. What is the importance of the distinction between these kinds of debts? Provide a brief example of each type of debt.

2. Explain the difference between an output and a requirements contract. Give at least one example of a business situation where each of these types of contracts might be useful.

CASE PROBLEMS

Answer the following problems, briefly explaining your answers.

1. Acme hired Sally as president for a fixed, three-year term. Sally's employment contract did not include a noncompetition clause. After Sally had worked for Acme for one year, Acme requested that Sally execute a noncompetition agreement to take effect after her employment with Acme ended. Sally did as requested. Acme did not promise anything pursuant to this agreement.
   a. Is Sally's noncompetition agreement supported by consideration?
   b. Is this agreement a legally binding contract?
   c. What should Acme have done differently?

2. Aries Inc. took the following actions regarding its employees: (a) Aries agreed to pay Randy a $5,000 bonus for extra services that Randy voluntarily performed the previous year; (b) Aries agreed to pay Fred a $1,000 bonus in exchange for his promise not to breach an existing contract with Aries; and (c) Aries refused to perform a one-year contract with Hill because Aries had contractually agreed to pay Hill $30,000 pursuant to this contract, but his services were worth only $15,000.
   a. Is the agreement with Randy legally binding?
   b. Is the agreement with Fred legally binding?
   c. Is Aries entitled to refuse to perform its contract with Hill because the consideration it is receiving is inadequate?

CHAPTER TWELVE
LEGALITY

CHAPTER OUTLINE

I. Contracts in Violation of a Statute

   A. Wagering

   B. Insurance

   C. Licensing Statutes

   D. Usury

II. Contracts in Violation of Public Policy

   A. Restraint of Trade

   B. Exculpatory Clauses

   C. Unconscionable Contracts

   D. Unconscionability and Sales Law

WHAT YOU SHOULD KNOW

After reading this chapter you should understand:

how illegality affects the validity of a contract;

when contracts involving gambling are legal;

when insurance policies may be legally obtained;

how licensing requirements affect the legality of contracts;

what usury is and how usury laws affect contracts;

what restraint of trade means and how it affects contracts;

the different kinds of exculpatory clauses and their legal effects;

what bailment means and how it relates to exculpatory clauses;

what unconscionable contracts are;

what adhesion contracts are; and

what the UCC says about unconscionable contracts.

REVIEW OF TERMS AND PHRASES

MATCHING EXERCISE

Select the term or phrase that best matches a statement or definition stated below. Each term or phrase is the best match for only one statement or definition.

Terms and Phrases

a. Adhesion contract

b. Ancillary

c. Exculpatory clause

d. Insurable interest

e. License

f. Noncompete agreement

g. Public policy

h. Unconscionable contract

i. Usury

Statements and Definitions

____ 1. Unjustifiably unfair or oppressive contract.

____ 2. Standard or policy that furthers or protects fundamental public and social values or interests.

____ 3. Term in a contract that releases one party from liability to another party.

____ 4. Being a part of something.

____ 5. Term in a contract whereby one party promises not to engage in competition against the other party.

____ 6. Financial stake in the life of another person or property sufficient to justify enforcing an insurance policy on the other person or property.

____ 7. Legal permission to engage in a given trade or profession.

____ 8. Lending money at a rate of interest greater than that permitted by law.

____ 9. Contract that involves one party who has dominant bargaining power over the other party and the contract is presented on a "take it or leave it" basis.

COMPLETION EXERCISE

Fill in the blanks with the words that most accurately complete each statement. Answers may or may not include terms used in the matching exercise. A term cannot be used to complete more than one statement.

1. A _______________ is an agreement giving possession and control of personal property to another party.

2. In the type of agreement referred to in the previous question, the _______________ receives possession of personal property from the _______________.

3. _______________ is the lending of money for an interest rate that exceeds the legal rate of interest.

REVIEW OF CONCEPTS

TRUE-FALSE QUESTIONS

Circle **T** (true) or **F** (false)

T F 1. A contract that is illegal is voidable at the option of the plaintiff.

T F 2. The U.S. Congress has recently passed the Internet Gambling Prohibition Act, which expressly forbids all gambling on the Internet.

T F 3. An exculpatory clause is generally invalid when it attempts to disclaim liability for an intentional tort or gross negligence.

T F 4. Donna owes you $10,000 and you take out a $10,000 life insurance policy on her life. If Donna dies, you will not be able to collect on the policy because you cannot prove that you had an insurable interest in her life.

T F 5. In some states, a creditor who charges a usurious rate of interest may lose the entire amount lent to the debtor.

T F 6. Lucy and Ricky run two of three dance studios in town. They meet one afternoon at lunch and agree to substantially cut the prices of dance lessons in order to drive the third studio out of business. This agreement is unenforceable.

T F 7. Noncompetition clauses may be for any time, area, and scope of activities if both parties freely and knowingly agree to such terms.

T F 8. Violation of any type of licensing statute renders an agreement illegal and unenforceable.

T F 9. One of the primary legal concerns underlying the concept unconscionable contracts is that the parties have not dealt at arms length.

T F 10. The UCC does not address unconscionability because it is designed for merchants who are more sophisticated in terms of business relations than are ordinary people.

MULTIPLE CHOICE QUESTIONS

1.____ Neal was hired as general manager for a food distributor doing business in Pork City, U.S.A. Neal managed all important customer accounts, he had access to the company's extensive customer lists, and was responsible for developing the company's confidential sales strategy. When hired, Neal agreed not to compete in the food distribution business after he quit. Under these facts, Neal's agreement would probably be:

a. Valid, if it prohibited Neal from competing in Pork City for one year after he quit.
b. Valid, if it prohibited Neal from competing anywhere in the state in which Pork City was located for ten years after he quit.
c. Valid regardless of its terms. All agreements not to compete are valid.
d. Void regardless of its terms. All agreements not to compete are illegal and void.

2.____ Chemco and Glen entered into an illegal agreement whereby Glen agreed to wrongfully acquire and copy a competitor's new chemical formula in consideration for $10,000. Performance of the agreement would be a crime. If Chemco paid the $10,000 to Glen, but Glen failed to perform:

a. A court would not require Glen to perform the agreement.
b. A court would make Glen repay the $10,000 to Chemco.
c. A court would make Glen pay for any damages Chemco suffered due to his failure to perform.
d. All of the above.

3.____ Assume that five companies distribute all of the gasoline in a certain state. Executives from the five companies meet and all agree to sell 87-octane gas for no less than $1.50 per gallon; 89-octane gas for no less than $1.65 per gallon; and, 93-octane gas for no less than $1.75 per gallon. Under these facts:

a. The agreement reflects legitimate competitive forces at work.
b. The agreement is void due to restraint of trade.
c. The agreement is void due to licensing requirements.
d. The agreement is valid due to noncompetition clauses.

4.____ Phil lives in a state that does not operate a lottery. This state does not have a statute expressly authorizing or prohibiting gambling. Phil feels that he can make a substantial profit from a lottery so he starts a private lottery within the state. Under these facts:

a. Phil's lottery is legal because it is not expressly prohibited by statute.
b. Contracts directly relating to Phil's lottery are void.
c. Contracts directly relating to Phil's lottery are valid.
d. a and c.

5.____ A noncompete clause in an employment contract is generally effective:

a. Always.
b. When it is stated in a written contract.
c. When it is essential to the employer, fair to the employee, and harmless to the general public.
d. Never.

6.____ Matt was a former partner of yours in a business long since ended. Although you and Matt no longer have any business, financial, or personal dealings with one another, you have kept in force a life insurance on Matt's life. This policy names you as the sole beneficiary. Matt ultimately died, but the insurance company refuses to pay you the life insurance benefits. Under these facts:

a. The life insurance contract is valid because you properly paid all required payments.
b. The life insurance contract is valid if Matt agreed to let you carry the policy on his life.
c. The life insurance contract is invalid because you don't have an insurable interest in Matt's life.
d. The life insurance contract is invalid because life insurance policies are illegal.

7.____ Carl is an excellent pilot and he contracted to serve as the personal pilot for Susan, flying her to meetings in her personal jet. Carl's contract states that he is to be paid an annual $50,000 salary. After flying Susan for four months without any problems, she fired him without notice when she discovered that he did not have the proper license to fly her jet. This license is intended to protect passengers, such as Susan, from the risk of injury or death that may result from the improper operation of jet planes. If Carl sues to enforce the contract and collect the balance of his annual salary, the court will:

a. Enforce the contract because Carl properly carried out his contractual duties.
b. Enforce the contract because the license is only intended to raise revenue for the government.
c. Enforce the contract because Susan should have investigated whether Carl had the required license.
d. Refuse to enforce the contract because Carl did not have the required license.

8. ____ Frank has asked to borrow $5,000 from you. Frank, however, is a very bad credit risk. You nonetheless decide to lend him the money provided he agrees to pay you 50% interest per month. The state in which this transaction occurs allows a maximum annual rate of interest of 24% on loans to individuals. Under these facts:

a. The loan that you made to Frank is usurious.
b. The loan you made to Frank is lawful since he knowingly and freely agreed to it.
c. In most states, you are entitled to be repaid the amount loaned and the agreed-upon interest.
d. b and c.

9.____ Permissible justifications for noncompetition clauses in employment contracts generally include:

a. Protect against competition from former employees whom you have trained.
b. Protect confidential information.
c. Protect trade secrets.
d. b and c.

10.____You live in a high-crime area. In order to encourage local police authorities to deal with this problem more aggressively, you and your neighbors sign an agreement with the police department stating that you will not sue the department for injuries or deaths that the police may cause during the normal course of crime prevention activities. Under these facts:

a. This agreement is valid because it serves an important public purpose.
b. This agreement is valid because you and your neighbors initiated it.
c. This agreement is valid because it is an exculpatory clause, which is always valid.
d. This agreement is an invalid exculpatory clause.

11.____ According to the Uniform Commercial Code:

a. Contracts that contain exculpatory clauses are voidable.
b. Contractual terms that are unconscionable may not be enforced.
c. Unconscionability is a matter of common law, not a matter for the UCC.
d. Adhesion contracts are always valid because they involve merchants.

SHORT ESSAY

Courts will occasionally choose not to enforce certain contracts even though the parties to the contract were both adults and were both of sound mind when they entered the contract. In what kinds of situations are courts likely to act in this fashion? Do you think that judges are in the best position to decide what contracts should and should not be enforced or should these decisions be left to individuals who enter such contracts?

CASE PROBLEMS

Answer the following case problems, explaining your answers.

1. Marjorie loves politics and closely follows important elections in her state. Marjorie's friend Beth also loves politics. On a brisk fall afternoon Marjorie and Beth share a bench outside the student union and discuss their mutual fascination with politics. At one point Beth says, "I think Herman Willow will win the upcoming election for state governor." Marjorie replies "What?! He isn't going to win – Ashley Dobbercoff is going to prevail." "Put your money were your mouth is" Beth sweetly responds. "All right," answers Marjorie, "I feel so certain that you're wrong that I'll pay you $500 if you're right, and you pay me $500 if I am right." As it turns out, Marjorie was wrong and Beth was right. Marjorie, however, refuses to pay.

   What is the most likely outcome if Beth sues Marjorie for the $500?

2. Luis agreed to employ Jim as an architect to design an addition to his house. Individuals are legally required to be licensed by the state to be architects, but Jim did not have this license. To assure the competency of architects, this license requires extensive education and successful completion of an exhaustive examination.
   a. What is the purpose of this license?
   b. Is the agreement between Luis and Jim valid or void?
   c. If Jim performs the work but Luis fails to pay him, can Jim collect his fee?

CHAPTER THIRTEEN
CAPACITY AND CONSENT

CHAPTER OUTLINE

I. Capacity

  A. Minors

  B. Mentally Impaired Persons

II. Reality of Consent

  A. Misrepresentation and Fraud

  B. Mistake - Bilateral Mistake

  C. Unilateral Mistake

  D. Duress

  E. Economic Duress

  F. Undue Influence

WHAT YOU SHOULD KNOW

After reading this chapter you should understand:

what capacity means;

the problems involved with minors entering into contracts;

the problems involved in mentally incompetent people entering into contracts;

the problems involved in drunk people entering into contracts;

the difference between fraud and misrepresentation (elements of each);

remedies for fraud and misrepresentation;

the difference between bilateral and unilateral mistakes and the effect of each on contracts;

the effects of duress on contracts; and

the effects of undue influence on contracts.

REVIEW OF TERMS AND PHRASES

MATCHING EXERCISE

Select the term or phrase that best matches a statement or definition stated below. Each term or phrase is the best match for only one statement or definition.

Terms and Phrases

a. Contractual capacity
b. Disaffirmance
c. Duress
d. Fraud
e. Innocent misrepresentation
f. Minor
g. Mutual mistake
h. Ratification
i. Undue influence
j. Unilateral mistake

Statements and Definitions

____ 1. Words or conduct indicating an intent to be bound by a contract.

____ 2. False statement regarding a material fact made by a party who reasonably believes it to be true.

____ 3. Misunderstanding by only one party.

____ 4. Intentional misrepresentation of fact reasonably relied on by another party to his or her harm.

____ 5. Domination by one contracting party of the other party that deprives the weaker party of his or her free will causing the weaker party to enter into an unfair contract.

____ 6. Misunderstanding of the same fact by both contracting parties.

____ 7. Ability to understand that a contract is being made and to understand its general meaning.

____ 8. In most states, a person under the age of eighteen.

____ 9. Wrongful threat or act that deprives a party of his or her free will thereby causing the party to make a contract.

____10. Avoidance or setting aside of a contract.

COMPLETION EXERCISE

Fill in the blanks with the words that most accurately complete each statement. Answers may or may not include terms used in the matching exercise. A term cannot be used to complete more than one statement.

1. An _______________ _______________ is a false statement that is made by a contracting party who honestly and reasonably believed that the statement was true.

2. In most states, a minor is a person who is under the age of _______________.

3. _______________ _______________ involves wrongful persuasion exerted on a person by a second person who is in a position of trust or domination.

4. Fraud, innocent misrepresentation, duress, and undue influence render a contract _______________.

5. _______________ _______________ is the type of duress that involves a wrongful threat that would cause severe financial hardship to a party.

6. Food, clothing, shelter, medical care, and other goods and services that are reasonably required for the proper care of a minor are called _________________.

7. Fraud and innocent misrepresentations involve a false statement of a material _______________.

8. A _______________ mistake occurs when only one party is mistaken about a fact.

9. A _______________ mistake occurs when both parties are mistaken regarding a fact.

10. _______________ is sales talk and is not a statement that can form the basis for a claim of fraud.

REVIEW OF CONCEPTS

TRUE-FALSE QUESTIONS

Circle **T** (true) or F (false)

T F 1. Capacity is the legal ability to enter into a contract.

T F 2. Persons who sell a good to a minor may disaffirm the sales contract at will.

T F 3. If a minor disaffirms a contract, then to the extent that the minor can, he or she must return any consideration the minor has received.

T F 4. When a minor contracts to buy necessaries the minor may disaffirm the contract, so long as she has her parent's permission.

T F 5. Every contract that is made by a person who has a mental impairment is voidable even if the impaired person understands the nature and consequences of the contract.

T F 6. Fraudulent, but not innocent, misrepresentations render contracts voidable.

T F 7. In order to prove fraud, an injured party must show that the fraudulent statement was material.

T F 8. In limited circumstances, nondisclosure of a fact may result in a fraud.

T F 9. The injured party may rescind contracts involving bilateral mistakes of a material fact.

T F 10. A key element that an injured party must prove in a case of undue influence is that both parties to the contract were mistaken about a material fact.

MULTIPLE CHOICE QUESTIONS

1. ____ Which contract is voidable due to mistake?
   a. Earl contracted to sell a cabin to Phil. Unknown to either party, the cabin had burned down the previous week.
   b. Subcontractor submitted a bid to Contractor for $15,000. Contractor accepted the bid, not knowing that Subcontractor had made a mistake and the bid should have been $16,000.
   c. Andie purchased stock of ABC, Inc. from Paul. Both Andie and Paul expected the stock to increase in value, but it did not.
   d. a and c.

2. ____ Mindy purchased a stereo when she was 16 years old. Mindy has used the stereo for one year, and she now wants to avoid the contract. (For purposes of this question, you may assume that 18 is the age of majority.) Under these facts:
   a. Mindy can disaffirm the contract, but she must do so before she turns 18.
   b. Mindy can disaffirm the contract, but she must pay for any depreciation to the stereo.
   c. Mindy can disaffirm the contract, and the seller must repay all money paid by Mindy.
   d. Mindy cannot under any circumstance disaffirm the contract.

3. ____ While Ken was a minor and living on his own without any support from his parents. In which situation did Ken contract for a necessary?
   a. Ken contracted to buy a motorcycle.
   b. Ken contracted to lease an apartment.
   c. Ken contracted to buy a raincoat.
   d. b and c.

4. ____ In which case did the party in question have the contractual capacity to make a valid contract?
   a. Irving contracted to buy a TV. Due to senility, Irving could not understand that the contract was a legal obligation and he could not understand the basic terms of the contract.
   b. Gary contracted to buy a VCR. Gary had been drinking, and he was intoxicated. However, Gary understood that he was making a contract and he understood the terms of the contract.
   c. Yin, 17 years old, contracted to buy a mountain bike.
   d. None of the above.

5. ____ Which contract is probably voidable due to fraud?
   a. Seller intentionally misrepresented to Buyer that a car being sold was a 1977 Mustang when it was actually a 1978 Mustang. However, Buyer did not rely on this misstatement because Buyer knew that the car was a 1978 Mustang.
   b. Kate contracted to sell her car to Sue. During negotiations, Kate told Sue that, in her opinion, the car was worth at least $2,000. In fact, the value of the car was only $1,500.
   c. Ali contracted to sell a store to Buyer. During negotiations, Ali intentionally lied to Buyer about the store's past profits stating that the profits were greater than they actually were, and Buyer reasonably relied on Ali's statement.
   d. a and c.

6. ____ Select the correct answer.

a. Robin and Tim, her son, are in a confidential relationship and Robin does whatever Tim says to do. Robin contracted to sell some stock to Tim for an unfairly low price because Tim demanded that she do so. In this case, this contract can be avoided due to undue influence.
b. Employer persuaded Ron to agree to an employment contract that paid a salary of $30,000, not $40,000 as Ron wanted. In this case, this contract can be avoided due to duress.
c. Rex threatened to injure Ina's child unless Ina lent $10,000 to Rex. Due to these threats, Ina felt compelled to agree to loan the money to Rex. This contract is voidable due to duress.
d. a and c.

7. ____ John goes out one afternoon to Tagrito's Cafe. He consumes too many margaritas, then leaves the cafe and heads to a local art gallery where he purchases an expensive painting. John takes the painting home, but when he sobers he decides to return the painting and get his money back. When he bought the painting he didn't notice the "FINAL SALE -- ABSOLUTELY NO RETURNS!" sign overhead. The store will not return John's money. Under these facts, is John entitled to rescind the purchase contract?

a. No, intoxication is never a defense to a contract.
b. No, because the sign said no returns.
c. Yes, because intoxicated persons can always rescind their contracts.
d. Yes, if he can prove that he was so intoxicated that he didn't understand the nature and consequences of his actions at the time he bought the painting.

8. ____ Suppose that you raise an extraordinarily attractive litter of beagle puppies. One of the puppies, a female, is especially lovely. When the puppy is 18 months old, a woman with a champion male beagle approaches you and asks whether your pup has been spayed or is capable of breeding. You tell her that the dog is in excellent health and will make a wonderful mother. The other beagle owner says "Oh, thank goodness! I want to breed Spike right away and your little female will be perfect." You sell the dog for $500. Two months later the buyer returns and she is furious: it seems that your female dog is sterile and cannot have puppies. You honestly but mistakenly believed that your dog was fertile. Under these facts:

a. The buyer may rescind the contract because of your fraudulent misrepresentation.
b. The buyer may rescind the contract because of your innocent misrepresentation.
c. The buyer may rescind the contract because of your duress.
d. The buyer cannot rescind the contract because you honestly believed that you were telling the truth.

9. ____ Carla takes care of her elderly aunt Fae. Carla is the only relative who lives close enough to help Fae and all of Fae's friends are deceased. Fae therefore relies completely on Carla to get her groceries, to take her to the doctor, and to otherwise care for her. Carla knows that Fae has $75,000 in savings. One day Carla told Fae: "Fae, you have got to give me the contractual power to take $50,000 from your savings or I'm going to leave you here all alone and no one will take care of you." Out of sheer terror and desperation, Fae signs a contract giving Carla the right to the money. Under these facts:

a. Carla has committed a fraud.
b. Carla has exerted undue influence on Fae.
c. Carla has committed a material misrepresentation.
d. Carla did nothing illegal.

10. ____ The majority of contracts that minors enter into are:
   a. Void.
   b. Voidable.
   c. Valid.
   d. Unaffirmed.

11. ____ In a case of fraud, the injured party must prove that:
   a. The other contracting party made a false statement of fact.
   b. The statement made by the other contracting party was fraudulent or material.
   c. The injured party justifiably relied on the statement.
   d. All of the above.

SHORT ESSAYS

1. Explain the difference between fraud and misrepresentation. What does an injured party need to show in each case? What is the key difference between the two? Under common law, what legal remedies are available to a party that suffers from either fraud or misrepresentation?

2. Explain the concept of ratification. Give two examples of how a party may ratify a contract.

CASE PROBLEMS

1. Lon is selling his home that has a severely damaged foundation. This damage is obvious. The home also has asbestos inside its walls, but this condition cannot be discovered without tearing the walls apart.
   a. Under traditional rules, does Lon have a duty to volunteer information to prospective buyers regarding the obviously damaged foundation?
   b. Can Lon plaster over the damaged foundation in order to hide the damage?
   c. Under modern rules, does Lon have a duty to disclose the asbestos to prospective buyers?

2. Laredo Ranch sold a parcel of land to Dynamic Developers. Prior to the sale, the parties retained Lawrence to do a survey and determine how many acres were in the parcel. Lawrence informed the parties that the parcel contained 100 acres. Unknown to the parties, the parcel actually contained only 75 acres. Laredo and Dynamic computed the contract price based on 100 acres.
   a. Can Dynamic rescind this contract based on mistake?
   b. What elements must Dynamic prove to establish this defense?

3. Seller contracted to sell an airplane to Buyer. Seller intentionally misrepresented to Buyer that the plane did not have any mechanical problems. In fact, the plane had serious defects that rendered the plane unsafe to operate. Buyer was unaware of these defects, and Buyer was induced into making this contract due to Buyer's reliance on Seller's misrepresentation.
   a. Did Seller commit fraud?
   b. Is the contract between Seller and Buyer voidable?
   c. What remedies can Buyer request under the UCC in this case?

CHAPTER FOURTEEN
WRITTEN CONTRACTS

CHAPTER OUTLINE

I. Statute of Frauds or Five Contracts That Must Be in Writing
   A. Contracts for an Interest in Land
   B. Contracts that Cannot be Performed Within One Year
   C. Contracts Involving a Promise to Pay the Debt of Another
   D. Contracts Involving a Promise Made by the Executor of an Estate
   E. Contracts Involving a Promise Made in Consideration of Marriage

II. What Written Contracts Must Contain
   A. Signature
   B. Reasonable Certainty of Terms

III. Sale of Goods under the U.C.C.
   A. UCC 2-201 (1) - The Basic Rule
   B. UCC 2-201 (2) - The Merchant's Exception
   C. UCC 2-201 (3) - Special Circumstances

IV. Parol Evidence
   A. Exception: An Incomplete or Ambiguous Contract
   B. Misrepresentation or Duress

WHAT YOU SHOULD KNOW

After reading this chapter you should understand:

what a statute of frauds is and its historical origins;

what kinds of contracts must be in writing;

exceptions to the general rule concerning written contracts;

the requirements for a writing that are necessary to satisfy the statute of frauds;

how the UCC deals with the requirement that some contracts be in writing;

exceptions to the basic UCC rule on written contracts;

what the parol evidence rule is; and

when courts will permit parol evidence to be introduced.

REVIEW OF TERMS AND PHRASES

MATCHING EXERCISE

Select the term or phrase that best matches a statement or definition stated below. Each term or phrase is the best match for only one statement or definition.

Terms and Phrases

a. Ambiguous term
b. Collateral promise
c. Integration clause
d. Leading object rule
e. Parol evidence
f. Parol evidence rule
g. Statute of frauds

Statements and Definitions

g 1. Rule that requires a contract to be evidenced by a sufficient writing in order to be enforceable.

f 2. Rule that prohibits altering a final, complete written contract by using parol evidence.

c 3. Contractual term stating that the written contract is the entire agreement of the parties.

b 4. Gratuitous promise to pay the debt of another.

e 5. Oral or written agreements or statements made prior to the execution of a written contract.

a 6. Contractual term that may reasonably have more than one meaning.

d 7. Rule which holds that a promise to pay the debt of another does not need to be in writing if the promise to pay is primarily intended to benefit the person making the promise.

REVIEW OF CONCEPTS

COMPLETION EXERCISE

1. Identify six types of contracts that must be in writing.

a. ______________________________.

b. ______________________________.

c. ______________________________.

d. ______________________________.

e. ______________________________.

f. ______________________________.

TRUE-FALSE QUESTIONS

Circle **T** (true) or **F** (false)

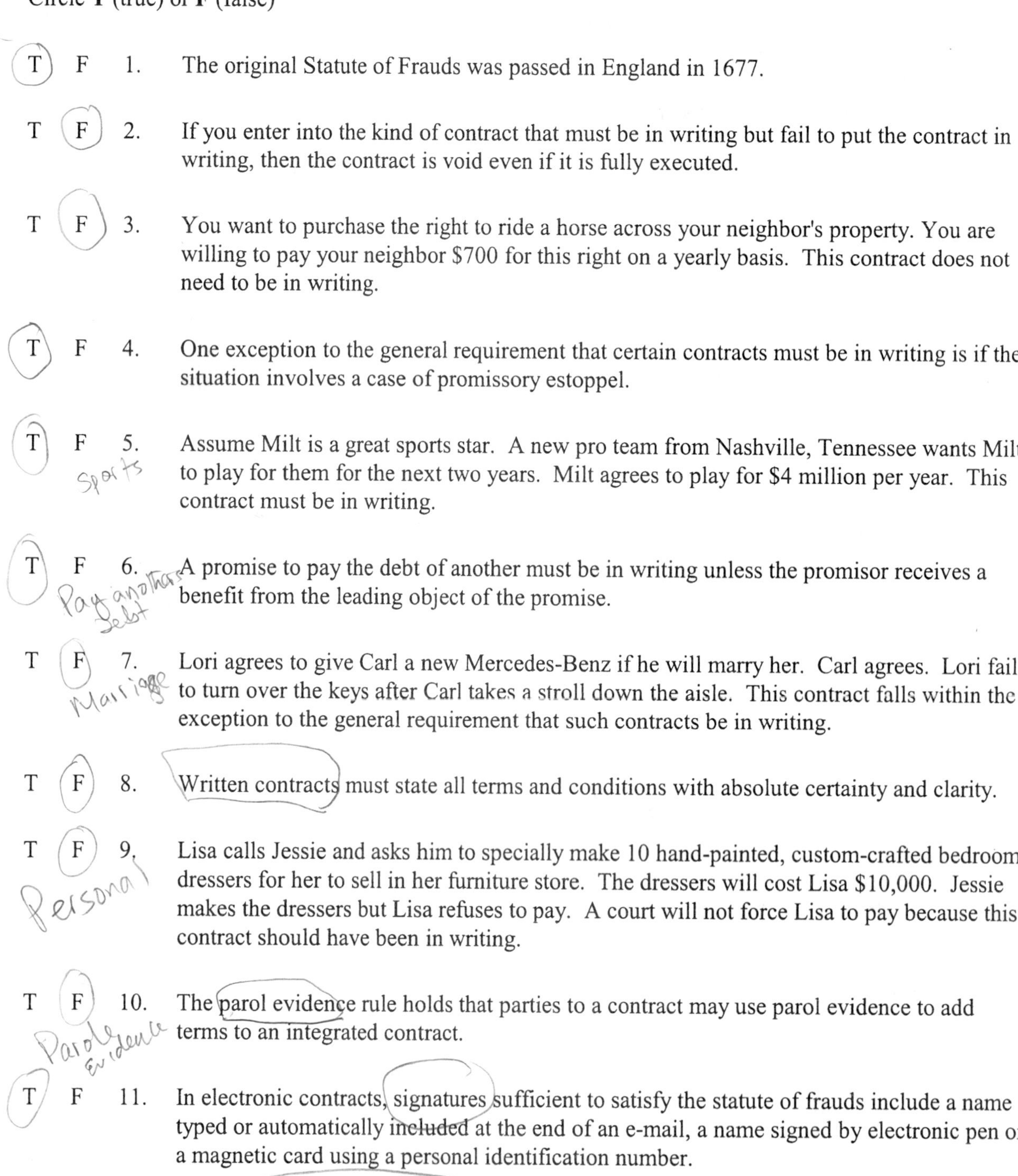

T F 1. The original Statute of Frauds was passed in England in 1677.

T F 2. If you enter into the kind of contract that must be in writing but fail to put the contract in writing, then the contract is void even if it is fully executed.

T F 3. You want to purchase the right to ride a horse across your neighbor's property. You are willing to pay your neighbor $700 for this right on a yearly basis. This contract does not need to be in writing.

T F 4. One exception to the general requirement that certain contracts must be in writing is if the situation involves a case of promissory estoppel.

T F 5. Assume Milt is a great sports star. A new pro team from Nashville, Tennessee wants Milt to play for them for the next two years. Milt agrees to play for $4 million per year. This contract must be in writing.

T F 6. A promise to pay the debt of another must be in writing unless the promisor receives a benefit from the leading object of the promise.

T F 7. Lori agrees to give Carl a new Mercedes-Benz if he will marry her. Carl agrees. Lori fails to turn over the keys after Carl takes a stroll down the aisle. This contract falls within the exception to the general requirement that such contracts be in writing.

T F 8. Written contracts must state all terms and conditions with absolute certainty and clarity.

T F 9. Lisa calls Jessie and asks him to specially make 10 hand-painted, custom-crafted bedroom dressers for her to sell in her furniture store. The dressers will cost Lisa $10,000. Jessie makes the dressers but Lisa refuses to pay. A court will not force Lisa to pay because this contract should have been in writing.

T F 10. The parol evidence rule holds that parties to a contract may use parol evidence to add terms to an integrated contract.

T F 11. In electronic contracts, signatures sufficient to satisfy the statute of frauds include a name typed or automatically included at the end of an e-mail, a name signed by electronic pen or a magnetic card using a personal identification number.

T F 12. The Uniform Electronic Transaction Act (UETA), which has been enacted by many states, provides that a contract or signature cannot be denied merely because it is in an electronic format.

MULTIPLE CHOICE QUESTIONS

1.____ On March 1, Julie orally contracted to work for Employer from April 1 through March 30 of the following year. Under these facts:

a. The contract violates the statute of frauds because it cannot be performed within one year from the date the contract was made.
b. The contract violates the statute of frauds because all employment contracts must be written.
c. The contract does not violate the statute of frauds because it can be performed within one year from when the work begins.
d. The contract does not violate the statute of frauds because it may be terminated at any time due to a party's breach.

2.____ Which of the following oral contracts is unenforceable?

a. Biff orally contracts to sell an apartment house to Marty.
b. Sue orally contracts to grant Finance Co. a mortgage on Sue's home.
c. Lin orally contracts to sell some land to Ashley
d. All of the above.

3.____ Phil orally contracts to sell land to Buyer. Buyer takes possession of the land, and Buyer makes valuable improvements, the value of which is hard to determine. This contract is:

a. Enforceable because the statute of frauds does not apply to land sale contracts.
b. Enforceable due to Buyer's part performance.
c. Voidable and cannot be enforced because the contract violates the statute of frauds.
d. Void and cannot be enforced because the contract violates the statute of frauds.

4.____ Which oral promise violates the statute of frauds?

a. Pete promises Lender that, if Lender loans $5,000 to Pete's father and Pete's father does not repay the loan, then Pete will repay the loan.
b. Personal representative promises Attorney that an estate will pay Attorney $100 per hour for services rendered to the estate.
c. Personal representative promises Attorney that the personal representative will pay Attorney $100 per hour for services rendered to the estate.
d. a and c.

5.____ Which oral contract violates the statute of frauds?

a. Dad and Jose make an oral contract whereby Dad promises to make Jose general manager of a company in exchange for Jose's promise to marry Dad's daughter.
b. Tom orally contracts to buy a TV for $400.
c. Osa orally contracts to buy a car for $10,000.
d. a and c.

6. 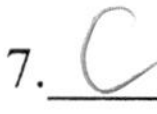 Which of the following oral contracts is unenforceable?

a. Bubba orally contracts with Madison to lease Madison's apartment for three years.
b. Lewis orally contracts to hire Charlie at will, i.e., for an unstated period of time.
c. Linda orally rents an apartment to Andy for three months.
d. All of the above.

7.  Leonard agreed to sell his boat to Jennifer for $5,000. Leonard wrote a letter stating, "I agree to sell my boat to you. You may take possession of the craft on June 1." Leonard and Jennifer signed the letter. Leonard delivered the boat to Jennifer as promised, but Jennifer refused to pay. Under these facts:

a. The contract is unenforceable because the writing does not state the contract price.
b. The contract is unenforceable because the writing does not state any terms regarding warranties.
c. The contract is enforceable because the writing satisfies the UCC statute of frauds.
d. The contract is enforceable because this type of contract need not be in writing.

8. 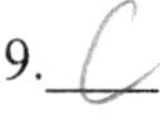 Wilson owns property close to the beach but his land does not have direct access to the beach. Wilson's neighbor, Greta, owns property that does have access to the beach. Wilson orally agrees to pay Greta $10,000 for the right to lay a 2-foot wide brick path from the edge of his property, across her land, and to the beach. Wilson pays the $10,000. After one year, Greta pulls up the path and tells Wilson that he can no longer go across her land. Under these facts:

a. The agreement is unenforceable because it must be in writing.
b. The agreement is unenforceable because it is illegal.
c. The agreement is enforceable because it is not required to be in writing.
d. The agreement is enforceable because Greta acted fraudulently.

9. c Suppose you want to take out a loan to help defray some of your college costs. You get your friend Gabriella to go with you to the loan office. Gabriella tells the loan officer that if you fail to repay the loan, she will pay it for you. The officer lends you $5,000. Eight months later you fail to make your loan payments and a loan officer demands payment from Gabriella. Under these facts:

a. Gabriella must pay because promises to pay the debt of another must be honored.
b. Gabriella must pay based on leading object exception.
c. Gabriella need not pay based on the one-year rule.
d. Gabriella need not pay because her promise wasn't in writing.

10. b Evia owns a sporting goods store. She calls Misha and offers to buy 15 top-quality stationary bicycles from him for $7,500. Misha agrees to sell the bicycles to Evia. Within two weeks Misha has sent Evia 10 of the bicycles. Evia changes her mind, however, and refuses to pay for any of the bicycles. Under these facts:

a. Evia does not have to pay for any of the bicycles because the contract was not in writing.
b. Evia must pay for the 10 bicycles that have been delivered.
c. Evia must pay for all 15 bicycles.
d. Evia must pay for all 15 bicycles plus punitive damages.

Delivery of goods

11. C Emmy manufactures textiles. Juan calls Emmy and orders $5,000 of a printed cotton cloth. Emmy agrees to send the cloth immediately, and Juan will pay in 30 days. That same day, Emmy faxes a sales receipt to Juan who receives it. The fax states what Juan is buying, the price, and payment terms. Emmy sends the cloth, but 30 days later Juan refuses to pay. Juan claims that this contract must have been in writing and, since there was no writing, the contract is unenforceable. Under these facts:

a. Juan is correct and the contract is unenforceable.
b. Juan is correct, but he should base his claim on the promissory estoppel doctrine.
c. Juan will lose based on UCC 2-201 (1). A contract for sale of goods $500 unenforceable unless in writing
d. Juan will lose based on UCC 2-201 (2).

12. a If a merchant sells goods worth $1,500, this sale must be in writing based on:

a. UCC 2-201.
b. UCC 3-314.
c. UCC 3-212.
d. The common law.

SHORT ESSAYS

1. Under the common law, what must a written contract contain in order to be enforceable? Analyze why the law establishes these requirements.

2. The UCC has several provisions dealing with writing requirements for contracts. What is the basic rule concerning written contracts made under the UCC? What are the exceptions to the rule? What is the rationale for both the basic rule and the exceptions?

CASE PROBLEMS

Answer the following case problems, explaining your answers.

1. Jim advertised a parcel of land for sale and Edna orally made a generous cash purchase offer, which Jim orally accepted. Eager to seal the deal and intending to evidence the transaction, Jim grabbed a piece of paper and wrote down his name as seller, Edna's name as buyer, a description of the land, and the cash purchase price, and scratched his initial "J" at the bottom. Edna took this paper with her as she left. After Edna left, Jim received a better offer and he told Edna that he would not sell the land to her.

   a. Does the contract between Jim and Edna come within the statute of frauds?
   b. If so, does the piece of paper satisfy the requirements of the statute of frauds?
   c. Does Edna have an enforceable contract against Jim?

2. Bob orally told his good friend and employee, Steve, "You have a job at my company for the rest of your life." Steve is 26 years old. The next month, Bob fired Steve and hired someone more qualified. Does this contract violate the statute of frauds?

CHAPTER FIFTEEN
THIRD PARTIES

CHAPTER OUTLINE

I. Third Party Beneficiary

II. Assignment and Delegation

   A. Assignment of Rights

   B. Delegation of Duties

WHAT YOU SHOULD KNOW

After reading this chapter you should understand:

what a third party beneficiary is;

the difference between incidental, creditor, and donee beneficiaries;

which beneficiaries may enforce contracts;

what an assignment is;

the legal limits placed on assignments;

how the UCC deals with assignments;

what a delegation is;

the legal limits placed on delegations; and

what a novation is.

REVIEW OF TERMS AND PHRASES

MATCHING EXERCISE

Select the term or phrase that best matches a statement or definition stated below. Each term or phrase is the best match for only one statement or definition.

Terms and Phrases

a. Assignee
b. Assignment
c. Assignor
d. Delegation
e. Incidental beneficiary
f. Obligor
g. Promisee
h. Promisor
i. Third-party beneficiary
j. Third-party beneficiary contract

Statements and Definitions

_a_ 1. Third party to whom a contract right is assigned.

_e_ 2. In general, any third party that may directly or indirectly benefit from a contract even though the contracting parties did not intend to contract for the benefit of the third party.

_b_ 3. Transfer of a contract right to a third party.

_d_ 4. Transfer of contract duties to a third party.

_i_ 5. Third party whom contracting parties intend to directly benefit by entering into a contract.

_f_ 6. Contracting party who has an obligation to perform a duty.

_j_ 7. Contract made by contracting parties with the intent to directly benefit a third party.

_h_ 8. Person who makes a promise.

_c_ 9. Contracting party who assigns a contract right to a third party.

_g_ 10. Person to whom a promise is made.

COMPLETION EXERCISE

Fill in the blanks with the words that most accurately complete each statement. Answers may or may not include terms used in the matching exercise. A term cannot be used to complete more than one statement.

1. The presence or absence of an _Intent_ to directly benefit a third party under a contract is a primary factor in deciding whether the third party is an intended or incidental beneficiary under the contract.

2. A Novation ________________ is a third party beneficiary to whom one of the contracting parties intends to bestow a benefit as a gift.

3. A donee beneficiary ________ clause generally shields an assignee from defenses that the obligor may try to assert in order to avoid performance of an obligation.

4. When assigning rights, an assignor creates three implied Warranties.

5. Identify three situations when an assignment may be prohibited:

   a. when assigment would Substantially change the Obligors contractual Rights or Duties

   b. when An Assigment is Forbidden law or Public Policy.

   c. when An " " validly forbidden by the Contract.

REVIEW OF CONCEPTS

TRUE-FALSE QUESTIONS

Circle **T** (true) or **F** (false)

T F 1. A third party beneficiary is a person who is a party to a contract.

T F 2. The intent of the parties to a contract is vital in determining whether or not a third party beneficiary will be able to enforce the contract.

T F 3. Incidental beneficiaries may always enforce contracts under the positive benefits rule.

T F 4. As a general rule, donee beneficiaries may enforce contracts if the parties to the contract intended to benefit the donee.

T F 5. By using vague or ambiguous language parties to a contract may inadvertently create contract rights in third parties.

T F 6. When a contracting party transfers rights to a third party this is known as a delegation.

T F 7. Any contractual right to a personal service may be assigned.

T F 8. Some contractual rights may not be assigned based on public-policy considerations.

T F 9. As a general rule, gratuitous assignments are irrevocable if written.

T F 10. Once a party delegates his or her duties under a contract, the party is relieved of liability to perform the contract.

MULTIPLE CHOICE QUESTIONS

1. a Dell owed Stark $9,000. As the result of an unrelated transaction, Stark owed Ball that same amount. The three parties signed an agreement that Dell would pay Ball instead of Stark, and Stark would be discharged from all liability. The agreement among the parties is best described as a:
   a. Novation.
   b. Accord and satisfaction.
   c. Assignment.
   d. Delegation of duties.

2. c Dalton and Kim own a car wash business together. One day while driving to work Kim is nearly hit head-on by a reckless driver. This near miss causes Kim to worry about what would happen to her son Sean, age 30, if she were to be die. At work that day, Kim asks Dalton to enter into a new contract, which makes Sean vice president of the company in case she dies while he is a minor. Dalton agrees and the two enter into the contract. In this case Sean is a:
   a. Third party obligee.
   b. Third party creditor.
   c. Third party beneficiary.
   d. Party to the contract.

3. c Assume the same facts as question No. 2 above with the additional fact that Kim dies two months later while the contract is still in effect. Under these facts, can Sean enforce the contract between Dalton and Kim?
   a. No, because Sean is an incidental beneficiary.
   b. No, because Sean is a creditor beneficiary.
   c. Yes, because Sean is a donee beneficiary.
   d. Yes, because Sean is a party to the contract.

4. d Select the third party who is a third-party beneficiary entitled to enforce the contract in question.
   a. Loan Co. lent Alice $500 to pay bills. The loan contract states that the parties do not intend for any of Alice's creditors to be third-party beneficiaries. Third party is a creditor of Alice.
   b. Ned contracted with Rock Insurance Co. whereby the insurance company agreed to pay $10,000 to Ned's sister (third party) upon Ned's death.
   c. Samantha contracts to sell her car to Tom for $1,000. The contract requires Tom to pay the $1,000 directly to Last Chance Bank (third party) to whom Samantha owes $1,000.
   d. b and c.

5. c Art sold a truck to Lucky on credit for $20,000. Art breached the contract with Lucky, and Lucky can claim a $5,000 set-off against Art. Art validly assigned to Stella all of Art's rights to receive money from Lucky. Lucky was informed of the assignment and was told to pay Stella. Lucky refuses to pay anything. Under these facts, how much can Stella collect from Lucky?
   a. $0.
   b. $5,000.
   c. $15,000.
   d. $20,000.

6. __a__ Sally lives in the Oak Ridge neighborhood in Copper City. The city council of Copper City contracted with Ace Sewer Corp. to build a new sewer system in Sally's neighborhood. This new sewer system would likely add to the value of Sally's property. The city, however, had the contractual right to terminate the contract if the final price for the system was too much. Ultimately, the city council exercised this right and terminated the contract because the final price tag for the new sewer system proved to be too expensive. Sally sues the city for the lost profits she would have made if the city had gone forward with the contract. Under these facts:

a. Sally will lose because she is an incidental beneficiary.
b. Sally will lose because she is a creditor beneficiary.
c. Sally will lose because she is a donee beneficiary.
d. Sally will win because she would be benefited by the contract.

7. __d__ You buy a new motorcycle from a dealer. You take out a bank loan to buy the motorcycle and you use the motorcycle as collateral for the loan. The agreement between you and the bank is that the bank may take and sell your motorcycle if you default on your loan payments. Under these facts, the bank has a:

a. Indebted interest in the motorcycle.
b. Debtor's interest in the motorcycle.
c. Delegation interest in the motorcycle.
d. Security interest in the motorcycle.

8. __b__ Mary Lou paints beautiful portraits in both oil and pastels. You have seen and admired her work for several years. You contact Mary Lou and agree to pay her $2,000 to do a portrait of your beloved pet cat in oils. Mary Lou agrees. However, after sitting with the cat for several hours she decides you own the nastiest cat in the world and she arranges for her friend Delia to paint Fluffy instead. Under these facts:

a. Mary Lou may not delegate her duty because the law forbids delegations of duties.
b. Mary Lou may not delegate her duty because it is for a personal service.
c. Mary Lou may not delegate her duty because delegations of duties can never be made without first obtaining the consent of the other contracting party.
d. Mary Lou may delegate her duty.

9. __d__ Cody owed Don $500. Don orally told Cody and Sylvia: "I transfer to Sylvia my right to be repaid the $500; Cody pay Sylvia the $500." Sylvia did not give Don anything in exchange for Don's right to receive this money. Under these facts:

a. The assignment by Don is invalid because assignments are illegal.
b. The assignment by Don is invalid because the assignment is oral.
c. The assignment by Don is invalid because Sylvia did not give any consideration.
d. The assignment by Don to Sylvia is valid.

10. __a__ Which right can be assigned without the consent of the other contracting party? (The agreements in question do not expressly prohibit assignments.)
   a. Donna agreed to pay $100 to Bret. Bret wants to assign the right to receive this money.
   b. Painter agreed to paint a portrait of Keri, and Painter guaranteed personal satisfaction. Keri wants to assign to her sister the right to have the portrait painted to her sister's personal satisfaction.
   c. D&D agreed to lend $500 to Fred. Fred wants to assign to Dee the right to borrow the $500.
   d. Central Airlines has an employment contract with Captain Buck, a pilot. Central Airlines wants to assign its right to Captain Buck's services to Air Asia, another airline.

11. __b__ When a contracting party transfers his or her duties under a contract to a third party this is known as a:
   a. Transformation.
   b. Delegation.
   c. Assignment.
   d. Obligation.

12. __d__ The general rule concerning the assignment of rights is that:
   a. Public policy forbids the assignment of rights.
   b. Statutory law prohibits the assignment of rights.
   c. Most rights are nonassignable.
   d. Most rights are assignable.

SHORT ESSAY

Explain the difference between donee, creditor, and incidental beneficiaries. Which of these beneficiaries may enforce contracts and why?

CASE PROBLEMS

Answer the following problems, briefly explaining your answers.

1. Erecto Construction Co. contracted to build an office building for Owner. Without Owner's consent, Erecto delegated its duty to do the excavation work to Gopher Inc., a subcontractor. The excavation work is standard, nonpersonal work that does not require any special skill. Gopher failed to do the work properly.
   a. Was Erecto legally entitled to delegate its duty to do the excavation work to Gopher without first obtaining Owner's consent? Yes he can Delegate
   b. Is Erecto liable to Owner because Gopher failed to properly do the work? Yes

2. Brent Auto Trades (BAT) sold Laurie a personal car on credit. The contract contained a standard waiver of defense clause, whereby Laurie agreed not to assert any defenses against an assignee of the contract. BAT assigned its rights under the contract to Third Bank. As it turns out, the car is defective and Laurie does not want to pay.
   a. Was the assignment to Third Bank valid? Yes (see 246)
   b. Can Laurie assert her defense of breach of contract against Last Bank in order to avoid paying for the car? Yes (see pg 246)

CHAPTER SIXTEEN
PERFORMANCE AND DISCHARGE

CHAPTER OUTLINE

I. Conditions

  A. How Conditions are Created

  B. Types of Conditions

II. Performance

  A. Strict Performance and Substantial Performance

  B. Personal Satisfaction Contracts

  C. Good Faith

  D. Time of the Essence Clauses

III. Breach

IV. Impossibility

  A. True Impossibility

  B. Commercial Impracticability and Frustration of Purpose

WHAT YOU SHOULD KNOW

After reading this chapter you should understand:

what conditions to contracts are and how they are created;

different kinds of conditions to contracts;

what strict and substantial performance mean;

what personal satisfaction contracts are;

what the common law and UCC require in terms of good faith;

what "time of the essence" clauses mean;

what it means to breach a contract and the kinds of breaches;

what the impossibility doctrine means; and

the difference between true impossibility, commercial impracticability, and frustration of purpose.

REVIEW OF TERMS AND PHRASES

MATCHING EXERCISE

Select the term or phrase that best matches a statement or definition stated below. Each term or phrase is the best match for only one statement or definition.

Terms and Phrases

a. Commercial impracticability	d. Frustration of purpose	g. Substantial performance
b. Condition	e. Material breach	h. Time is of the essence
c. Discharge	f. Rescission	i. True impossibility

Statements and Definitions

i 1. Doctrine discharging a contract because an unforeseen event has made performance impossible.

c 2. Extinguishment of a contract resulting from performance, actions of parties, or operation of law.

d 3. Doctrine discharging a contract because its value to at least one party has been destroyed by an unforeseen event.

g 4. Doctrine authorizing a party to enforce a contract if the party has almost completely performed his or her contractual obligations.

b 5. Event, the occurrence or nonoccurrence of which, may discharge a contract.

a 6. Doctrine discharging a contract because an unforeseen event has made performance by one or both parties unreasonably expensive or burdensome.

f 7. Termination of a contract and return of the parties to the position they were in prior to contracting.

e 8. Breach of contract that substantially harms one party and deprives that party of what he or she was to receive under the contract.

h 9. Timely performance is vital; timely performance is required to discharge a contractual duty.

COMPLETION EXERCISE

Fill in the blanks with the words that most accurately complete each statement. Answers may or may not include terms used in the matching exercise. A term cannot be used to complete more than one statement.

1. Concurrent Coditions are events that must occur or be performed at the same time.

2. An event that must occur prior to the time that a contracting party must perform is called a Codition Precedent.

3. An event that must occur after a duty of performance has arisen or else the duty is discharged is called a Condition Subsequent.

4. Strict Performance is precise or perfect performance in contrast to Substantial Performance, which is performance that delivers most of what the other party bargained for with minor defects.

REVIEW OF CONCEPTS

TRUE-FALSE QUESTIONS

Circle **T** (true) or **F** (false)

T F 1. Parties are discharged from contracts when they have performed the majority of their duties under the contract.

T F 2. In cases of commercial impracticability a party may be discharged from a contract even though the party has not performed his or her obligations.

T F 3. Kyla agrees to represent Bubba in a lawsuit, but only if he brings his case to her within the next two weeks (she's a very busy lawyer). Bubba is immediately obligated to bring his case to Kyla.

T F 4. Pia promises to pay Ellen $2,500 per month if she attracts two new clients a month to Pia's advertising agency. This is an example of a condition subsequent.

T F 5. The reason why distinguishing between conditions precedent and subsequent is important is because you can tell who has the burden of proof based on the kind of condition that exists.

T F 6. In general, a party to a contract is not required to strictly perform the contract unless the contract expressly demands such performance and the demand is reasonable.

T F 7. Jeff contracts with Leila to build her a set of bookcases. Leila will pay Jeff $1,200 for the bookcases and she wants them in two months. At the end of the two months Jeff has picked out the wood for the job. In this case Jeff has substantially performed.

T F 8. Under both the common law and the UCC, parties to contracts have positive obligations to deal with each other on a basis of good faith and fair dealing.

T F 9. An anticipatory breach occurs after a party partially performs, then informs the other party to the contract that additional performance will take place late.

T F 10. Frank contracts to sell Bill his prize sow, Bessie. Bill is going to pay a whopping $1,000 for the porky beauty. Frank agrees to deliver Bessie on Thursday morning. On Wednesday evening a tornado hits Frank's farm and Bessie is killed. This contract is discharged based on material breach.

MULTIPLE CHOICE QUESTIONS

1. c William, a CPA, contracted to provide accounting services for Tyler. William promised to perform the work to Tyler's personal satisfaction. William rendered the required services. A reasonable person in Tyler's position would be satisfied with the services, but Tyler is not. Under these facts:
   a. Tyler's contractual duties are discharged because he is dissatisfied with William's services.
   b. Tyler's contractual duties are discharged because personal satisfaction contracts are illegal.
   c. Tyler's contractual duties are not discharged because a reasonable person would be satisfied with William's services.
   d. a and b.

2. c Which contract would be discharged under the doctrine of impossibility?
   a. Ventricle Corp. contracted to sell a heart medicine to Aorta. The contract was legal when made. Prior to performance, the FDA unforeseeably declared sale of the medicine illegal.
   b. Acme contracted to sell a standard Yomo stereo to Bob. Prior to performance, a fire destroyed Acme's inventory of stereos. Acme can obtain a replacement Yomo stereo elsewhere, but doing so will diminish Acme's profits on the contract.
   c. Larry contracted to buy a house. Prior to either party performing, Larry died.
   d. All of the above.

3. a Juan contracted to sell coffee beans to the Wide-Eye Café each week. Delivery was required to be made every Friday. One week, Juan failed to deliver the beans until Saturday, a minor breach of contract. Under these facts:
   a. Wide-Eye Café is not discharged due to Juan's breach.
   b. Wide-Eye Café is discharged due to Juan's breach.
   c. Wide-Eye Café is discharged due to Juan's breach if Wide-Eye Café lost any sales because of the late delivery.
   d. b and c.

4. b Penelope agreed to reupholster Flynn's couch and chair by May 1. The contract does not state that time is of the essence, and timely performance is not vital to this contract. Penelope completed the work on May 7, a reasonable time under the circumstances. Under these facts:
   a. Time is not of the essence in this contract. Penelope cannot enforce the contract.
   b. Time is not of the essence in this contract. Penelope can enforce the contract.
   c. Time is of the essence in this contract. Penelope cannot enforce the contract.
   d. Time is of the essence in this contract. Penelope can enforce the contract.

5. b JR contracted to renovate an historical home for June for $50,000. The renovations were completed as required, except JR unintentionally failed to refinish one oak banister. It will cost $250 to have someone else do this refinishing. Under these facts, JR is entitled to recover:
   a. $0. JR failed to completely perform his duties. Thus, JR cannot enforce the contract.
   b. $49,750. JR substantially performed his duties. Thus, JR can enforce the contract. June must pay the contract price, less damages caused by JR's imperfect performance.
   c. $50,000. JR substantially performed his duties. Thus, JR is entitled to the full contract price.
   d. Only such amount, if any, that June may decide to pay JR.

6._c_ Silas contracts with Elmer to buy a used tractor. Elmer agrees to sell the tractor to Silas for $750. Silas turns over the cash and Elmer turns over the tractor. This is an example of:

a. Discharge by breach
b. Discharge by impossibility.
c. Discharge by full performance.
d. Discharge by substantial performance.

7._b_ Mark enters into a contract with old Mr. Jefferson. The contract states that if Mr. Jefferson is unable to walk without the aid of a walker, Mark will come to his house five times a week to do chores. Mr. Jefferson will pay Mark $200 per week for this service. This is an example of:

a. A novation.
b. A condition.
c. A discharge.
d. A performance.

8._d_ John contracts with Evangeline to mow her yard all summer long, once a week for $30 each cut. John is scheduled to start this job on May 1. On February 20, he calls Evangeline to tell her that he has decided to backpack through Borneo the remainder of the year and, therefore, he will not mow her lawn. This is an example of:

a. A strict performance.
b. A substantial performance.
c. A material breach.
d. An anticipatory breach.

9._d_ Megan contracts with Aristide to put a new bathroom into his house. The work includes demolishing the existing bathroom, replacing all of the fixtures and plumbing, installing new drywall, and repainting the room. The contract price was $15,000. By the time for completion of the contract work, Aristide had only partially demolished the existing bathroom. When Aristide proceeded to walk off the job, Megan had to hire another contractor to finish the work and pay the replacement contractor $17,000 for his work. Under these facts:

a. Megan must pay Aristide for the value of his demolition work.
b. Megan must pay Aristide the $15,000 contract price.
c. Aristide must pay $0 to Megan.
d. Aristide must pay $2,000 to Megan.

10._a_ Same facts as question No. 9 above. Under these facts:

a. Megan was discharged from the contract with Aristide due to his material breach of contract.
b. Megan was discharged from the contract with Aristide due to his immaterial breach of contract.
c. Megan was discharged from the contract with Aristide because of the doctrine of impossibility.
d. Megan was not discharged from the contract with Aristide because he substantially performed the contract.

11. <u>d</u> Gina has a beautiful voice. Eric wants Gina to sing at his parent's 50th wedding anniversary. Gina and Eric enter into a contract the terms of which are that Gina will sing for four hours and Eric will pay her $400. In a terrible turn of events Gina is killed when a tractor-trailer runs into her car while she is on her way to the anniversary party. Two weeks later Gina's estate contacts Eric, wanting the $400 he promised to pay. Under these facts:

a. The contract was discharged by true impossibility.
b. The contract was discharged by full performance.
c. The contract was discharged by commercial impracticability.
d. The contract was discharged by accord and satisfaction.

SHORT ESSAY

Explain what is meant by a condition to a contract. How are conditions created? What kinds of conditions exist and how do they affect contracting parties? Provide an example of a contract with a condition.

Event that must occur

CASE PROBLEMS

Answer the following case problems, explaining your answers.

1. Theo contracted to build storage shelving for Casey. The shelving is not unique, and any carpenter can perform the work. While Theo was working on the shelving, he severely cut his hand and he cannot complete the work.
   Is the contract discharged under the doctrine of impossibility?

2. Leonardo, a sculptor, contracted with Albert, an eccentric millionaire, to cast a bronze sculpture of Albert and to do so to Albert's personal satisfaction. Albert told Leonardo how much the sculpture meant to him. The sculpture was a masterpiece; it received world acclaim. However, Albert is not pleased with the sculpture.
   Must Albert accept the sculpture and pay for it?

3. Mark contracted to purchase a business that drills for natural gas. After the parties entered into this contract, the price for natural gas declined significantly, making it unprofitable to operate the business. It is well known in the natural gas industry that prices can rise and fall sharply and unpredictably, although prices had never before fallen this low.
   Is this contract discharged under the doctrine of impossibility or commercial frustration?

CHAPTER SEVENTEEN
REMEDIES

CHAPTER OUTLINE

I. Expectation Interests
   - A. Compensatory Damages
   - B. Consequential Damages
   - C. Incidental Damages
   - D. Sale of Goods

II. Reliance Interests
   - A. Reliance Damages and Promissory Estoppel
   - B. Law and Equity

III. Restitution Interests
   - A. Restitution and Valid Contracts
   - B. Restitution and Quasi-Contract

IV. Other Equitable Interests
   - A. Specific Performance
   - B. Injunction
   - C. Reformation

V. Special Issues of Damages
   - A. Mitigation of Damages
   - B. Nominal Damages
   - C. Liquidated Damages
   - D. Punitive Damages

WHAT YOU SHOULD KNOW

After reading this chapter you should understand:

what an expectation interest is;

the kinds of damages a party may seek when expectation interests have been harmed;

how the UCC treats expectation interests;

what a reliance interest is;

the kinds of damages a party may seek when reliance interests have been damaged;

what a restitution interest is;

how restitution relates to fraud, misrepresentation, duress, and undue influence;

the different kinds of equitable interests;

when court may award specific performance or an injunction;

when a court will reform a contract;

what a duty to mitigate means;

what liquidated damages are and the limits on recovering such damages; and

what punitive damages are.

REVIEW OF TERMS AND PHRASES

MATCHING EXERCISE

Select the term or phrase that best matches a statement or definition stated below. Each term or phrase is the best match for only one statement or definition.

Terms and Phrases

a. Compensatory damages
b. Consequential damages
c. Incidental damages
d. Injunction
e. Liquidated damages
f. Mitigation of damages
g. Nominal damages
h. Punitive damages
i. Reformation
j. Specific performance

Statements and Definitions

__a__ 1. Loss that is the natural result of a breach.

__h__ 2. Damages awarded to punish a party.

__g__ 3. Token damages that are awarded when a party proves a breach of contract, but the party cannot prove any actual loss.

__e__ 4. Contractually agreed-upon damages to be paid if a party breaches a contract.

__f__ 5. Doctrine prohibiting recovery of damages that a party can reasonably avoid.

__i__ 6. Equitable remedy whereby a court rewrites a contract to reflect the true understanding of the parties.

__b__ 7. Loss occurring because of the particular circumstances of the injured party.

__c__ 8. Relatively minor, out-of-pocket expenses a contracting party incurs as a result of the other party's breach of contract.

__d__ 9. Court order directing a party to do or not to do something.

__j__ 10. Equitable remedy requiring performance of a contract.

COMPLETION EXERCISE

Fill in the blanks with the words that most accurately complete each statement.

1. A ________________ ____ ______________ occurs when a party wrongfully fails to perform a contractual duty.

2. When one contracting party breaches a contract, the other party generally has a duty to ______________ its losses if it can reasonably do so.

3. An ______________ is a legal right in something.

4. The ______________ ______________ of a party refers to what a party anticipated receiving from performance of a contract.

5. The ______________ ______________ of a party refers to what a party spent in anticipation that a contract would be properly performed.

REVIEW OF CONCEPTS

TRUE-FALSE QUESTIONS

Circle **T** (true) or **F** (false)

T F 1. In breach of contract cases, courts focus on compensating the injured parties rather than punishing the breaching parties.

T F 2. Expectation damages include compensatory, consequential, and punitive damages.

T F 3. Janice accidentally backs her car into Michelle's car. In order to prove her compensatory damages, Michelle must be able to prove with reasonable certainty what it will cost her to repair her damaged car.

T F 4. Like compensatory damages, consequential damages may always be recovered.

T F 5. Under the UCC, the buyer of goods is never entitled to consequential damages.

T F 6. The main type of damages awarded in a promissory estoppel case are reliance damages.

T F 7. When a court rescinds a contract it rewrites the contract to reflect greater fairness.

T F 8. Jenna contracts to supply Paul with ordinary paper products for his office. Paul breaches the contract when he arranges a better deal with Ella. In this case, a court will order Paul to specifically perform his contract with Jenna.

T F 9. Under the UCC, a buyer must first try to cover in order to recover any damages.

T F 10. A liquidated damages clause will be enforced even if the actual damages could have been estimated with reasonable certainty.

MULTIPLE CHOICE QUESTIONS

1.____ Beth agreed to repair a computer for AAA Tax Service. Beth unintentionally breached the contract. As a result of Beth's breach, the computer suffered $250 damage, and AAA lost profits of $500 because it could not complete certain tax returns without the computer. The lost profits were reasonably foreseeable. Mitigation was not possible. Under these facts, can AAA recover any damages from Beth?

a. AAA cannot recover any damages. Beth did not agree to pay for losses caused by a breach.
b. AAA can recover only $250 compensatory damages.
c. AAA can recover $250 compensatory damages and $500 consequential damages.
d. AAA can recover $250 compensatory damages, $500 consequential damages, and $1,000 punitive damages.

2.____ Juan can obtain specific performance of which contract?

a. Seller contracted to sell Juan a farm. Seller wrongfully refuses to convey title.
b. Juan bought a bull. Seller wrongfully failed to deliver the bull. The bull is a unique, hybrid bull that is to be used for breeding and it cannot be replaced. Damages cannot be measured.
c. Juan contracted to purchase an ordinary Sony stereo from ABC Inc. ABC wrongfully refuses to perform.
d. a and b.

3.____ Larry is a professional magician. He has a wonderful reputation as an outstanding entertainer and as a great draw for crowds. Thomas contracts to have Larry present seven shows at Thomas's comedy club, Chez T. In their contract, Thomas includes a clause that states that if Larry is unable to perform any show, Thomas will reduce his total payment by $3,000 per show (the amount of money Thomas expects to lose as a result of having a different act in the club on a given evening). As a result of flight delay, Larry in fact misses the first show. At the end of the week Thomas gives Larry a check for $11,000 ($2,000 per show as agreed minus $3,000 for the missed show). Larry is furious because the flight delay wasn't his fault. If Larry sues, the most likely outcome will be:

a. The court will not enforce the clause because it is a penalty clause.
b. The court will probably enforce the clause because it is a valid liquidated damages clause.
c. The court will probably enforce the clause because it is a valid unliquidated damages clause.
d. The court will probably not enforce the contract because the clause is clearly unreasonable.

4.____ In breach of contract cases courts seek to protect the legal interests of parties who have been harmed by the breach. Among the legal interests that courts seek to protect are:

a. Extinguished interests.
b. Reliance interests.
c. Expressive interests.
d. Equivalency interests.

5.____ Don sees a sales advertisement for land in the beautiful mountains of a western state. Don lives in the East, but he now decides to opt for a change of scenery. He sends for information regarding the land and the seller sends him literature showing land with breathtaking mountain views and babbling brooks. Don is hooked and he arranges through the mail to buy 10 acres of this land. After the deal is completed and Don sends his $250,000, he flies out to see his new estate. When he arrives he finds that his land is mostly unusable wetland in the prairie, with no mountain views and stagnant water instead of babbling brooks. Don not only deeply regrets his purchase decision, he also wants to get out of this awful contract. What should Don request from a court if the seller will not return his money?

a. Rescission of the contract and restitution damages.
b. An injunction and reliance damages.
c. Compensatory damages based on substantial performance.
d. Nominal damages based on the benefit the land has conferred on him.

6.____ Mary walks into the Uptown Gallery and sees an oil painting by an American impressionist painter that she loves. She immediately asks the gallery owner how much the painting costs. Once she learns the price she cries, "I'll take it!" The gallery owner informs her that the painting is an integral part of her current show and, therefore, she can't give Mary the picture until the show is over in two weeks. Mary says "That's fine, but let me go ahead and pay for it now." Mary pays for the painting. In two weeks, Mary returns to pick up the picture only to learn that the Uptown Gallery has contracted to sell it to someone else and won't give it to Mary. Mary is furious - she paid for and wants <u>that</u> painting. If Mary sues the gallery in order to get the painting, then Mary should request what remedy?

a. An injunction.
b. Compensatory damages.
c. Reliance damages.
d. Specific performance.

7.____ Your neighbor Filbert has an annoying habit of walking across your backyard at all hours of the day and night. Several times you have mistaken Filbert for a burglar and almost died of fright. After repeatedly telling Fil to keep off your land, you are considering more serious action. You are thinking about filing a lawsuit in order to obtain a court order to keep Filbert off your property. If you file this action, you should request:

a. An injunction.
b. Consequential damages.
c. Rescission.
d. Specific performance.

8.____ If you ask a court to rewrite all or part of a contract, you are asking the court for:

a. Restitution.
b. Specific performance.
c. An injunction.
d. Reformation.

9. d Toni is injured when the driver of a municipal bus loses control of her vehicle and plows onto a sidewalk and into a small women's clothing store where Toni works. Toni's legs are broken and she suffers numerous cuts and some internal bleeding. If Toni sues the city for the injuries she suffered as a result of the bus accident, her medical expenses would be categorized as:
   a. Restitution damages.
   b. Equitable damages.
   c. Consequential damages.
   d. Compensatory damages.

10. C Same facts as question No. 9 above. Toni needs to take a taxi from the hospital to her home once she is released. If she sues the city for the harms she has suffered as a result of the bus driver losing control of her bus, the taxi fare would be categorized as:
   a. Remedial damages.
   b. Injunctive relief.
   c. Incidental damages.
   d. Punitive damages.

SHORT ESSAY

Explain the difference between expectation interests and reliance interests. What kinds of damages will a person ask for whose expectation interests have been damaged? What kinds of damages will a person ask for whose reliance interests have been damaged?

CASE PROBLEMS

Answer the following problems, briefly explaining your answers.

1. Mica Co. agreed to build a commercial storage building by September 1 for Pack Rat Storage. It was hard to predict Pack Rat's losses if the building was not completed on time. The parties estimated that Pack Rat would lose $200 in storage fees per day if the building was not completed on time. Thus, the contract required Mica to pay liquidated damages of $200 per day if the work was completed late. Mica finished ten days late. Pack Rat actually lost $1,800 due to the breach.
   a. Is the liquidated damage amount stated in the contract between Mica Co. and Pack Rat Storage valid, or is it an invalid penalty?
   b. How much in damages can Pack Rat Storage recover from Mica Co.?

2. Kendra manufactures wooden blinds for use in homes or offices. She contracts to sell $60,000 worth of blinds to a major home supply store. Kendra completes the order and ships the goods to the supply store's distribution center. When the blinds arrive, a manager at the supply store tells the delivery person that his company will not accept the blinds.
   a. Explain what Kendra must now do, according to the terms of the UCC.
   b. What damages may Kendra recover?

CHAPTER EIGHTEEN
INTRODUCTION TO SALES

CHAPTER OUTLINE

I. Development of Commercial Law

II. Basics of Commercial Law

- A. The Purpose of the Uniform Commercial Code
- B. The Scope of Article Two of the UCC
- C. Merchants
- D. Good Faith and Unconscionability

III. Contract Formation

- A. Formation Basics - Section 2-204
- B. The Statute of Frauds
- C. Additional Terms - Section 2-207
- D. Open Terms - Sections 2-305 and 2-306
- E. Modification
- F. Code Provisions that Change the Common Law

WHAT YOU SHOULD KNOW

After reading this chapter you should understand:

briefly, how commercial law developed in Europe and England;

the genesis of the UCC;

the purpose of the UCC;

what Article 2 applies to;

what a merchant is, according to the UCC;

obligations imposed upon merchants by the UCC;

how contracts may be validly formed under the UCC;

what kinds of statute of frauds provision the UCC contains;

how contracts may be validly modified under the UCC; and

what open terms mean for contracts under the UCC.

REVIEW OF TERMS AND PHRASES

MATCHING EXERCISE

Select the term or concept that best matches a definition or statement set forth below. Each term or concept is the best match for only one definition or statement.

Terms and Concepts

a. Additional term

b. Confirmation

c. Good faith

d. Merchant

e. Mixed contract

f. Non-merchant

g. Open term

h. Output contract

i. Requirements contract

j. Unconscionable

Definitions and Statements

____ 1. Term in an acceptance that deals with a matter not covered by the offer.

____ 2. Contract that requires the seller to both sell goods and provide a service.

____ 3. Contract that requires a seller to provide all of the goods that a buyer needs.

____ 4. Typically, one who does not regularly deal in a particular type of goods.

____ 5. Written memorandum of an agreement.

____ 6. Honesty in fact for non-merchants.

____ 7. Term that is omitted from a contract.

____ 8. Typically, one who regularly deals in a particular type of goods.

____ 9. Contract that requires a buyer to purchase all goods that a seller produces.

____ 10. Grossly unfair.

COMPLETION EXERCISE

Fill in the blanks with the words that most accurately complete each statement. Answers may or may not include terms used in the matching exercise. A term cannot be used to complete more than one statement.

1. Parties to a sales contract are required to act in _______________ _______________.

2. ____________________ ____ governs contracts for the sale of goods.

3. ____________________ ____ governs contracts for the lease of goods.

4. The ______________ ____ ______________ requires contracts for the sale of goods for $500 or more to be evidenced by a writing to be enforceable.

5. The ______________ ______________ test is used to determine what law governs a mixed contract.

6. A ______________ ______________ is a practice that has become a standard in a specific industry or trade.

REVIEW OF CONCEPTS

TRUE-FALSE QUESTIONS

Circle **T** (true) or F (false)

T F 1. The law merchant was a body of rules and customary practices developed by merchants for use in commercial transactions.

T F 2. The Uniform Commercial Code was created by English lawyers in the nineteenth century to meet the changing needs of an industrialized society.

T F 3. The UCC is a national law, adopted by the federal government to manage commercial transactions across state borders.

T F 4. One of the stated purposes of the UCC is to simplify the law governing commercial transactions in the United States.

T F 5. A sales agreement may be a legally binding contract even if certain important terms are not stated in the parties' agreement.

T F 6. The UCC states that a contract between merchants always includes any new terms that are stated in the acceptance.

T F 7. Merchants are oftentimes held to a higher standard of conduct than are non-merchants under the UCC.

T F 8. Under the UCC all terms of a contracts must be defined with reasonable clarity.

T F 9. If a price term in a contract is left open, under the UCC the contract is void as a result of this ambiguity.

T F 10. Merchants may include clauses in sales contracts prohibiting oral modifications. Such clauses are valid in sales contracts between merchants and non-merchants only if the non-merchant signs the clause separately.

MULTIPLE CHOICE QUESTIONS

1. ____ Jessica is an attorney. She has created a software package that predicts the outcome of civil lawsuits with a high degree of certainty. Matthew is the president of a pharmaceutical company. His company is often involved in litigation. Matthew decides that it would be a good idea to buy Jessica's software. Therefore, Matthew enters into a contract to buy Jessica's software for $100,000. As part of the contract, Jessica also agrees to conduct a two-day seminar to demonstrate to the company's attorneys how to use this software. Under these facts:
   a. This is a mixed contract.
   b. Article 2 governs this contract.
   c. Common law governs this contract.
   d. a and b.

2. ____ In the early part of the twentieth century a movement got underway to change the commercial law of the United States. This movement resulted in the creation of the Uniform Commercial Code. Among the reasons why a change in commercial law was desired were:
   a. A perceived need to make commercial law less uniform.
   b. A perceived need to increase commercial predictability.
   c. A perceived need to increase the costs of contracting.
   d. A perceived need to provide jobs to academic lawyers.

3. ____ According to UCC § 1-102, the purposes of the Code include:
   a. Introducing more complicated commercial provisions into American law.
   b. Replacing American commercial law with European legal rules.
   c. Permitting the continued expansion of commercial practices through custom.
   d. Creating a variety of commercial rules and regulations across the country.

4. ____ One of your friends offers to sell you her CD player for a very reasonable price. You know she bought the CD player three months ago and has taken good care of it since. However, she wants to buy an airline ticket to go visit her out-of-state boyfriend and now wants to sell her CD player to get the cash necessary for the ticket. Under these facts, your friend is a:
   a. Merchant according to the UCC.
   b. Merchant according to the merchant law.
   c. Non-merchant according to the UCC.
   d. Person who is not subject to the UCC.

5. ____ The UCC places an obligation on parties to deal in good faith. For merchants, good-faith dealing means:
   a. A good faith attempt to act honestly.
   b. Honesty in fact.
   c. Honesty in fact plus the exercise of reasonable standards of fair dealing.
   d. Not acting fraudulently.

6. ____ Lin and Nola enter into a sales agreement for the purchase of swimsuits. Lin manufactures the designer suits and Nola wants to sell them at her boutique. Lin agrees to sell Nola 100 suits at $50 per suit and Nola accepts this offer. However, the agreement does not state the time or place of delivery. Under these facts:
   a. This is not a valid contract.
   b. This is a valid contract.
   c. If Lin and Nola do not subsequently agree to the time and place of delivery, the UCC will supply these missing terms.
   d. b and c.

7. ____ Joe would like to buy 500 yards of canvas cloth for his upholstery business and he contacts Ed, a textile manufacturer, regarding this purchase. Ed offers to sell Joe the cloth that he needs at $2 per yard. Joe writes a short letter telling Ed that he accepts Ed's offer to sell 500 yards of canvas cloth at $2 per yard, and adds that the cloth is to be delivered in 3 weeks, a standard term in the industry. Ed does not object to this term. Under these facts:
   a. There is a contract and Ed must deliver the cloth within 3 weeks.
   b. There is a contract and Ed must deliver the cloth when he decides to do so.
   c. There is a contract and the court will determine when Ed must deliver the cloth.
   d. There is no contract under the UCC mirror-image rule.

8. ____ Carl's Fish Markets contracts to purchase all of the cod that Cannery Row is able to catch and process. Under these facts, this is:
   a. A requirements contract.
   b. An output contract.
   c. A void contract
   d. An illegal contract.

9. ____ Felicia wants to buy a new computer for her bakery from Terry's store. Terry offers to sell Felicia a computer for $3,000. Felicia accepts Terry's offer by signing a contract. Later that evening, Felicia remembers that she wanted to ask Terry to include in her purchase a new software package called "Doughs and Don'ts of the Bakery Biz." Felicia calls Terry and tells her that she forgot to request the software to be included and would Terry include it in light of their long-term business relationship. Terry agrees. Under these facts:
   a. The modification is invalid based on UCC § 2-214.
   b. The modification is invalid based on UCC § 2-104.
   c. The modification is valid based on UCC § 2-209.
   d. The modification is valid based on UCC § 2-306.

10. ____ When a sales contract is made between two merchants, a new term that is stated in the acceptance is not be part of the contract:
   a. If the new term is objected to by the offeror within a reasonable time.
   b. If the new term may require the offeror to do or pay anything.
   c. If the new term would materially alter the contract.
   d. a and c.

11. ____ Rick orally offered to sell his personal auto to Basil for $10,000 and Basil accepted. Later, Basil recanted, stating that he refused to perform the contract. In which situation would this oral contract be enforceable?

a. Rick had delivered the auto to Basil who had accepted it.
b. When Rick sued Basil to enforce the contract, Basil admitted at trial that the parties made this contract, but defended that the contract was oral.
c. In a signed writing, Rick stated that he sold the auto to Basil. Basil did not sign the writing.
d. a and b.

12. ____ LaDonna agreed to purchase a case of CDs from Roger. The parties did not state the price. Under these facts:

a. There is a contract and the price to be paid is whatever price LaDonna wants to pay.
b. There is a contract and the price to be paid is whatever price Roger demands.
c. There is a contract and the price to be paid is a reasonable price at time of delivery.
d. There is no contract because the agreement does not state the price for the goods.

SHORT ESSAY

Explain the difference between good-faith dealing and unconscionability. How does the UCC deal with each? What obligations concerning good faith dealing does the UCC impose on merchants and non-merchants?

CASE PROBLEMS

Answer the following case problems, explaining your answers.

1. Centrex Equipment Manufacturers Inc. offered to sell a harvester to Carl for $50,000. The Centrex president made this offer in a signed writing. The offer stated that it would be held open for two days. Carl did not pay anything for Centrex's promise to keep its offer open. The next day, the Centrex president called Carl, stating that Centrex could not honor its offer and it was revoked.
Was Centrex legally entitled to revoke its offer? BAD FAITH ON SIDE OF CENTREX

2. Geneva orally contracted to buy her bridal gown from Michelle's Bridal Shoppe for $2,000. The dress was custom designed for Geneva and made from specially-ordered fabric. After the dress was partially done, Geneva called off the wedding and called Michelle's stating: "I don't need him, and I don't want the dress." Michelle's cannot resell the dress.
Is the oral contract legally enforceable? - BAD FAITH ON SIDE OF BRIDE HOWEVER BAD FAITH CONTRACTS ARE NOT USUALLY ENFORCED

3. Shawna's Supply House orally agreed to sell Kim's Hair Salon 10 cases of shampoo for $500 per case. Shawna sent a signed, written letter to Kim, confirming the sale. Two weeks after receiving the letter, Kim wrote back, stating that she did not want the shampoo. Is the oral contract legally enforceable?

CHAPTER NINETEEN
OWNERSHIP AND RISK

CHAPTER OUTLINE

I. Identification, Title, and Insurable Interest

- A. Existence and Identification
- B. Passing of Title
- C. Insurable Interest

II. When the Seller has Imperfect Title

- A. Bona Fide Purchasers
- B. Entrustment

III. Creditor's Rights

- A. Ordinary Sales
- B. Bulk Sales
- C. Returnable Sales

IV. Risk of Loss

- A. When the Parties Do Allocate the Risk
- B. When Either Party Breaches

WHAT YOU SHOULD KNOW

After reading this chapter you should understand:

what an interest is;

how goods are identified;

when title to goods can pass under the UCC;

when parties to a contract obtain insurable interests;

what a bona fide purchaser is;

what void and voidable title means;

what entrustment involves;

rights of creditors in cases of ordinary sales;

rights of creditors in cases of bulk sales;

rights of creditors in cases involving returnable goods;

how parties may allocate risk of loss under the UCC, and how the UCC allocates this risk if the parties fail to do so themselves; and

what the various shipping terms mean.

REVIEW OF TERMS AND PHRASES

MATCHING EXERCISE

Select the term or phrase that best matches a statement or definition stated below. Each term or phrase is the best match for only one statement or definition.

Terms and Phrases

a. CIF
b. Existing goods
c. F.O.B. place of destination
d. F.O.B. place of shipment
e. Identified goods
f. Risk of loss
g. Sale on approval
h. Unidentified goods
i. Voidable title

Statements and Definitions

____ 1. Shipping term that means the seller is obligated to deliver the goods to the buyer at the place named.

____ 2. Goods that have not been designated as being for a particular buyer.

____ 3. Legal responsibility for a financial loss that may result from a casualty to goods.

____ 4. Specific goods designated as being for a particular buyer.

____ 5. Transaction that permits a buyer to test out goods and to return them to the seller if the buyer decides not to purchase them.

____ 6. Goods that exist and are owned by a seller at the time of contracting.

____ 7. Defective title to goods that is acquired by a person who pays for the goods with a "bad" check, who fails to pay the cash purchase price for the goods, or who obtains the goods by fraud.

____ 8. Shipping term which means that the seller is obligated to put the goods in the hands of the carrier at the place named.

____ 9. Shipping term which means that the contract price includes the cost of goods, and insurance and freight expense to the named destination.

COMPLETION EXERCISE

Fill in the blanks with the words that most accurately complete each statement.

1. A ____________________ _______________ is a sale of a business or its assets that includes most or all of the inventory of that business.

2. An __________________ is a transaction whereby the owner of goods turns over possession of such goods to a merchant who deals in goods of that kind.

3. In a _________________ ________________ the seller has a duty to deliver the goods to the buyer at a stated location.

4. In a _________________ ________________ the seller must deliver the goods to a carrier who is then responsible for delivering the goods to the buyer.

5. ____________________ means the normal rights of ownership.

REVIEW OF CONCEPTS

TRUE-FALSE QUESTIONS

Circle **T** (true) or **F** (false)

T F 1. A security interest is a creditor's interest in goods that secures performance of an obligation by the owner, such as payment of the purchase price for the goods.

T F 2. Under the common law, a court would determine who had a legal interest in a good by looking at which party had the insurable interest in that good.

T F 3. Title to goods passes before the goods are identified to the contract.

T F 4. Identification occurs if the parties enter into a contract that describes existing, specific goods that are to be delivered to the buyer.

T F 5. When goods are being moved, title passes when the seller and the buyer agree on a price.

T F 6. A seller has an insurable interest in goods so long as the seller has title to or a security interest in the goods.

T F 7. A buyer and a seller may have simultaneous insurable interests.

T F 8. A thief who steals goods obtains voidable title to the stolen goods.

T F 9. A good-faith purchaser of goods that have been entrusted to a merchant who deals in goods of that kind has a superior right to the goods over the original owner.

T F 10. A person who has voidable title has the power to transfer valid title to a BFP.

MULTIPLE CHOICE QUESTIONS

1. ____ On July 15, Seller contracted to sell a shipment of tools to Acme Co. The tools were not yet identified to the contract. As required by the contract, Seller duly delivered the tools to a carrier for shipment to Buyer on August 15. (Seller was not required to deliver the tools at the destination.) On September 15, the shipment was delivered to Acme at the destination. Under these facts, when did title and risk of loss pass to Acme?
   a. July 15
   b. August 15
   c. September 15
   d. Never.

2. ____ On May 1, John contracted to buy an existing, identified filing cabinet from Seller, a merchant. Documents of title were not involved. Seller was required to deliver the cabinet to John's place of business, which was located in another city. On June 1, Seller delivered the cabinet to a carrier for shipment to John. On June 15, the cabinet was tendered to John at his place of business. Under these facts:
   a. Title passed to John on May 1.
   b. Title passed to John on June 1.
   c. Title passed to John on June 15.
   d. Title never passed to John.

3. ____ On September 1, Darrin contracted to buy an existing, identified bed from Seller, a merchant. Documents of title were not involved. Delivery was required to be made at Seller's business. On October 1, Seller tendered delivery of the bed to Darrin, but Darrin did not take the bed. On November 1, Darrin took physical possession of the bed. Under these facts:
   a. Darrin had an insurable interest in the bed on September 1.
   b. Risk of loss passed to Darrin on October 1.
   c. Risk of loss passed to Darrin on November 1.
   d. a and c.

4. ____ Select the right answer. (The damage to the goods in question was not the fault of either party.)
   a. Walt contracted to buy a one-of-a-kind statue from Seller. The statue was identified and existing at time of contracting. Before risk of loss passed to Walt, the statue was destroyed. In this case, the contract is not avoided, and Seller is in breach if Seller fails to perform.
   b. Seller contracted to sell a desk to Bill. After risk of loss had passed to Bill, the desk was destroyed. In this case, the contract is avoided, and Bill is not required to pay for the desk.
   c. Seller contracted to sell an unidentified General Electric oven to Lisa. Before risk of loss passed, Seller's inventory of ovens was destroyed. In this case, the contract is not avoided, Seller bears the loss, and Seller is liable for breach if an appropriate oven is not delivered to Lisa.
   d. b and c.

5. ____ Fran received a hair dryer from Seller pursuant to a sale on approval agreement. The agreement allows Fran to test the dryer for 14 days, and Fran may return the dryer at any time during this period if she is not satisfied. Fran received the dryer on June 1. Fran tested the dryer for seven days, and she shipped it back to Seller on June 9. During return shipment, the dryer was damaged. Under these facts:
   a. Title and risk of loss passed to Fran on June 1.
   b. Title and risk of loss never passed to Fran.
   c. Fran must pay for the return shipment of the dryer.
   d. Fran was not entitled to return the dryer because she used it; Fran must pay for the dryer.

6. ____ Nicki sold a fax machine to Jasper. Jasper paid Nicki with a "bad" check, and Jasper's bank refused to pay the check due to insufficient funds. Prior to Nicki's rescinding the sale, Jasper took the fax and sold it to Gary for value. Gary was unaware of the transaction between Nicki and Jasper. Under these facts:
   a. Gary received only voidable title to the fax.
   b. Gary received valid title to the fax.
   c. Nicki cannot recover the fax from Gary.
   d. b and c.

7. ____ Samantha and Darren agree, in their written contract for the sale of one mastiff puppy, that title to the puppy will pass at the time that the puppy is three months old. Under the rules of the UCC, this agreement is:
   a. Valid according to Section 2-401.
   b. Valid according to Section 1-102.
   c. Invalid because title may only pass when the goods are identified.
   d. Invalid because title may only pass when the goods are delivered.

8. ____ Malcolm sees a beautiful woman walking down the street. She has on an expensive Rolex watch. Malcolm watches her draw closer to him, then he darts forward, grabs her by the shoulders, swings her around and yanks the watch from her wrist. She screams and runs after him, but she's unable to catch him. So too are the police. Eluding capture, Malcolm drives a few hours to a big city. He changes into a beautiful stolen men's suit, and walks into a jewelry store. He tells the owner that he would like to sell his Rolex. The jewelry-store owner looks at Malcolm, who now appears very respectable, and gives him $5,000 for the watch. Fortunately, the mysterious beautiful woman is able to track her stolen watch to the jewelry store in the distant city. Under these facts, who has title to the watch?
   a. The mysterious beautiful woman.
   b. Malcolm, the well-dressed thief.
   c. The jewelry-store owner.
   d. No one does, because the theft destroyed title.

9. ____ After talking to Julie on the telephone and agreeing to sell her horse feed that she needs, Gaylord walks into his warehouse in Athens Georgia and sets aside 50 bags of horse feed. Gaylord puts a small sticker on each bag with the words, "Sold/Julie P./Greenville SC" on each bag. Two days later the feed is shipped to Julie. It arrives in Greenville three days later. Under these facts, when does Julie get an insurable interest in the feed?
   a. The day the feed arrives in Greenville.
   b. The day the feed leaves Athens.
   c. The day Gaylord marks the bags.
   d. The moment on the phone when she places her order.

10. ____ Louise agrees to sell 100 magnolia trees to Matt, a nursery owner. Louise agrees to ship the trees from her tree farm in Mississippi to Matt who is located in California. Louise agrees to get the trees to the train station in Montgomery, Alabama, for shipment to California. In their sales contract, Louise and Matt fail to specify which one of them would bear the risk of loss. Under these facts:
   a. Matt bears the risk once Louise agrees to the sales price.
   b. Matt bears the risk once the bill of sale is written.
   c. Louise bears the risk until she delivers the magnolias to the shipper in Montgomery, Alabama.
   d. Louise bears the risk until the trees arrive safely in California.

SHORT ESSAY

The common law and the UCC have different ideas about when title to a good passes. Explain the common law and UCC rules regarding the passage of title. When does a person have good title under the UCC? What does it mean to have voidable title?

CASE PROBLEMS

Answer the following case problems, explaining your answers.

1. Fran delivered her computer to Computer Traders, a merchant who regularly bought and sold used computers. Computer Traders was supposed to repair the computer. Instead, Computer Traders sold Fran's computer to Ted in the ordinary course of business. Did Ted receive title to the computer?

2. Jim, in Atlanta, contracted to sell peaches to Cindy in Chicago. The contract states that the peaches are sold "F.O.B. Atlanta." If the peaches are damaged during shipment, who bears the risk of loss?

3. Kathy received an exercise bike from Seller pursuant to a sale on approval agreement. The agreement allows Kathy to test the bike for 14 days, and Kathy may return the bike at any time during this period. Kathy received the bike on June 1. Kathy shipped the exercise bike back to Seller on June 9. During shipment, the exercise bike was damaged. Does Kathy bear the risk of loss for the exercise bike?

CHAPTER TWENTY
WARRANTIES AND PRODUCT LIABILITY

CHAPTER OUTLINE

I. Express Warranties

II. Implied Warranties

- A. Implied Warranty of Merchantability
- B. Implied Warranty of Fitness for a Particular Purpose
- C. Warranties of Title and Infringement

III. Disclaimers and Defenses

- A. Disclaimers
- B. Remedy Limitations
- C. Privity
  1. Personal Injury
  2. Economic Loss
- D. Buyer's Misconduct
- E. Statute of Limitations and Notice of Breach

IV. Negligence

V. Strict Liability

- A. Time Limits - Tort versus Contract

VI. Other Legislation

WHAT YOU SHOULD KNOW

After reading this chapter you should understand:

what an express warranty is and how it is created;

what is meant by "basis of the bargain;"

what a warranty of merchantability is;

how implied warranties are arise;

what a warranty of fitness for a particular purpose is;

how warranties may be modified;

what warranties of title and of infringement are;

how sellers can legally disclaim warranties;

what privity is and why it's important;

the role of negligence in compensating persons hurt by goods;

the role of strict liability in compensating persons hurt by goods; and

other statutes that deal with defective or unsafe products.

REVIEW OF TERMS AND PHRASES

MATCHING EXERCISE

Select the term or phrase that best matches a statement or definition stated below. Each term or phrase is the best match for only one statement or definition.

Terms and Phrases

a.	Conspicuous	f.	Statutes of limitation
b.	Disclaimer	g.	Warranty against infringement
c.	Express warranties	h.	Warranty of fitness for a particular purpose
d.	Implied warranties	i.	Warranty of merchantability
e.	Privity	j.	Warranty of title

Statements and Definitions

____ 1. Broad category of warranties that automatically arise when a sales contract is made.

____ 2. Noticeable to a reasonable person.

____ 3. Broad category of warranties that arise due to the words or conduct of a seller.

____ 4. Disavowal or elimination of a warranty.

____ 5. Direct contractual relationship between two parties.

____ 6. Warranty that a buyer will receive good title and that the seller has the right to transfer title.

____ 7. Implied warranty that a good is fit for the ordinary purposes for which the good is sold.

____ 8. Laws that limit the time within which a lawsuit must be brought or else it is barred.

____ 9. Implied warranty that a good can perform an unusual use that is intended by a buyer.

____10. Warranty that a good does not violate the patent or trademark rights of others.

COMPLETION EXERCISE

Fill in the blanks with the words that most accurately complete each statement. Answers may or may not include terms used in the matching exercise. A term cannot be used to complete more than one statement.

1. A seller's statement of fact or promise regarding a good does not create an express warranty unless the statement or promise is part of the ______________ ____ ____ ______________.

2. A _______________ is a specimen or portion of the actual goods to be furnished to a buyer.

3. A replica or example of what purchased goods will be like is called a _______________.

4. Two implied warranties that are generally made by merchant sellers are the _______________ _______________ _______________ and _______________ ____ _______________.

5. The theory of product liability that holds a manufacturer liable for personal injuries caused by a defective and unreasonably dangerous product is known as _______________ _______________.

6. The term "______ _____" will effectively exclude the implied warranties of merchantability and fitness for a particular purpose.

7. A _______________ _______________ is a contract that is created when a consumer opens a wrapped product which contains contractual terms inside, and a _______________ _______________ is a contract that is created when a buyer clicks on an Internet icon, which states "I agree to all terms" as part of an online purchase.

8. List the principal factors in the risk utility test:

   a. ____.

   b. ____.

   c. ____.

   d. ____.

   e. ____.

REVIEW OF CONCEPTS

TRUE-FALSE QUESTIONS

Circle **T** (true) or **F** (false)

T F 1. A seller may create an express warranty by merely describing goods.

T F 2. When a buyer argues that he or she has received an express warranty, the buyer must prove that what the seller told the buyer became part of the basis of the bargain.

T F 3. Statements of fact about the goods being sold that are stated in written contracts typically become binding warranties.

T F 4. In general, a seller's opinion creates an express warranty if the buyer relies on this opinion.

T F 5. Warranties of merchantability are implied in sales contracts if a merchant sells similar goods as a matter of course.

T F 6. Implied warranties may be created by the actions of the seller.

T F 7. A seller may *specifically* disclaim the implied warranty of merchantability, but only if the seller actually uses the word "merchantability."

T F 8. When a product is sold "as is" this means that express, but not implied, warranties are disclaimed.

T F 9. Under negligence standards, a seller who acts unreasonably in manufacturing, designing, or selling a product has breached the seller's duty.

T F 10. In strict liability cases, the plaintiff must show that the defendant acted carelessly in manufacturing a defective product that caused the plaintiff's harm.

MULTIPLE CHOICE QUESTIONS

1. ____ In which situation does Seller make an express warranty?
   a. During negotiations, Seller gave Byron a brochure regarding a ring that Byron was considering purchasing. The brochure stated that the ring was sterling silver.
   b. During negotiations for the sale of a drill, Seller stated to Buyer: "This drill is the best little drill on the market today." Seller did not say or do anything else.
   c. During negotiations for the sale of a chair to be specially manufactured, Seller showed Buyer a model of what the chair would be like. Seller did not say or do anything else.
   d. a and c.

2. ____ Select the correct statement.
   a. Kit sold an engine to Buyer. Unknown to the parties, Kit did not have title to the engine. In this case, Kit breached the warranty of title.
   b. Kim sold an RV to Sam. Sam knew that the RV was subject to a lien. In this case, Kim breached the warranty of title.
   c. John sold a car to Sam. Unknown to Sam, the car was subject to a lien. In this case, John breached the warranty of title.
   d. a and c.

3. ____ In which case is an express warranty made?
   a. The salesman for PainBgone aspirin states that, in his opinion, PainBgone aspirin is the best painkiller in the world.
   b. The salesman for the Belchfire 500 automobile states: "This car will go from zero to 60 miles per hour in six seconds."
   c. The salesman in a tool shop says "This chain saw has 38 teeth."
   d. b and c.

4. ____ In which case is the implied warranty of fitness for a particular purpose breached?
   a. Manufacturer sold an egg incubator to a zoo. At time of contracting, Manufacturer knew the zoo needed an incubator for hatching ostrich eggs (an unusual purpose), and that the zoo was relying on Manufacturer to select an appropriate incubator. (The zoo did in fact rely on Manufacturer.) The incubator delivered did not hatch ostrich eggs; it baked them.
   b. Buyer needed a paint that could withstand unusual, prolonged heat. Buyer developed a paint formula and furnished Manufacturer with specifications for the paint. The paint was made in accordance with the specifications, but it failed to perform the unusual task.
   c. Seller sold Buyer a lawn mower. Unknown to Seller, Buyer intended to use the mower to cut three-foot-tall salt marsh grass, an unusual purpose. The mower failed to cut this grass.
   d. a and c.

5. ____ The implied warranty of merchantability is breached in which case?
   a. Juanita (a nonmerchant) sold Buyer a new toaster that Juanita had received as a gift. The toaster cannot toast bread.
   b. Seller (a merchant) sold an ordinary private airplane to Buyer. The airplane operates safely and it is fit for ordinary private use. However, the plane cannot perform acrobatic stunts.
   c. Manufacturer, a merchant, sold a portable plastic pool to Buyer. The pool leaks badly, and it cannot be repaired. However, Manufacturer was not negligent in making the pool.
   d. All of the above.

6. ____ Devon sells fabric to retail fabric stores. He stops into Carmen's store and shows her some fabric samples. Devon's samples are beautiful, high-quality linen. Carmen places an order for $500 worth of the fabric, which she will use to upholster several chairs for sale. When Carmen's fabric arrives, it is cheap, low-quality material. Under these facts:
   a. Devon has breached his duty of care.
   b. Devon has breached an express warranty.
   c. Devon has breach a warranty of fitness for a particular purpose.
   d. Devon is strictly liable for his breach.

7. ____ Which of the following statements would a court be most likely to consider to be express warranties?
   a. General statements that express opinions about products.
   b. Statements made by sellers with similar expertise to buyers.
   c. Statements concerning obvious defects.
   d. Statements made in a written contract.

8. ____ Lari's Manufacturing Company developed a revolutionary new hammock, which it sells to home-supply stores. When Mark comes to Lari's showroom to look at her hammock, Lari tells him, "these hammocks are priceless - worth far more than purchase price." Mark buys 100 hammocks to sell in his store. Which of the following warranties did Lari make regarding the hammocks sold to Mark?
   a. Express warranty created by Lari's words.
   b. Implied warranty of merchantability.
   c. Warranty of infringement.
   d. b and c.

9. ____ Same facts as question No. 8 above, except Mark also says to Lari: "You know, I like these hammocks. But what I really want is something I can use to pick up small cows and lift them from my pasture into a trailer. Will your hammocks be good for that?" Lari looks Mark straight in the eye and says, "Oh yes, our hammocks work well as cow movers." Lari means it, and based on Lari's statement, Mark buys 10 hammocks for this purpose. Which of the following warranties did Lari make under these new facts?
   a. Warranty of coverage.
   b. Warranty of title.
   c. Warranty of fitness for a particular purpose.
   d. b and c.

10. ____ Acme Hardware sold a shovel to Wilson. The purchase contract for the shovel states: "This shovel is guaranteed to withstand 200 lbs of pressure." Further down in the contract, it states: "All warranties express or implied associated with this product are disclaimed, specifically including the IMPLIED WARRANTY OF MERCHANTABILITY." The disclaimer is printed in bold face and a different color from the rest of the tag. Under these facts:
   a. The disclaimer effectively disclaims the implied warranty of merchantability.
   b. The disclaimer effectively disclaims the express warranty regarding the shovel's strength.
   c. The disclaimer does not effectively disclaim the express warranty regarding the shovel's strength.
   d. a and c.

SHORT ESSAY

Explain the difference between an express warranty, a warranty of merchantability, and a warranty of fitness. How is each warranty created? What obligations does each warranty create for sellers?

CASE PROBLEM

Answer the following problem, briefly explaining your answer.

Aqua Boats manufactured a boat, and it sold the boat to Crest Sales Co. Aqua disclaimed all warranties. Crest sold the boat to Gary for family use. Crest expressly warranted to Gary that the boat's hull was shatterproof. While Gary was boating one day, the boat struck a small rock. The rock shattered the boat's hull, causing the boat to sink. Gary was seriously injured and the boat itself was lost. Not only did the boat not satisfy the warranties made by Crest, but the boat was also defective and unreasonably dangerous. However, both Aqua Boats and Crest Sales Co. exercised due care in designing, manufacturing, and selling the boat.

a. Analyze whether Aqua Boats is liable to Gary and, if so, on what theory or theories.
b. Analyze whether Crest Sales Co. is liable to Gary and, if so, on what theory or theories.

CHAPTER TWENTY-ONE
PERFORMANCE AND REMEDIES

CHAPTER OUTLINE

I. Contract Performance - Good Faith

II. Contract Performance - Seller's Obligations and Rights

A. Perfect Tender Rule

B. Restrictions on the Perfect Tender Rule

III. Contract Performance - Buyers Obligations and Rights

A. Inspection and Acceptance

IV. Remedies - Assurance and Repudiation

V. Sellers' Remedies

VI. Buyers' Remedies

WHAT YOU SHOULD KNOW

After reading this chapter you should understand:

what is meant by conforming and non-conforming goods;

the seller's obligation to tender conforming goods;

what the perfect-tender rule means;

exceptions or restrictions to the perfect-tender rule;

what the seller's right to cure means;

what happens when a seller tenders substantially impaired goods;

what happens when goods identified to a contract are wholly or partially destroyed;

buyers' rights to inspect and accept goods;

buyers' rights to revoke acceptance or reject goods;

what assurance and repudiation mean;

what a seller may legally do once a buyer breaches a contract;

what a buyer may legally do once a seller breaches a contract; and

the kinds of damages the non-breaching party may expect.

REVIEW OF TERMS AND PHRASES

MATCHING EXERCISE

Select the term or concept that best matches a definition or statement set forth below. Each term or concept is the best match for only one definition or statement.

Terms and Concepts

a. Assurance
b. Consequential damages
c. Course of dealing
d. Course of performance
e. Cover
f. Good faith
g. Reject
h. Revoke acceptance
i. Specific performance
j. Substantial impairment
k. Tender
l. Usage of trade

Definitions and Statements

____ 1. Promise or guarantee that a party will perform as promised.

____ 2. Offer to perform.

____ 3. Buying substitute goods from another source within a reasonable time of the breach.

____ 4. A common practice or understanding in a particular trade or profession.

____ 5. Refusal to accept goods.

____ 6. For merchants, honesty in fact and observing reasonable commercial standards of fair dealing.

____ 7. Repeated prior dealings between the parties to a contract.

____ 8. Court order directing a seller to perform a contract relating to unique goods.

____ 9. Buyer retracts acceptance of goods and refuses to take or keep goods.

____ 10. Significant reduction in the value of goods.

____ 11. Damages that arise due to the particular circumstances of the parties.

____ 12. Repeated performances by the parties in carrying out the contract in question.

REVIEW OF CONCEPTS

COMPLETION EXERCISE

Fill in the blanks with the words that most accurately complete each statement. Answers may or may not include terms used in the matching exercise. A term cannot be used to complete more than one statement.

1. ________________ ____________________ is a contractually agreed upon sum of money that will be the amount of damages to be paid to a contracting party in the event that the other contracting party breaches.

2. An _________________ _________________ is a contract for the sale of goods that requires the goods to be delivered in separate shipments.

3. A seller may reclaim goods from a buyer if the buyer is insolvent and the seller reclaims the goods within ________________ _________________ after delivery of the goods to the buyer.

4. ________________ means that the seller has corrected an improper performance by tendering conforming goods to the buyer.

5. A buyer may revoke his or her acceptance of nonconforming goods only if the nonconformity __________________ ________________ the value of the goods.

TRUE-FALSE QUESTIONS

Circle **T** (true) or **F** (false)

T F 1. Goods are conforming when they satisfy the terms of the contract of sale.

T F 2. According to the perfect-tender rule, a buyer may reject goods that fail in any respect to conform to the terms of the contract of sale.

T F 3. The primary obligation of the seller is to insure that the goods are properly advertised.

T F 4. In certain situations when a buyer has breached a contract, the seller may go ahead and identify goods to the contract and sue for damages.

T F 5. In general, a seller has a right to cure an imperfect tender if the seller notifies the buyer that the seller intends to cure and the seller does in fact cure within the original contract time for performance.

T F 6. The obligation to act in good faith applies to all contracts for the sale of goods whether the parties are merchants or non-merchants.

T F 7. If a seller refuses to deliver goods, a buyer is always entitled to specific performance.

T F 8. If a buyer breaches a contract before the goods are delivered, a seller may refuse to deliver the goods.

T F 9. If a seller tenders conforming goods and is unable to resell these goods after a buyer breaches, then the seller may recover the original contract price from the buyer.

T F 10. A seller can never stop a shipment of goods that has already been handed over to a carrier for shipment to the buyer, even if the buyer has already breached the contract.

MULTIPLE CHOICE QUESTIONS

1.____ Seller sold his personal motorcycle to Buyer for $5,000. Prior to delivery or payment, Buyer breached the contract and refused to take the cycle. After the breach, Seller properly held a public sale and sold the cycle for $4,500. Seller had to pay a $500 commission to the auctioneer who conducted the sale. Under these facts, Seller can recover how much in damages?

a. $0.
b. $500.
c. $1,000.
d. $5,000.

2.____ Ike sold his personal record collection to Brie for $500. Brie refused the records and breached the contract. The market price of the records was $200 at the time they were tendered to Brie. Ike did not try to resell the records. Under these facts, Ike can recover how much in damages?

a. $0.
b. $200.
c. $300.
d. $500.

3.____ Mary bought and paid for a sewing machine. Mary accepted the machine, unaware that the machine was nonconforming. Soon afterwards, the machine's engine seized due to the nonconformity, and the machine was rendered worthless. Seller failed to cure. Under these facts:

a. Mary cannot revoke her acceptance because she accepted the sewing machine.
b. Mary can revoke her acceptance.
c. If Mary revokes her acceptance, she may sue for damages.
d. b and c.

4.____ Ralph bought a power sander from Seller for $500. *Prior to paying*, Ralph properly rejected the sander due to Seller's breach. An identical sander can be purchased elsewhere for $550. The market price of the sander at the time Ralph learned of the breach was $600. Ralph did not buy a replacement sander. Under these facts, Ralph can recover how much in damages?

a. $0.
b. $50.
c. $100.
d. $500.

5.____ Acme Wares sold a stove to Kitty for $600. Kitty refused to accept the oven and breached the contract. Acme would have made a profit of $300 on the sale. At the time the oven was tendered to Kitty, the oven's market price was $500. Under these facts, Acme can recover how much in damages?

a. $0.
b. $100.
c. $300.
d. $500.

6.____ Seller sold a set of encyclopedias to Betty for $1,000. Betty accepted the encyclopedias and loves reading them, but she refuses to pay any portion of the purchase price. The market price for the encyclopedias is $900. Under these facts, Seller may sue for:

a. $0.
b. $100.
c. $900.
d. $1,000.

7.____ On Saturday, Joan contracts to sell Ned four specific female horses and their young offspring. Joan is obligated under the contract to ship the horses and colts to Ned on Friday. On Thursday, a tornado hits and three of the mares and two colts are killed. Under these facts:

a. Joan is in breach of contract because she cannot deliver conforming goods.
b. Ned may choose to accept the remaining horse and colts and reduce the price accordingly.
c. Ned may choose to void the entire contract.
d. b or c.

8.____ Alvin contracts to sell Max 100 pairs of ballet tights and 50 pink, size 4 leotards for the women in his ballet company. The contract requires the goods to be delivered by March 7. On February 29 (it's a leap year), the goods arrive at Max's door. Although Alvin sent Max the tights and leotards, the leotards are all size 10, much too big for Max's petite ballerinas. Under these facts:

a. Max may reject the tender because it is nonconforming.
b. Max must inform Alvin of the defective performance so that Alvin may send conforming, replacement goods.
c. Max must accept and pay for conforming, replacement goods if they are delivered by March 7.
d. All of the above.

9.____ Acme Manufacturing agreed to sell 100 shovels and 200 grass clippers to Gardners' Warehouse Store. The goods were required to be delivered in a single shipment on April 1 for a special weekend sale starting the next day. Acme delivered 100 conforming shovels, but the grass clippers were the wrong size. Acme was unable to cure. Under these facts:

a. Gardners' may accept all of the goods but, if it does this, it cannot sue Acme for whatever damages it suffers due to Acme's breach.
b. Gardners' may accept all of the goods and sue Acme for whatever damages it suffers due to Acme's breach.
c. Gardners' may accept the shovels, reject the grass clippers, and sue Acme for whatever damages it suffers due to Acme's breach.
d. b or c.

10. ___ Lucia Inc. is a hat manufacturer and Alan's Shop is a men's clothing store. Lucia and Alan have a 10-year, on-going business relationship. During this time, Alan has placed 20 different orders for 100 men's hats. For each order, Lucia has always tendered and Alan has always accepted 46 black hats and 54 off-white hats. Alan's last order was like all the previous ones, i.e. 100 hats. However, Alan rejected Lucia's tender of 46 black hats and 54 off-white hats because Alan argued that Lucia should have delivered 50 hats of each color. Under these facts:

a. Based on the perfect-tender rule, Lucia's performance was nonconforming.
b. Based on the substantial impairment rule, Lucia's performance is nonconforming.
c. Based on the course of dealings between the parties, Lucia's performance is conforming.
d. b and c.

SHORT ESSAY

Explain what a buyer must do in case a seller of goods breaches a contract. What are the buyer's obligations? What options does the buyer have in this situation? Explain how a buyer can obtain damages and what kinds of damages the buyer may request.

CASE PROBLEM

Answer the following problem, briefly explaining your answer.

During a promotional sale, Alicia bought a used car from Seller for $10,000. Seller warranted that the car had no defects. The car would have been worth $11,000 had it complied with Seller's warranty. In fact, the car's transmission was defective, a breach of warranty. As a result, the actual value of the car was only $9,000. Alicia spent $200 for a rental car when the transmission of the car she purchased failed and she could not drive the car. Alicia has accepted the car, and she intends to keep the car.

a. Is Alicia required to give Seller notice of the breach?
b. What are the consequences if Alicia does not give notice of the breach?
c. If Seller refuses to cure the breach, how much in damages can Alicia recover?

CHAPTER TWENTY-TWO
CREATING A NEGOTIABLE INSTRUMENT

CHAPTER OUTLINE

I. Commercial Paper

II. Types of Negotiable Instruments

   A. Notes v. Drafts

III. Negotiability

   A. Requirements for Negotiability

   B. Interpreting Ambiguities

IV. Negotiation

V. Holder in Due Course

   A. Requirements for Being a Holder in Due Course

      1. Holder

      2. Value

      3. Good Faith

      4. Notice of Outstanding Claims or Other Defects

   B. Shelter Rule

   C. Defenses Against a Holder in Due Course

      1. Real Defenses

      2. Personal Defenses

      3. Claims in Recoupment

   D. Consumer Exception

WHAT YOU SHOULD KNOW

After reading this chapter you should understand:

the fundamental rule of commercial paper;

the functions that commercial paper serves in our society;

the types of negotiable instruments and their differences;

what makes an instrument negotiable;

how the law interprets ambiguities in negotiable instruments;

how a negotiable instrument may be negotiated;

what a holder in due course is, and the requirements for being such a holder;

when a person is not a holder in due course;

what the shelter rule is;

the defenses that may be used against holders in due course and ordinary holders; and

the consumer exception to the rules concerning holders in due course.

REVIEW OF TERMS AND PHRASES

MATCHING EXERCISE

Select the term or phrase that best matches a statement or definition stated below. Each term or phrase is the best match for only one statement or definition.

Terms and Phrases

a. Bearer paper
b. Blank indorsement
c. Certificate of deposit
d. Check
e. Commercial paper
f. Dishonored
g. Drawee
h. Drawer
i. Holder
j. Judgment rate
k. Maker
l. Negotiable draft
m. Negotiable promissory note
n. Order paper
o. Payee

Statements and Definitions

____ 1. Broad category of contracts to pay money that may serve as a substitute for money or as a loan of money.

____ 2. Special type of draft that orders a drawee bank to pay the draft on demand.

____ 3. Party who originally signs and issues a promissory note.

____ 4. Signature on the back of an instrument that does not designate anyone to whom payment is to be made.

____ 5. An unconditional signed, written promise to pay on demand or at a definite time a sum certain in money to order or to bearer.

____ 6. Party whom a drawer orders to pay a draft or check.

____ 7. Unconditional signed, written order by one person ordering another party to pay on demand or at a definite time a sum certain in money to order or to bearer.

____ 8. Instrument originally made payable to the order of a named person, or an instrument that is specially indorsed to a named indorsee.

____ 9. Party who originally signs and issues a draft or check.

____10. Instrument issued to bearer or to cash, or one that is indorsed in blank.

____11. Instrument issued by a bank, which acknowledges receipt of funds and contains a promise by the bank to repay this sum when the instrument becomes due.

____12. Party who has possession of an instrument that is payable to or indorsed to the party or who properly has possession of bearer paper.

____13. Party to whom an instrument is made payable.

____14. Legal rate of interest that is paid on judgments.

____15. Refusal to pay an instrument.

REVIEW OF CONCEPTS

COMPLETION EXERCISE

Fill in the blanks with the words that most accurately complete each statement.

1. A ______________ instrument is one that fails to satisfy one or more of the requirements for negotiability.

2. A negotiable promissory note must be signed by the __________________, and a negotiable draft must be signed by ______________________.

3. In order to be a negotiable instrument, commercial paper must state that it is payable in some form of ________________.

4. A ______________ __________________ is an indorsement that directs payment to be made to a specified party.

5. If the typed terms of an instrument conflict with preprinted terms, then the ______________ terms will generally prevail.

6. A ____________ _______________ is an indorsement that limits how the proceeds from an instrument are to be used.

7. ______________ means that someone other than the issuer has transferred an instrument to a holder.

TRUE-FALSE QUESTIONS

Circle **T** (true) or F (false)

T F 1. In order to be used as a substitute for money, commercial paper must be payable on demand.

T F 2. A holder who possesses a commercial paper has an unconditional right to be paid as long as the paper was negotiated to the holder.

T F 3. A note is a promise by the person signing the note to pay money to someone else.

T F 4. There are two parties to a draft: the maker and the payee.

T F 5. If a person is a holder in due course of commercial paper, then that person takes the paper free of personal defenses that anyone else may assert as a defense to having to pay.

T F 6. In order for an instrument to be negotiable, it must be state: "Pay To Bearer."

T F 7. By their very definition, all checks are negotiable.

T F 8. A special indorsement occurs when the person creating a negotiable instrument specifies one particular person to whom the paper is payable.

T F 9. A holder in due course may give a promise of future performance in exchange for the negotiable instrument.

T F 10. You cannot be a holder in due course if you know that the original parties to the instrument have a dispute amongst themselves.

T F 11. If an issuer transfers an instrument to a holder, then the instrument has not been negotiated and the issuer can raise any defenses against the holder that arise out of the underlying contract that gave rise to issuance of the instrument in the first place.

MULTIPLE CHOICE QUESTIONS

1. ____ Which of the following are required in order for the possessor of commercial paper to have an unconditional right to be paid?
   a. The paper must be based on an oral agreement.
   b. The possessor must know that the original parties have a dispute.
   c. The paper must be negotiated to the possessor.
   d. The paper must be negotiated to the original parties.

2. ____ James borrows $6,000 from his uncle Wallace in order to buy a car. When Wallace gives James the $6,000, James gives Wallace a piece of paper that says, "I, James, promise to pay to the order of my dear uncle Wallace $6,000 in two years." James' piece of paper is a:
   a. Note.
   b. Draft.
   c. Check.
   d. Bearer instrument.

3. ____ Carl issues to the order of Burt a negotiable promissory note. The note is for the principal amount of $10,000 and is payable in five years from date of issue. Burt indorsed the note to Sally who paid Burt $11,000 for the note. Under these facts, Sally's rights to be paid are:
   a. Unconditional so long as she is a holder in due course.
   b. Unconditional so long as she is a holder.
   c. Limited if Carl doesn't know that Burt sold the paper to her.
   d. Limited if Carl didn't give his prior approval to the sale of the paper to her.

4. ____ James issues his promissory note to the order of Caroline but he forgot to sign it. Under these facts:
   a. The note is negotiable as it is.
   b. The note is negotiable if Caroline noticed that James forgot to sign it.
   c. The note is negotiable if Caroline did not notice that James forgot to sign it.
   d. The paper is not negotiable.

5. ____ Larry issues his check payable to the order of Juanita. Larry wrote the number $5,000.00 but he wrote in long hand the amount as "Fifty Thousand Dollars and no/100." Under these facts, how much does Larry have to pay Juanita?
   a. $0.
   b. $5,000.
   c. $50,000.
   d. A reasonable sum.

6. ____ Paul issues a negotiable promissory note to Sam who is a holder in due course. Sam in turn gives the note to his favorite niece Judy as a present. On the back of the note, Sam signs and writes, "Pay to Judy." Judy may best be described as a:
   a. Drawer.
   b. Maker.
   c. Holder in due course.
   d. Holder who enjoys the rights of a holder in due course.

7.____ Mac issued a negotiable note to Peg to pay for goods. Peg negotiated the note to Chris, who negotiated the note to Herb. Herb paid value for the note, and he took it in good faith. Which additional fact would not prevent Herb from being a holder in due course?

a. The note was due June 1, and Chris negotiated the note to Herb on July 1.
b. At the time the note was negotiated to Herb, Herb knew that the note had become due and that Mac had refused to pay it.
c. At the time the note was negotiated to Herb, Herb knew that Peg claimed ownership of the note because she had been defrauded into transferring it to Chris.
d. One day after the note was negotiated to Herb, Mac informed Herb that the goods delivered to Mac were defective, and he had a breach of contract defense.

8.____ In which case does Denise have a personal defense that cannot be used against a holder in due course?

a. Denise issued a check to Contractor in payment for certain remodeling work. Contractor performed the work improperly, a breach of contract.
b. Denise issued a check to Payton. Denise issued the check due to wrongful physical abuse by Payton. Under state law, the duress exerted by Payton would render the obligation void.
c. Thief stole Denise's checkbook. Thief forged Denise's signature to a check.
d. When Denise was a minor, she issued a check in payment for a magazine subscription.

9.____ In which case does Dana have a real defense that can be asserted against all holders?

a. While intoxicated, Dana bought a painting and she issued a check in payment. Under state law, Dana's lack of capacity due to intoxication would render the obligation voidable.
b. Dana issued a check in payment for illegal drugs. Under state law, negotiable instruments issued for illegal drugs are void.
c. Dana issued a check to Perry as payment for landscaping services that Perry agreed to perform. Perry wrongfully failed to perform the services.
d. Dana issued a check to Stockbroker. Delivery of the check was conditioned on Stockbroker's delivery of certain stock to Dana. Stockbroker failed to deliver the stock to Dana.

SHORT ESSAY

Explain the difference between real defenses and personal defenses. Who may use a real defense, and who may use a personal defense? Identify the primary real and personal defenses? Should the UCC allow such defenses? Why or why not?

CASE PROBLEM

Answer the following case problem, explaining your answer.

Builders West, a contractor, hired Sparky, an electrician, to do the electrical work on an office project. According to their contract, Builders is obligated to pay Sparky $4,000 upon signing of the contract, with the balance payable upon completion of the project. The balance to be paid is undetermined and will be computed on an hourly rate after Sparky has completed his work. At Sparky's request, Builders issued a promissory note that stated, "Builders West promises to pay to the order of Sparky all sums due under its subcontract. Payment to be made 10 days after completion of the office project. /signed/Builders West.

a. Is the promissory note negotiable?
b. Does the promissory note represent a legal obligation to pay?
c. Does it matter whether the promissory note is negotiable or non-negotiable?

CHAPTER TWENTY-THREE
LIABILITY FOR NEGOTIABLE INSTRUMENTS

CHAPTER OUTLINE

I. Signature Liability
   - A. The Maker
   - B. The Drawer
   - C. The Drawee
   - D. The Indorser
   - E. The Accommodation Party
   - F. The Agent

II. Warranty Liability
   - A. The Basic Rules of Warranty Liability
   - B. Transfer Warranties
   - C. Comparison of Signature Liability and Transfer Warranties
   - D. Presentment Warranties

III. Other Liability Rules
   - A. Conversion Liability
   - B. The Impostor Rule
   - C. The Fictitious Payee Rule
   - D. The Employee Indorsement Rule
   - E. Negligence
   - F. Crimes

IV. Discharge
   - A. Discharge of the Obligor
   - B. Discharge of an Indorser or Accommodation Party

WHAT YOU SHOULD KNOW

After reading this chapter you should understand:

the difference between signature and warranty liability;

how the payment process works with negotiable instruments;

what the difference is between primary and secondary liability;

the liability of the maker, drawer, drawee, and indorser respectively;

exceptions to the rule of indorser liability;

what an accommodation party is and what kind of liability such a person has;

liabilities of agents for negotiable instruments;

the basic rules of warranty liability;

what a person warrants when they transfer a negotiable instrument;

what a person warrants when they present a negotiable instrument for payment;

how conversion relates to liability for negotiable instruments;

what the impostor rule means;

what the fictitious-payee rule means;

what the employee-indorsement rule means;

how negligent behavior may result in liability for a negotiable instrument;

crimes related to negotiable instruments; and

how negotiable instruments are discharged.

REVIEW OF TERMS AND PHRASES

MATCHING EXERCISE

Select the term or phrase that best matches a statement or definition stated below. Each term or phrase is the best match for only one statement or definition.

Terms and Phrases

a. Accommodation party
b. Certified check
c. Dishonor
d. Impostor rule
e. Indorser
f. Presentment
g. Primary liability
h. Secondary liability
i. Transfer warranties
j. Unauthorized indorsement

Statements and Definitions

____ 1. Demand for payment of an instrument made by a holder upon a person who has liability to pay.

____ 2. Maker's or drawee's refusal to pay an instrument.

____ 3. Anyone, other than an issuer or acceptor, who signs an instrument.

____ 4. Indorsement that is made by an agent who has no authority to make the indorsement.

____ 5. Party who voluntarily signs an instrument to strengthen its collectability.

____ 6. Unconditional liability to pay an instrument.

____ 7. Check that the drawee has signed, agreeing to pay it.

____ 8. Liability to pay an instrument only if the person with primary liability fails to pay.

____ 9. Guarantees regarding certain matters that are impliedly made by an indorser who makes an unqualified indorsement for consideration.

____10. Exception to the general rule that order paper cannot be negotiated by a forged indorsement.

REVIEW OF CONCEPTS

COMPLETION EXERCISE

Fill in the blanks with the words that most accurately complete each statement.

1. The _______________ of a note has primary liability to pay it.

2. A drawee does not have any liability to pay a draft or check until the drawee _______________ the instrument.

3. _______________ means that someone has stolen an instrument or that a bank has paid an instrument that has a forged, required indorsement.

4. Persons who transfer or present instruments may incur contractual liability to pay the instrument and also _______________ _______________ to pay damages if certain matters turn out to be false.

5. List the five transfer warranties:

   a. ____.

   b. ____.

   c. ____.

   d. ____.

   e. ____.

TRUE-FALSE QUESTIONS

Circle **T** (true) or **F** (false)

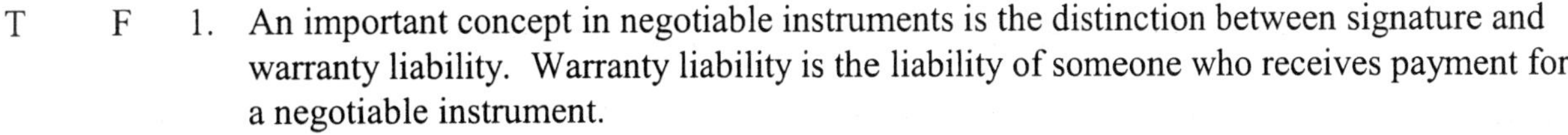

T F 1. An important concept in negotiable instruments is the distinction between signature and warranty liability. Warranty liability is the liability of someone who receives payment for a negotiable instrument.

T F 2. Once someone in payment for a debt accepts a negotiable instrument, the debt is immediately extinguished.

T F 3. The maker of a note is primarily liable for payment of the note, and if a note has more than one maker, then the makers are jointly and severally liable for payment.

T F 4. Indorsers of notes are primarily liable for payment of the notes and must pay immediately once a note is presented.

T F 5. Larry wants to borrow $5,000 from his bank. The bank feels uneasy about Larry's creditworthiness and requests that Larry's father, Frank, also sign the note. Frank is known as an indorser.

T F 6. In general, an agent who signs a negotiable promissory note on behalf of a principal may be personally liable for payment of the note unless the agent indicates that he or she is signing as an agent and states the name of the principal.

T F 7. Susan steals one of Carol's blank checks. Susan forges Carol's name as drawer on the check and makes it out to "CASH" in the amount of $1,000. Susan then takes the check to Carol's bank and cashes it. Under these facts, Carol must bear the loss for this forgery.

T F 8. When you present a check for payment you warrant that the check has not been altered. In this situation, if the check has been altered, then the bank may demand that you repay the sum it paid to you.

T F 9. According to the fictitious-payee rule, if someone issues a negotiable instrument to someone pretending to be the named payee, then any indorsement in the name of the payee is valid so long as the person who pays is not aware of the fraud.

T F 10. If a bank clerk carelessly fails to check the identification of a person who cashes a check, and if it turns out that the check was in fact forged, then the bank will be liable.

T F 11. Employer is fraudulently induced by Employer's agent to issue a check to a fictitious (nonexistent) creditor, and Employer gives the check to the agent. In this case, the agent can negotiate the check by indorsing the fictitious creditor's name.

MULTIPLE CHOICE QUESTIONS

1. ____ In which case may Nick have secondary liability to pay if the instrument in question is subsequently dishonored?
   a. Nick issued a check to Clint.
   b. Nick issued a negotiable promissory note to Lonnie.
   c. Ed issued a check for cash to Nick. Nick negotiated the check to Kate without indorsing it.
   d. a and c.

2. ____ In which case does Drake have primary liability to pay the instrument in question?
   a. Drake issued a check to Rhonda.
   b. Sally sold goods to Drake, and Sally issued a sales draft ordering Drake to pay the $500 purchase price to First Bank. Drake signed the draft, thereby accepting it.
   c. Dorothy issued a check to Drake. Drake indorsed the check "Drake Soren," and then negotiated the check to Frank.
   d. a and b.

3. ____ Max issued Irene a $9,000 note. Irene sold the note to Fair Factors, indorsing it "without recourse." Max failed to pay the note because of a lack of funds. Under these facts:
   a. Irene has secondary liability to pay the note.
   b. Irene has warranty liability to pay the note.
   c. Irene has no liability to pay the note.
   d. a and b.

4. ____ Abe issued a negotiable note to Kay. Certain collateral secured payment of the note. Kay indorsed the note "Kay Jones," and negotiated the note and security interest to Bart. In which situation is Kay discharged from liability on the note?
   a. Bart extended the time for payment of the note without Kay's consent.
   b. Bart accepted an early partial payment from Abe without Kay's consent.
   c. Bart terminated the security interest in the collateral without Kay's consent.
   d. a and c.

5. ____ Maker issued and delivered her negotiable promissory note to Perry Mills. Perry negotiated the note to Hans who took it in good faith and for value. Perry indorsed the note "Without recourse, Perry Mills." Under these facts:
   a. Perry's indorsement is an unqualified indorsement.
   b. Perry's indorsement is a qualified indorsement that destroys the negotiable nature of the note.
   c. If Maker fails to pay the note, Perry does not have secondary liability to pay it.
   d. a and c.

6. ____ B&K Inc. wanted to borrow $5,000 from Myra. A written promissory note stated that B&K Inc. promised to pay $5,000 on demand to the order of Myra.
Tim Blue, President of B&K Inc., was authorized to sign the note and he signed it:

B&K Inc.

By *Tim Blue*

President of B&K Inc.

a. Tim Blue is personally liable to pay the note Myra.
b. Tim Blue is not personally liable to pay the note to Myra.
c. B&K Inc. is liable to pay the note to Myra.
d. b and c.

7. ____ Sarah issues her check for $250 payable to the order of Claire. Claire indorses the check in blank to Sam to whom she owes $250. When Sam attempts to cash the check at Sarah's bank, the bank teller informs him that Sarah does not have sufficient funds in her account to pay the check and refuses to pay the check. Who has liability to pay the check to Sam?
a. Sarah.
b. Claire.
c. Sarah's bank.
d. a and b.

SHORT ESSAY

Explain how a negotiable instrument may be discharged. Give a brief example of each kind of discharge. Also, provide at least two examples of invalid discharges.

CASE PROBLEMS

Answer the following case problems, explaining your answers.

1. Wally issued a check to Jake, and the check was drawn on Wally's bank, Peoria Bank. Jake presented the check to Peoria Bank and it accepted the check for payment. The next day, Peoria Bank discovered that Wally had no money in his account and it refused to disburse the funds to Jake. Must Peoria Bank pay the check to Jake?

2. Allison posed as James' landlord, Michelle. For two months, James wrote out his rent checks payable to Michelle, but gave them to Allison thinking she was Michelle. Allison indorsed and cashed these checks at Check-Rite Service.
Discuss the rights of Michelle, James, and Check-Rite in this case.

CHAPTER TWENTY-FOUR
LIABILITY FOR NEGOTIABLE INSTRUMENTS: BANKS AND THEIR CUSTOMERS

CHAPTER OUTLINE

I. Checking Accounts

II. The Customer's Right to Withdraw Funds

  A. The Payment Process for a Check

  B. Funds Availability

III. Electronic Banking

  A. The Electronic Fund Transfer Act

  B. Wire Transfers

WHAT YOU SHOULD KNOW

After reading this chapter you should understand:

the different roles that banks may play in relation to their customers;

the duties of a bank in a checking-account relationship;

the problems associated with stop-payment orders;

when a customer has a right to withdraw funds from a checking account;

the protections provided to consumers by the Electronic Funds Transfer Act;

what a wire transfer is and how it works; and

a bank's liability in cases of incorrect transfers.

REVIEW OF TERMS AND PHRASES

MATCHING EXERCISE

Select the term or phrase that best matches a statement or definition stated below. Each term or phrase is the best match for only one statement or definition.

Terms and Phrases

a. Article 4A

b. Beneficiary

c. Beneficiary's bank

d. Collecting bank

e. Depository bank

f. Electronic Fund Transfer Act (EFTA)

g. Funds transfer

h. Originator

i. Payment order

j. Postdated check

k. Stale check

l. Stop payment order

Statements and Definitions

____ 1. Instruction by a drawer to a drawee bank not to pay a check.

____ 2. Check that is dated later than the date on which it is actually issued.

____ 3. Request to pay money to or for the credit of a party without physically transferring money.

____ 4. Any bank that handles a check during the collection process (not including the payor bank).

____ 5. Party who initiates a funds transfer request.

____ 6. First bank to take a check.

____ 7. Law that generally regulates electronic funds transfers that are made by nonconsumers.

____ 8. Direction or request made by an originator or subsequent bank to make a funds transfer.

____ 9. Final bank that makes payment or gives credit to a beneficiary in accordance with payment order.

____10. Party who ultimately receives funds pursuant to a funds transfer.

____11. Law that governs electronic fund transfers by consumers.

____12. Check presented more than six months after the date on which it was issued.

REVIEW OF CONCEPTS

COMPLETION EXERCISE

Fill in the blanks with the words that most accurately complete each statement. Answers may or may not include terms used in the matching exercise. A term cannot be used to complete more than one statement.

1. Under Article 4, the ______________ ______________ is the bank that ultimately pays its customer's check.

2. An oral stop payment order is effective for ______________ ______________ and a written stop payment order is effective for ______________ ______________.

3. ______________ is a drawee bank's agreement that it will pay a check when it is presented for payment, regardless of the balance in the drawer's account at the time the check is presented.

4. A drawer cannot require a drawee bank to recredit its account due to a forged drawer's signature or alteration of a check unless the drawer gave the bank notice of such matters within ______________ ______________ after the drawer received his or her bank statement.

5. In the bank collection process, a bank must exercise ______________ ______________ in handling checks.

6. The EFTA regulates electronic fund transfers made by ______________.

7. Two examples of electronic fund transfer systems are ______________________________ and ______________________________.

TRUE-FALSE QUESTIONS

Circle **T** (true) or **F** (false)

T F 1. A depository bank is the first bank to take a check.

T F 2. Banks are required by law to return all canceled checks to their customers.

T F 3. If First Sun Bank wrongfully fails to honor a customer's checks, then the customer may sue the bank for both actual and consequential damages.

T F 4. Once a bank discovers that one of its customers suffers from mental incompetence, the bank legally must take responsibility for paying that customer's bills.

T F 5. Lila writes a check to Bill for $300. Without Lila'a knowledge, Bill very cleverly and skillfully alters the amount of the check to read $390. Lila's bank pays the check. Under these facts, the bank may deduct $390 from Lila's account.

T F 6. Fred writes a check to Karen for $1,500. Two days after writing the check Fred puts a written stop-payment order on the check. Under these facts, Fred's bank is legally entitled to cash this check ten months later without incurring liability to Fred.

T F 7. Mell deposits with a teller a $4,000 cashier's check that is to be deposited into his checking account with the bank. Under these facts, Mell's bank is legally obligated to make all of these funds available for withdrawal on the next business day.

T F 8. Charlie deposits a $500 personal, out-of-state check issued by a distant cousin into his checking account. Under these facts, Charlie's bank is legally obligated to make all of these funds available for withdrawal on the next business day.

T F 9. In emergencies, banks may make automatic transfers of funds from customer's accounts without their customers' prior approval.

T F 10. If a customer's ATM card is stolen and used to withdraw $2,000 from the customer's checking account, the customer is liable for a maximum of $50 provided that the customer reports the card stolen within two days.

T F 11. A drawer may be criminally prosecuted for issuing a bad check if the drawer's account has insufficient funds to pay the check and the check was issued with the intent to defraud a payee.

T F 12. Drawer issued a postdated check and informed Drawee Bank of this fact. Nonetheless, Drawee Bank paid the check before the date of the check. In this case, Drawee Bank cannot be held liable for damages that Drawer may suffer due to the early payment the check.

T F 13. A drawer may be barred from asserting a forged signature or alteration against a drawee bank if the drawer failed to exercise proper care in examining a bank statement or canceled checks and in notifying the drawee bank of any improper payment.

T F 14. The EFTA governs consumers' funds transfers that are accomplished by issuance of checks.

T F 15. The Gramm-Leach-Liley Privacy Act of 1999 authorizes banks and other financial institutions to disclose non-public information regarding their consumer clients to third parties without having to inform their clients or having to first obtain their clients' permission to do so.

MULTIPLE CHOICE QUESTIONS

1. _____ Oscar issued a check to Juan. Juan negotiated the check to Laura, a holder in due course. On April 2, Oscar gave his bank an oral stop payment order on the check because the check had been issued as payment for goods that breached certain warranties (a personal defense). On April 4, Laura presented the check for payment, and Oscar's bank paid the check. Under these facts:

a. The stop payment order was not binding. Stop payment orders must be made in writing.
b. The stop payment order was not binding. A bank has three days before it must act in accordance with a stop payment order.
c. The stop payment order was binding, but Oscar is still liable to pay the check to Laura.
d. The stop payment order was binding, and it terminated Oscar's liability to pay the check.

2.____ Cody has a checking account with State Bank. Cody has $10,000 in his checking account. Cody issued a check to Paul for $5,000. Paul properly presented the check for payment to State Bank, but the bank dishonored the check. As a result, Cody incurred $100 damages and Paul incurred $50 damages. Under these facts:

a. State Bank is not liable to Cody or Paul.
b. State Bank is liable to Paul for $50 in damages, but it is not liable to Cody.
c. State Bank is liable to Cody for $100 in damages, but it is not liable to Paul.
d. State Bank is liable to Cody for $100 in damages, and it is liable to Paul for $50 in damages.

3.____ Dan's checkbook was stolen by Thief. Thief forged Dan's signature on a check and issued it to Penny, who was unaware of the forgery. Penny presented the check for payment to First Bank, the drawee bank. First Bank paid the check and charged Dan's account for the amount of the check. Under these facts:

a. First Bank was entitled to charge Dan's account for the check, and it has no obligation to recredit his account.
b. First Bank must recredit Dan's account for the amount of the check.
c. Between First Bank and Dan, First Bank must bear any loss that may occur due to its payment of the check.
d. b and c.

4.____ Sal has a checking account with SunBank. There is $43,057 in his account on June 2 when he dies. At the time of his death, Sal has two checks outstanding: one for $350 to his auto mechanic and one for $47.89 to the local grocery store. On June 4, the mechanic learns that Sal is dead and he immediately goes to SunBank and demands payment of the $350 check. Under these facts:

a. SunBank must pay the check no matter what.
b. SunBank must not pay the check no matter what.
c. SunBank bank may pay the check if a stop payment order has not been received from someone claiming an interest in the account.
d. SunBank must do what it thinks Sal would have wanted it to do.

5.____ Drew issued an incomplete check. Drew gave the check to Ginger, telling Ginger to complete it for $100. Ginger instead completed the check for $500 and she negotiated it to Hank, a holder in due course. Hank presented the check to Drew's bank for payment and it paid $500 to Hank. The bank did not know about the unauthorized completion. Under these facts, the bank may charge Drew's account for:

a. $0.
b. $100.
c. $500.
d. Any amount that the bank deems reasonable.

6. ____ Mia issued a check for $500 and delivered it to Paul, the payee. Paul artfully raised the amount to $5,000 and presented the altered check to Mia's bank for payment. The bank was unaware of the alteration. The bank paid $5,000 to Paul and charged Mia's account for this amount. Assuming that the money cannot be recovered from Paul, who ultimately is responsible for the $5,000 paid to Paul?

a. Mia is responsible for the entire $5,000.
b. Mia is responsible for $500 and Mia's bank is responsible for $4,500.
c. Mia's bank is responsible for the entire $5,000.
d. No one is responsible for anything.

7. ____ Consumer electronic fund transfers are governed by:

a. Common law of contracts.
b. UCC Article 4.
c. Electronic Funds Transfer Act.
d. All of the above.

SHORT ESSAY

Discuss briefly the process by which businesses make large wire transfers of money. What law governs these transactions?

CASE PROBLEM

Answer the following problem, briefly explaining your answer.

Greg has a bank account with First Federal Bank. First Federal issued Greg an ATM card that allowed him to withdraw funds from his personal bank account through the use of automated teller machines. On Monday, Greg's ATM card is stolen by a thief who uses it to withdraw $750 from Greg's account. Greg discovers the theft on Thursday, and he immediately informs First Federal of the theft.

a. What law governs Greg's rights in this case?
b. Describe a consumer's liability for the unauthorized use of a lost or stolen EFT card.
c. For how much of the unauthorized transfer is Greg liable?

CHAPTER TWENTY-FIVE
SECURED TRANSACTIONS

CHAPTER OUTLINE

I. Revised Article 9: Terms and Scope
   A. Article 9 Revisions
   B. Scope of Revised Article 9

II. Attachment of a Security Interest
   A. Agreement
   B. Control and Possession
   C. Value
   D. Debtor Rights in the collateral
   E. Attachment to Future Property

III. Perfection
   A. Nothing Less than Perfection
   B. Perfection by Filing
   C. Perfection by Possession or Control
   D. Perfection of Consumer Goods
   E. Perfection of Movable Collateral and Fixtures

IV. Protection of Buyers
   A. Buyers in Ordinary Course of Business
   B. Buyers of Consumer Goods
   C. Buyers of Chattel Paper, Instruments and Documents
   D. Liens

V. Priorities Among Creditors
   A. Filing versus Control or Possession
   B. Priority Involving a Purchase Money Security Interest

VI. Default and Termination
   A. Default
   B. Termination

WHAT YOU SHOULD KNOW

After reading this chapter you should understand:

what the term "secured transaction" means;

what the terms used in Article 9 of the UCC mean;

what kinds of goods and property Article 9 applies to;

how a security interest attaches;

the various ways in which a security interest may be perfected;

how a security interest in consumer goods may be perfected;

what a purchase money security interest (PMSI) is;

the respective rights of a buyer in ordinary course of business and a secured party;

the respective rights of a buyer of consumer goods and a secured party;

ways that buyers are protected from the security interests of others;

which creditors take priority when two or more creditors have a security interest in the same collateral;

what legal options secured parties have when debtors default; and

how a secured transaction is terminated.

REVIEW OF TERMS AND PHRASES

MATCHING EXERCISE

Select the term or phrase that best matches a statement or definition stated below. Each term or phrase is the best match for only one statement or definition.

Terms and Phrases

a. Attachment
b. Collateral
c. Consumer goods
d. Continuation statement
e. Equipment
f. Filing
g. Financing statement
h. Fixtures
i. Inventory
j. Perfected security interest
k. Pledge
l. Proceeds
m. Purchase money security interest
n. Security agreement
o. Termination statement

Statements and Definitions

____ 1. Goods that have become attached to real property.

____ 2. Recordation of a financing statement to perfect a security interest.

____ 3. Goods used or bought primarily for personal, family, or household purposes.

____ 4. Property that is subject to a security interest.

____ 5. Document that is filed with an appropriate government office, thereby giving third parties notice of a security interest and perfecting a security interest in many kinds of collateral.

____ 6. Document that is filed to continue perfection of a security interest for an additional five years.

____ 7. Goods used or bought primarily for use in a business.

____ 8. Statement filed to give notice of payment of a secured debt and termination of a security interest.

_____ 9. Goods held primarily for sale or lease by a debtor.

_____10. Agreement signed by debtor that grants a secured party a security interest in described collateral.

_____11. Security interest that secures repayment of either the unpaid purchase price for collateral or a loan that was used to purchase the collateral.

_____12. Security interest that gives a creditor priority to collateral over most creditors who subsequently acquire a security interest in the collateral or buyers who subsequently purchase the collateral.

_____13. Creation of an enforceable security interest in collateral.

_____14. Secured transaction pursuant to which a creditor takes possession of the collateral.

_____15. Cash, property, and other value received from a debtor's sale or other disposition of collateral.

REVIEW OF CONCEPTS

TRUE-FALSE QUESTIONS

Write **T** if the statement is true, write **F** if it is false.

T F 1. Article 9 of the UCC governs secured transactions in personal property.

T F 2. A security agreement may be oral if the secured party retains possession of the collateral.

T F 3. Collateral is classified according to the debtor's primary intended use of the collateral.

T F 4. Only creditors with a perfected security interest can repossess collateral upon a debtor's default.

T F 5. In general, a perfected security interest gives a secured party a superior right to collateral over most subsequent security interests in the collateral and most buyers of the collateral.

T F 6. If a security interest is perfected in one state and the collateral is then moved to another state, nothing is required to be filed in the second state to continue perfection of the security interest.

T F 7. In most states, if a title is issued for a motor vehicle, a creditor can perfect a security interest in the motor vehicle only by filing a financing statement.

T F 8. Article 9 prohibits a creditor from taking a security interest in after-acquired inventory.

T F 9. A financing statement must be signed by a debtor, but it need not describe the collateral.

T F 10. If a financing statement is filed in the wrong office, it does not perfect a security interest.

T F 11. Filing a financing statement perfects a security interest for ten years.

T F 12. If two creditors each have an unperfected security interest in the same collateral, then each creditor has priority to one-half of the collateral.

T F 13. *A* perfected a security interest in Debtor's after-acquired equipment. *B* later sold new equipment to Debtor on credit. *B* took a purchase money security interest in the equipment, *B* perfected this interest two days after Debtor received the equipment, and *B* gave *A* proper notice of its interest. In this case, *B*'s security interest in the new equipment has priority over *A*'s security interest.

T F 14. Al sold equipment to Dan on credit. Dan properly granted Al a security interest in the equipment to secure the unpaid price. Al filed a financing statement, perfecting the security interest. Dan sold the equipment to Jim. In this case, Jim takes the equipment free from Al's security interest.

T F 15. Unless otherwise agreed, a secured party must always resell or otherwise dispose of collateral.

T F 16. Perfection is the series of steps that a secured party must take to protects its rights in collateral against people other than the debtor.

T F 17. Article 9 does not cover security interests in intangible property, such as trademarks, goodwill, stocks and bonds.

T F 18. Security interests in inventory or equipment can usually be perfected by filing a financing statement with the Secretary of State in the state where the collateral is located.

T F 19. In order for a security interest to attach, the secured party must have given something of value to the debtor.

T F 20. Security interests cannot be taken in a business's account receivables.

T F 21. In general, a secured party may perfect a security interest in tangible goods by possession.

T F 22. State laws typically require that security interests in automobiles be filed with the Secretary of State.

T F 23. Even if a security interest is perfected in a debtor's inventory, a buyer in ordinary course of business takes such goods free of any security interest created by the seller.

T F 24. In general, a mechanic's lien attaches to personal property when someone makes improvements to that property.

T F 25. Article 9 does not cover security interests in real property, such as land.

MULTIPLE CHOICE QUESTIONS

1. ____ Barney sold a large screen TV to Raymond on credit and required Raymond to sign a security agreement. Which of the following items must be included to make the security agreement valid?
   a. The cost of the TV.
   b. Description of the TV.
   c. Requirement that Raymond carry insurance on the TV.
   d. The length of time for Raymond to complete payments.

2. ____ Select the collateral that is consumer goods:
   a. Debtor grants a security interest in an oven Debtor intends to use in Debtor's restaurant.
   b. Debtor grants a security interest in a stereo that Debtor intends to sell in Debtor's store.
   c. Debtor grants a security interest in a table saw that Debtor intends to use at home.
   d. All of the above.

3. ____ Giuseppe bought a portable fan to help cool off his restaurant. How is the fan categorized under the UCC?
   a. Inventory.
   b. Consumer goods.
   c. Fixtures.
   d. Equipment.

4. ____ Max sold Darla a new intercom system on credit and he permanently installed it into her office building. What type of collateral is the intercom system?
   a. Inventory.
   b. Consumer goods.
   c. Fixtures.
   d. Equipment.

5.____ IKR Finance loaned $1,000 to Debtor. Debtor agreed to repay the $1,000 in one year, and Debtor signed a written security agreement granting IKR a security interest in an item of equipment owned by Debtor to secure this debt. IKR did not perfect the security interest. In this case:
   a. The security interest is attached. If Debtor defaults, IKR can repossess and sell the collateral.
   b. The security interest has not attached because IKR does not have possession of the collateral.
   c. The security interest has not attached because IKR did not give value.
   d. The security interest has not attached because IKR failed to perfect the security interest.

6.____ Spokes Inc. sold a bike to Dee on credit for Dee's personal use. Dee granted Spokes a security interest in the bike to secure payment of the unpaid purchase price. Spokes did not file a financing statement. Under these facts:
   a. Spokes' security interest in the bike is perfected.
   b. Spokes' security interest in the bike is not perfected.
   c. If Dee sells the bike to Phil for his personal use, Phil pays value, and Phil does not know of the security interest, then Phil will take the bike free from Spokes' security interest.
   d. a and c.

7.____ Leo lent $10,000 to B&B, a tire dealer. B&B signed a security agreement granting Leo a security interest in B&B's existing tire inventory. Leo did nothing to perfect this security interest, and B&B kept possession of the inventory. Under these facts:

a. Leo's security interest is perfected; a security interest in inventory is automatically perfected.
b. Leo's security interest is unperfected; Leo cannot repossess the inventory if B&B defaults.
c. Leo's security interest is unperfected; Leo's security interest has priority over a subsequent unperfected security interest that another creditor may take in the inventory.
d. Leo's security interest is unperfected; Leo's security interest has priority over a subsequent perfected security interest that another creditor may take in the inventory.

8.____ On May 1, First Bank perfected a security interest in Debtor's inventory. On June 1, Bob bought an item of the secured inventory from Debtor for cash in the ordinary course of business. On July 1, Second Bank acquired a perfected security interest in Debtor's same inventory. In this case:

a. Bob took the item of inventory subject to First Bank's security interest.
b. First Bank has a security interest in the proceeds received from the sale of inventory to Bob.
c. First Bank's security interest has priority over Second Bank's security interest.
d. b and c.

SHORT ESSAY

A secured party may be able to perfect its security interest in a number of different ways. Please explain the possible ways in which a security interest may be perfected. Give a brief example of at least three of these ways.

CASE PROBLEM

Answer the following problem, briefly explaining your answer.

Acme has a perfected security interest in Debtor's inventory to secure repayment of a $50,000 loan. Debtor has defaulted on three $1,000 monthly payments, and Acme has accelerated the entire debt.

1. Can Acme repossess the inventory without obtaining a court order to do so?
2. Can Acme commit a breach of the peace if necessary to repossess the inventory?
3. Can Debtor redeem the collateral?
4. How are proceeds from the sale to be applied?
5. Would Debtor be liable for any deficiency?

CHAPTER TWENTY-SIX
BANKRUPTCY

CHAPTER OUTLINE

I. Introduction to the Bankruptcy Code

II. Chapter 7 Liquidation

   A. Filing a Petition

   B. The Trustee

   C. Creditors

   D. Automatic Stay

   E. The Bankruptcy Estate

   F. The Payment of Claims

   G. Discharge

III. Chapter 11 Reorganization

   A. Debtor in Possession

   B. Creditor's Committee

   C. Plan of Organization

   D. Confirmation of the Plan

   E. Does Chapter 11 Work?

   F. Discharge

IV. Chapter 13 Consumer Reorganizations

   A. Beginning a Chapter 13 Case

   B. The Plan of Payment

   C. Discharge

V. Fairness Under the Code

WHAT YOU SHOULD KNOW

After reading this chapter you should understand:

the origin of the Bankruptcy Code;

the goals of the Bankruptcy Code;

how someone files for Chapter 7 bankruptcy;

the roles played by different parties in Chapter 7 bankruptcy;

the meaning of an automatic stay in bankruptcy proceedings;

the kinds of property that may be exempt from a bankruptcy estate;

when trustees can void transfers;

how creditor's claims are paid and the priority of these claims;

the kinds of debts that cannot be discharged;

the process involved in filing for Chapter 11 bankruptcy;

the effect of a discharge under Chapter 11 bankruptcy;

the process involved in filing a Chapter 13 bankruptcy;

the effect of a discharge under Chapter 13;

why some commentators believe the current Bankruptcy Code is unfair; and

the problems posed by debtors who owe creditors in more than one country.

REVIEW OF TERMS AND PHRASES

MATCHING EXERCISE

Select the term or phrase that best matches a statement or definition stated below. Each term or phrase is the best match for only one statement or definition.

Terms and Phrases

a. Automatic stay
b. Confirmation of plan
c. Debtor
d. Discharge
e. Exempt assets
f. Insider
g. Involuntary case
h. Liquidation proceeding
i. Preference
j. Priority
k. Proof of claim
l. Voluntary case

Statements and Definitions

____ 1. Creditor's written statement that alleges a claim against a debtor and the basis for the claim.
____ 2. Chapter 7 bankruptcy proceeding.
____ 3. Relative, business partner, director, or controlling person of an insolvent debtor.
____ 4. Court decree that releases a debtor from unpaid debts upon conclusion of a bankruptcy action.
____ 5. Bankruptcy proceeding that is commenced by the filing of a petition by a debtor.
____ 6. Approval of a Chapter 11 or Chapter 13 rehabilitation plan.
____ 7. Automatic prohibition that prevents a creditor from starting or continuing any legal action to collect a debt after a petition for bankruptcy has been filed.
____ 8. Assets that may be retained by a debtor despite the debtor's filing for Chapter 7 bankruptcy.
____ 9. The order in which payment is to be made under the Bankruptcy Act for certain unsecured claims.
____10. Bankruptcy proceeding that is commenced by the filing of a petition by creditors against a debtor.
____11. Party who files for bankruptcy.
____12. Improper transfer of property by a debtor to a creditor that allows the creditor to recover more than would be paid to the creditor pursuant to a bankruptcy liquidation.

REVIEW OF CONCEPTS

COMPLETION EXERCISE

Fill in the blanks with the words that most accurately complete each statement. Answers may or may not include terms used in the matching exercise. A term cannot be used to complete more than one statement.

1. Bankruptcy law is primarily _______________ law.

2. In a Chapter 7 bankruptcy, the bankruptcy estate is administered by a _______________.

3. Individuals, partnerships, and corporations in business can reorganize their businesses pursuant to a _______________ ____ bankruptcy.

4. Individuals with regular income who want to extend the time for payment of their debts may use a _______________ ____ bankruptcy.

5. If a debtor has more than twelve creditors, then at least _______________ unsecured creditors, with total unsecured claims of at least _______________ must sign an involuntary bankruptcy petition.

6. A transfer of assets by a debtor is a _______________ _______________ if it is made within one year and filing of the petition and the transfer is done to hinder, delay, or defraud creditors.

7. A debtor who has received a discharge under Chapter 7 or 11 bankruptcy cannot receive another discharge under Chapter 7 for at least _______________ years after the prior filing.

TRUE-FALSE QUESTIONS

Write **T** if the statement is true, write **F** if it is false.

T F 1. In a Chapter 13 bankruptcy, the court cannot approve a debtor's plan of payment unless all classes of creditors first approve such plan.

T F 2. An unsecured creditor must file a proof of claim within 90 days following the meeting of creditors in order to qualify for payment from the bankruptcy estate.

T F 3. A debtor cannot contest an involuntary bankruptcy petition that is filed by the debtor's creditors.

T F 4. Money owed for alimony, maintenance, and child support cannot be discharged in bankruptcy.

T F 5. In a Chapter 7 bankruptcy, a trustee generally assumes control of all nonexempt property belonging to the debtor at the time of filing of the petition for bankruptcy.

T F 6. A trustee may set aside a preferential transfer of property made to an insider by an insolvent debtor if the transfer was made within one year prior to the filing of a bankruptcy petition.

T F 7. In general, a payment of any past debt may be set aside if payment was made by an insolvent debtor within ninety days prior to the filing of a petition for bankruptcy and the payment enables the creditor to receive more than would be received in a Chapter 7 liquidation.

T F 8. A debtor has the duty to file a list of creditors and a list of the debtor's assets and liabilities.

T F 9. Employees have priority to payment for all unpaid wages, regardless of amount.

T F 10. In general, a debtor can claim only the exempt property that is permitted by the Bankruptcy Act. States do not have the power to specify property that may be exempt in a bankruptcy action.

T F 11. A discharge does not release a debtor from liability for unpaid student loans that came due within 7 years prior to filing for bankruptcy unless the debtor has acted in good faith and payment would cause an undue hardship.

T F 12. A discharge releases a debtor from liability for all unpaid income and property taxes.

T F 13. A debtor may reaffirm a debt that would have been discharged in a bankruptcy proceeding.

T F 14. In a Chapter 11 bankruptcy, the business of a debtor is discontinued and the assets of the debtor are liquidated in order to pay the creditors.

T F 15. A debtor is not discharged from a debt that arises from a judgment based on liability that was incurred as a result of the debtor's driving while legally intoxicated.

T F 16. A debtor's Chapter 11 rehabilitation plan may be approved even if some of the creditors' classes reject the plan.

T F 17. In general, a Chapter 11 plan that has been confirmed by the court is binding on all creditors and the creditors have only the rights stated in the plan.

T F 18. An individual whose unsecured or secured debts exceed certain limits may not be entitled to file a petition for Chapter 13 bankruptcy.

T F 19. A Chapter 13 plan of payment cannot be confirmed by the court unless all of the unsecured creditors receive at least as much as they would receive in a Chapter 7 bankruptcy of the debtor.

T F 20. State exempt property laws oftentimes widely differ regarding property that is exempt in bankruptcy proceedings.

MULTIPLE CHOICE QUESTIONS

1. ____ B&B Bakery just filed for Chapter 7 bankruptcy. B&B is in default on a loan from Arco Finance. Arco has a perfected security interest in B&B's equipment to secure payment of this debt. Under these facts:
   a. Arco can file a lawsuit against B&B in state court to collect the loan.
   b. Arco can immediately repossess and sell B&B's equipment pursuant to its security interest.
   c. Arco cannot sue B&B in state court and it cannot immediately repossess the equipment due to an automatic stay, but Arco will have priority to the equipment in the bankruptcy action.
   d. Arco no longer has a right to be paid; the bankruptcy filing terminated this right.

2. ____ Barbara was unemployed and insolvent. On June 10, Barbara sold her gold watch to a jeweler for $1,500, a fair value. On June 11, Barbara paid: $300 to her landlord for the current month's rent; $1,100 to her grandmother in payment of an old loan that would not have been paid in a Chapter 7 liquidation; and $100 in payment of the minimum monthly amount due on her personal credit card. On August 1, Barbara filed a petition for Chapter 7 bankruptcy. Which transfer or payment can be set aside by the bankruptcy trustee?
   a. Sale of the watch.
   b. Rent payment.
   c. Credit card payment.
   d. Loan payment that was made to Barbara's grandmother.

3. ____ Joyce filed a voluntary petition for Chapter 7 bankruptcy. Which of the following facts would *not* be a sufficient ground to deny Joyce a discharge in bankruptcy?
   a. Joyce was discharged in bankruptcy four years prior to filing the present bankruptcy petition.
   b. One month prior to filing for bankruptcy, Joyce transferred a rare coin collection to her brother with the intent to conceal the coin collection from her creditors.
   c. At the meeting of her creditors, Joyce lied under oath regarding her assets.
   d. Two months prior to filing for bankruptcy, Joyce sold her condo for a fair price.

4. ____ Ramon filed for Chapter 7 bankruptcy, and he received a discharge. Certain debts were not paid in Ramon's bankruptcy. Which of the following unpaid debts was discharged?
   a. $2,000 in child support owed for the support of Ramon's minor children.
   b. $1,500 owed to MasterCard.
   c. $1,000 in federal income taxes owed for the prior year.
   d. $5,000 judgment resulting from Ramon's embezzlement of money from a former employer.

5. ____ ARK Co. has filed a petition for Chapter 11 bankruptcy. ARK is indebted to ten unsecured creditors who are included in the same class of creditors. Under these facts:
   a. ARK Co. will serve as the debtor in possession and will continue to operate its business.
   b. A trustee will be appointed to operate the debtor's business.
   c. For one year after filing its bankruptcy petition, ARK Co. has the exclusive right to propose a plan of reorganization.
   d. a and c.

6. ____ Select the correct answer regarding Chapter 13 bankruptcy.
   a. In general, the debtor's plan of payment may extend up to seven years.
   b. The debtor's plan of payment must be feasible.
   c. As soon as the debtor's plan of payment is confirmed, all pre-petition debts that are not to be paid are permanently discharged.
   d. All of the above.

7. ____ The primary job of the trustee in a Chapter 7 bankruptcy is to:
   a. Create a reorganization plan for the debtor.
   b. Meet the needs of shareholders of the debtor.
   c. Gather the bankrupt's assets and divide them among creditors in the manner stated in the Bankruptcy Code.
   d. Determine on his or her own who should be paid and in what order.

8. ____ Liza borrows $60,000 to buy a boat. Her bank takes a security interest in the boat. Unfortunately Liza's finances fizzle and she files for Chapter 7 bankruptcy. At the time of filing for bankruptcy, the boat is worth only $30,000. Under these facts, Lisa's bank will probably:
   a. Recover the entire $60,000 as a secured creditor.
   b. Recover the entire $60,000 as a priority creditor.
   c. Recover $30,000 as a secured creditor and have an unsecured claim for the remaining $30,000.
   d. Recover nothing.

SHORT ESSAY

Briefly explain the Chapter 11 bankruptcy process. What does a debtor do in order to file for this type of bankruptcy? What role do creditors play in a Chapter 11 bankruptcy?

CASE PROBLEM

Answer the following case problem, explaining your answer.

Tarco Inc. filed for Chapter 7 bankruptcy. Tarco's assets are a building and $10,000 cash. Tarco has these creditors: (a) First Bank is owed $50,000. This debt is fully secured by the building. (b) Bud is owed $500 for a deposit he paid Tarco for consumer goods that he never received. (c) Mr. Atkins, the bankruptcy trustee, is owed a $6,000 fee. (d) Tina is owed $1,000 for wages she earned thirty days prior to Tarco's filing for bankruptcy. (e) Fuller Co. has a $5,000 unsecured claim for goods that it sold to Tarco.

Discuss the rights of Tarco Inc.'s creditors to be paid.

CHAPTER TWENTY-SEVEN
AGENCY

CHAPTER OUTLINE

I. Creating An Agency Relationship

   A. Consent

   B. Control

   C. Fiduciary Relationship

   D. Elements Not Required For An Agency Relationship

II. Duties Of Agents To Principals

   A. Duty of Loyalty

   B. Other Duties of an Agent

   C. Principal's Remedies When the Agent Breaches a Duty

III. Duties Of Principals To Agents

   A. Duty to Reimburse the Agent

   B. Duty to Cooperate

IV. Terminating An Agency Relationship

   A. Termination by Agent or Principal

   B. Principal or Agent Can No Longer Perform Required Duties

   C. Change in Circumstances

   D. Effect of Termination

V. Liability

   A. Principal's Liability for Contracts

   B. Agent's Liability for Contracts

   C. Principal's Liability for Torts

   D. Agent's Liability for Torts

WHAT YOU SHOULD KNOW

After reading this chapter you should understand:

- what is required to create an agency relationship;
- what a fiduciary duty is;
- what elements are not required to form an agency relationship;
- the agent's duty of loyalty and what it entails;
- the agent's duty to obey instructions;
- the agent's duty to act with reasonable care;
- the agent's duty to provide information;
- the duties of a gratuitous agent;
- the remedies that are available to a principal when an agent breaches a duty;
- the principal's duty to reimburse an agent in various situations;
- the principal's duty to cooperate with the agent;
- the various ways in which an agency relationship may be terminated;
- when a principal is liable for contracts made by his or her agent;
- the difference between express, implied, and apparent authority;
- the legal implications of ratification;
- when an agent is liable for contracts made on behalf of a principal;
- what the doctrine of *respondeat superior* involves;
- the difference between a servant and an independent contractor;
- when a principal is liable for torts committed by his or her agents;
- what is meant by "scope of employment;"
- the rules relating to a principal's liability for agents' negligent and intentional torts;
- what happens if an agent defrauds or defames a third party; and
- the agent's responsibility for his or her own torts.

REVIEW OF TERMS AND PHRASES

MATCHING EXERCISE

Select the term or concept that best matches a definition or statement set forth below. Each term or concept is the best match for only one definition or statement.

Terms and Concepts

a. Abandonment
b. Agency at will
c. Agent
d. Apparent authority
e. Duty of care
f. Duty of obedience
g. Equal dignities rule
h. Express authority
i. Fiduciary duty
j. Fully disclosed principal
k. Implied authority
l. Indemnify
m. Independent contractor
n. Partially disclosed principal
o. Principal
p. Ratification
q. Term agreement
r. Undisclosed principal

Definitions and Statements

____ 1. Obligation of an agent to follow all lawful instructions of a principal in all matters relating to the agency relationship.

____ 2. Person who is employed to accomplish a task. The person employed has the right to control how to accomplish the assigned work.

____ 3. Legal doctrine that requires the appointment of an agent to be in writing if the agent is to enter into a contract that must be in writing.

____ 4. Agency contract that establishes a fixed period of time for the agency relationship.

____ 5. Obligation of an agent to act in good faith and to act in the best interest of a principal in all matters relating to the agency relationship.

____ 6. Person who empowers another to negotiate contracts on his or her behalf.

____ 7. Agency relationship that may be terminated by either party at any time.

____ 8. Person who is empowered to negotiate contracts on behalf of another.

____ 9. Reimburse someone for expenses that have been incurred or may be incurred.

____ 10. Servant's act of forsaking any intent to act on behalf of his or her master.

____ 11. Authority that is orally or in writing given by a principal to an agent.

____ 12. Principal's express or implied agreement to be bound by an unauthorized contract made by an agent.

____ 13. Principal whose existence and identify are known by a third party.

____ 14. Obligation of an agent to exercise reasonable prudence and judgment when acting on behalf of a principal.

____ 15. Principal whose existence, but not identity, is known by a third party.

____ 16. Authority that arises because a principal falsely creates the impression that an agent has authority to act.

____ 17. Principal whose existence and identity are not known to a third party.

____ 18. Authority that arises because of an agent's position.

COMPLETION EXERCISE

Fill in the blanks with the words that most accurately complete each statement. Answers may or may not include terms used in the matching exercise. A term cannot be used to complete more than one statement.

1. Three elements that must be present to establish an agency relationship are ________________, __________________, and ________________ ________________.

2. In general, the duty of care requires an agent to act with _____________ ______________ and the agent's failure to do so may render the agent liable to the principal for any damages suffered.

3. In a ________________ ________________, an agent voluntarily agrees to perform a task for a principal.

4. The _______________ of ______________ requires the agent to look out for the principal's best interests.

5. A principal's two primary duties to an agent are the duty to ______________ and the duty to ________________.

6. Identify five general ways that an agent and principal may terminate their agency relationship:

   a. ____.

   b. ____.

   c. ____.

   d. ____.

   e. ____.

7. An _______________ is a relationship pursuant to which one party negotiates and makes contracts on behalf of another party.

8. When an agent represents a ______________ principal, the agent does not ordinarily incur any personal liability on the contract in question.

9. When agents represent an ______________ principal, the other contracting party actually believes that the agents are acting on their own behalf.

10. The doctrine of ______________ ______________ generally holds masters liable for torts that their servants commit while acting within the course and scope of their employment.

11. In general, principals are liable for nonphysical torts of their agents, such as misrepresentation, only when their agents had some type of ______________ to act on behalf of the principals.

12. Two major issues associated with determination of whether a person is a servant acting within the scope of employment are ______________ and ______________.

13. Robert hired Nell to negotiate and make contracts on his behalf. Robert is a ______________ and Nell is an ______________.

14. Larry hired AAA Tax Service to prepare his personal tax returns. AAA has complete control over how it will prepare the returns. AAA is not a servant; instead it is an ______________ ______________.

15. Describe three circumstances when a principal may be held liable for contracts made on its behalf by an agent:

   a. ____.

   b. ____.

   c. ____.

TRUE-FALSE QUESTIONS

Circle **T** (true) or **F** (false)

T F 1. In general, agents are liable on contracts that they make on behalf of disclosed principals.

T F 2. A contract is not essential in order to create an agency relationship.

T F 3. A primary feature of the agency relationship is that all agents are paid for their services.

T F 4. In general, a principal has the power to terminate an agency relationship even if the termination breaches a contract between the principal and agent.

T F 5. An agent breaches the duty to obey the principal's instructions when the agent refuses to do something illegal that the principal requested.

T F 6. If the agency agreement does not specify a time limit, either party generally has the legal right and power to terminate the relationship at any time.

T F 7. In general, when a principal dies, the agency terminates.

T F 8. If the principal wrongfully discharges an agent, the agent may have the right to recover damages from the principal.

T F 9. In an agency relationship, the principal agrees to perform a task for and under the control of the agent.

T F 10. In an agency relationship, the agent has a fiduciary relationship with the principal.

T F 11. Absent an agreement to the contrary, an agent may compete against a former principal once the agency relationship is terminated.

T F 12. Karen is an agent of Mrs. Smith's Cookies, her principal. During the agency relationship, Karen learns the secret recipe for Mrs. Smith's famous chocolate chip cookies. If Karen quits Mrs. Smith's she may use the recipe so long as she calls her cookies "Karen's Cookies."

T F 13. An agent's duty to provide his or her principal with information requires an agent to provide accurate information regarding any matters that the agent should think that the principal might want to know.

T F 14. If an agent makes an unauthorized purchase for the principal, the principal is never responsible for reimbursing the agent because the agent acted beyond the scope of his or her duties.

T F 15. Jennie is the agent of Cliff and the goal of the agency relationship is to acquire five women's clothing stores in Denver, Colorado. Under these facts, the agency relationship will terminate once Jennie helps Cliff to acquire the fifth such store.

T F 16. As a general rule, the principal is bound by a contract that is entered into on its behalf by a properly authorized agent.

T F 17. The law assumes that an agent has the authority to do anything reasonable that will contribute to the accomplishment of the agent's assigned task.

T F 18. In a case of apparent authority, the principal has given the agent express powers to act, but the agent has refused to do so.

T F 19. Sub-agents are people hired by intermediate agents to perform a delegated task.

T F 20. In the case of an undisclosed principal, the third party may recover only from the agent.

T F 21. Bob works for Denise. While Bob is driving home after a hard day's work, he accidentally drives his pick-up truck into Fred, injuring him. Under these facts, Denise is liable for the harm to Fred.

T F 22. If an agent makes an unauthorized contract on behalf of a principal, the principal may choose to ratify all or only a portion of the contract.

T F 23. A principal is liable for every contract that is made on the principal's behalf by an agent.

T F 24. If a principal ratifies a contract, the contract is treated as if it were valid from its inception.

T F 25. Builders Inc. hired Jim as supervisor for a building project. Jim hired, trained, supervised, and fired workmen as needed to complete the project. Jim is exercising implied authority.

T F 26. Principals are not responsible for the actions of agents unless their authority is stated in writing.

T F 27. A principal cannot be held liable on a contract that is made by an agent who acted with only apparent authority.

T F 28. Masters may be held liable for torts committed by servants while they are on a reasonably foreseeable detour from their assigned tasks.

MULTIPLE CHOICE QUESTIONS

1. ____ General Contractors Unlimited (GCU) hired Piper Plumbing, Inc. to install the plumbing for an apartment building that GCU was building for an owner. Piper is obligated to install the plumbing in accordance with certain building plans, but Piper may otherwise control its own workers, method of construction, tools, supplies, etc. In this case, Piper is an:
   a. Employee of GCU.
   b. Agent for GCU.
   c. Independent contractor for GCU.
   d. Servant for GCU.

2. ____ Zsa Zsa, a circus performer, employed Eddie as her agent to find her engagements for the next five years. Under these facts, the parties' agency relationship would terminate by operation of law after one year if:
   a. Eddie does merely an average job in finding engagements for Zsa Zsa.
   b. Zsa Zsa declares bankruptcy.
   c. Zsa Zsa decides that she no longer wants Eddie to represent her.
   d. Zsa Zsa decides to limit the number of engagements she will accept each year.

3. ____ Jenni owns a construction company that builds custom houses. She hired Steve as her agent to solicit new business. Steve was approached by a celebrity who wanted to have a $3 million custom house built. Steve did not disclose this information to Jenni so that he could take advantage of this opportunity himself. Under these facts, Steve has:
   a. Breached his duty of loyalty.
   b. Breached his duty to give notice.
   c. Not breached any duty.
   d. a and b.

4. ____ There are several requirements for creating an agency relationship. In general, which of the following is *not* a requirement?
   a. The agent and principal mutually consent that the agent will act on behalf of the principal.
   b. The appointment of the agent must be in writing.
   c. The agent and principal create a fiduciary relationship.
   d. The agent be subject to the principal's control.

5. ____ Kyle wanted to get a job as purchasing agent for Ace Sporting Goods Store. Kyle wants to impress Ace with his business skills in hopes of gaining the desired position. To impress Ace and on behalf of Ace, Kyle orders 250 pairs of hot pink sneakers from a manufacturer with whom Ace had never done business. When the sneakers arrive, Ace refuses to accept them. Does Ace have the right to reject the sneakers?
   a. No, Kyle intended to represent Ace in making this contract.
   b. No, the manufacturer thought that it was selling the sneakers to Ace.
   c. Yes, Ace never consented to Kyle being its agent.
   d. a and b.

6. ____ Arlen is a divorce lawyer. Cathy asks Arlen to represent her in a divorce and he agrees. Several days later, Cathy's estranged husband, Hubert, comes to Arlen's office. Hubert says that it makes more sense for Arlen to represent both Cathy and Hubert in order to streamline the process. Arlen agrees and undertakes representation of Hubert in the divorce matter without first consulting Cathy. Under these facts:
   a. Arlen has violated his duty to compete.
   b. Arlen is not permitted to represent both Cathy and Hubert because they have conflicting interests.
   c. Arlen has violated his duty not to engage in secret self-dealing.
   d. Arlen has done nothing improper and he may represent both Cathy and Hubert.

7. ____ Principal hired Alex as general manager for a fixed two-year term. One year has now passed, and Principal no longer wants Alex to be general manager even though Alex has properly performed all of his contractual and agency duties. Under these facts:
   a. Principal has the legal right and power to terminate Alex as general manager.
   b. Principal has the legal right, but not the power, to terminate Alex as general manager.
   c. Principal has the power, but not the legal right, to terminate Alex as general manager.
   d. Principal does not have the legal right or the power to terminate Alex as general manager.

8. ____ Juan was the new car sales manager for Rev Car Sales. Juan was authorized to sell Rev's cars, but he was told not to accept promissory notes as payment. In good faith and with the intent to benefit Rev, Juan sold a car to Buyer in exchange for Buyer's promissory note. Buyer subsequently failed to pay the note, and Rev suffered a $3,000 loss. Under these facts:
   a. Juan is liable to Rev for $3,000 because he breached his duty of obedience when he accepted the promissory note from Buyer.
   b. Juan is not liable to Rev because Juan acted in good faith in accepting the note.
   c. Juan is not liable to Rev because Juan intended to benefit Rev when he accepted the note.
   d. Juan is not liable to Rev because an agent can disobey a principal's instructions if the agent believes that it is in the principal's best interest to do so.

9.____ Barbara works as an agent for Martin. Barbara's job is to travel throughout the Southeast looking for new artistic talent. In this case:

a. Martin has a duty not to impede Barbara's efforts.
b. Martin has a duty to pay Barbara's travel expenses.
c. Martin does not have a duty to pay for Barbara's travel expenses.
d. a and b.

10.____ Niles, as agent for an undisclosed principal, entered into a contract to buy and sell land with LandHo!, Inc. Which of the following is a true statement?

a. LandHo! can sue both Niles and the principal if the principal breaches.
b. LandHo! can sue Niles or the principal if the principal breaches.
c. LandHo! cannot sue Niles or the principal because the principal was undisclosed.
d. The principal can sue Niles for making the contract on its behalf.

11.____ In which situation is Pat (the principal) liable on the contract in question?

a. Pat signed a written power of attorney, authorizing an agent to sell his house. On Pat's behalf, the agent contracted with a third party for the sale of the house.
b. An agent signed a contract to sell Pat's car, but Pat had not authorized this sale. Later Pat decided to accept the contract as written and signed it.
c. Pat appointed an agent as general manager of a retail store. The agent hired a cashier who was necessary for the proper operation of the store and for the agent to carry out her duties as general manager.
d. All of the above.

12.____ Sue applied for a job at Paul's Cafe. When Sue arrived for her job interview, Paul was busy with other business. To avoid having to interview Sue, Paul told her: "Go see Agnes, the head cashier. Agnes is responsible for all hiring decisions." Paul lied (Agnes was not supposed to hire anyone on her own), but Sue did not know this. After the interview, Agnes hired Sue to work at the cafe. What type of authority did Agnes have in this case?

a. Express authority
b. Implied authority
c. Apparent authority
d. No authority

13.____ Lynn is the purchasing agent for Patty, owner of a medical supply business. Lynn was expressly authorized to buy all necessary inventory on Patty's behalf. Acting pursuant to this authority, Lynn contracted to purchase some inventory from BandageCo. Patty breached this contract and failed to pay the purchase price. In this case, BandageCo. may hold Lynn personally liable on the contract if:

a. Patty's existence and identity were disclosed to BandageCo. at the time of contracting.
b. Patty's existence, but not identity, was disclosed to BandageCo. at the time of contracting.
c. Patty's existence and identity were undisclosed to BandageCo. at the time of contracting.
d. b and c.

14.____ In which scenario is Lupe, the owner of Lupe's Dress Shop, liable for her employee's tort?

a. Ellen, an employee, struck her ex-husband, who had come into the store, because he told her that he was getting remarried.
b. Ed, who was a janitor for the store and under Lupe's direction and control, failed to put away a ladder. Later, a customer was injured when the ladder fell on her.
c. Edger, an in-store salesperson, was driving his own car to a restaurant for lunch when he struck a pedestrian. At the time, Edger was not running any errands for Lupe.
d. All of the above.

15.____ Todd was a delivery person for Kar World. While driving to deliver a part to a customer, Todd negligently damaged Kip's car. Todd was speeding at the time of the accident, a violation of a Kar World work regulation. Under these facts, who is liable to Kip?

a. Only Todd.
b. Only Kar World.
c. Todd and Kar World.
d. No one.

16.____ In which case would a principal be directly liable for a worker's tort?

a. Norm, the principal, instructed Al, his agent, to assault Tim, a person who owed Norm's business a great deal of money.
b. Zoe hired an independent contractor to put a new roof on her home. While transporting material to Zoe's house, the contractor negligently injured a third party.
c. Kevin, owner of Children Day Care Center, hired Carl as a staff worker. One day, Kevin snuck out of work and was driving 50 miles away to visit his girlfriend when he negligently drove his personal vehicle into a third party's vehicle.
d. All of the above.

SHORT ESSAY

When is a master liable for torts committed by its servant? Please explain this issue as fully as possible, being sure to cover both intentional and negligent torts.

CASE PROBLEM

Answer the following case problem, explaining your answer.

Singh and Ratou are partners in a small turban manufacturing business. In their partnership agreement, the parties agreed that they may each act on behalf of the partnership in making partnership contracts. On behalf of the partnership, Ratou contracted with California Fabrics to buy muslin that was needed for making turbans. Ratou, however, agreed to a higher price than normal because California Fabrics promised to pay her a secret commission on the sale. Under these facts:

1. What relationship exists between the individual partners and the partnership?
2. What is the nature of this relationship?
3. Did Ratou breach any duty owed to the partnership?

CHAPTER TWENTY-EIGHT
EMPLOYMENT LAW

CHAPTER OUTLINE

I. Employment Security

   A. National Labor Relations Act

   B. Family Medical and Leave Act

   C. Wrongful Discharge

      1. Public Policy

      2. Contract Law

      3. Tort Law

II. Safety and Privacy in the Workplace

   A. Workplace Safety

   B. Employee Privacy

III. Financial Protection

   A. Fair Labor Standards Act

   B. Workers' Compensation

   C. Social Security

   D. Pension Benefits

IV. Employment Discrimination

   A. Equal Pay Act of 1963

   B. Title VII

      1. Proof of Discrimination

      2. Religion

      3. Defenses to Charges of Discrimination

      4. Affirmative Action

      5. Sexual Harassment

      6. Procedures and Remedies

      7. Pregnancy

   C. Age Discrimination

   D. Americans with Disabilities Act

WHAT YOU SHOULD KNOW

After reading this chapter you should understand:

the common-law rule of employment at will;

the general provisions of the National Labor Relations Act;

what the Family Medical and Leave Act provides;

the possible bases for a wrongful discharge claim;

special protections for government workers from wrongful discharge;

how contracts may provide a basis for a wrongful discharge claim;

how employers may be liable to employees under tort law;

general provisions of the Fair Labor Standards Act;

what Worker's Compensation provides;

the benefits provided by the Social Security system;

what ERISA is and what it protects;

what OSHA is and what it does;

when employers do and do not have a right to test employees for drugs or alcohol use;

what the Equal Pay Act requires;

what Title VII of the Civil Rights Act provides;

how a plaintiff brings a Title VII case;

the possible defenses to a Title VII case;

what sexual harassment is and the different forms of harassment that are prohibited;

what constitutes age discrimination; and

what the Americans with Disabilities Act requires.

REVIEW OF TERMS AND PHRASES

MATCHING EXERCISE

Select the term or phrase that best matches a statement or definition stated below. Each term or phrase is the best match for only one statement or definition.

Terms and Phrases

a. Covenant of good faith and fair dealing
b. Electronic Communications Privacy Act of 1986
c. Employee Polygraph Protection Act of 1988
d. Employment-at-will doctrine
e. Equal Pay Act of 1963
f. ERISA
g. Fair Labor Standards Act
h. Family and Medical Leave Act
i. Just (good) cause for job termination
j. National Labor Relations Act
k. OSHA
l. Public policy rule
m. Social security
n. Title VII
o. Workers' compensation law
p. Wrongful discharge

Statements and Definitions

____ 1. An employee's theft, failure to perform duties, or other serious misconduct.

____ 2. Federal law that established employees' right to collectively bargain with employers.

____ 3. Federal law that requires the same pay for male and female workers who perform the same work.

____ 4. Federal program that pays benefits to workers who are retired, disabled, or temporarily unemployed.

____ 5. Legal principle that generally authorizes an employer at any time and for any reason to discharge an employee who is not hired for a fixed term.

____ 6. Administrative agency that enforces federal laws relating to health and safety in the workplace.

____ 7. Federal law that generally requires vesting of employee pension rights after five years of service.

____ 8. State law that provides benefits for work-related injuries and certain occupational illnesses.

____ 9. Federal law that allows employers to monitor workers' telephone calls and e-mail if certain conditions are met.

____10. Federal law that requires employers to pay most employees at least a specified minimum wage.

____11. Federal law that prohibits the use or suggestion of lie detector tests in most employment situations.

____12. Federal law that generally forbids employment discrimination based on race, religion, national origin, color, or gender.

____13. Doctrine that forbids discharging an employee for a reason that violates a fundamental public value or interest.

____14. Implied obligation that an employer will not deny an employee an opportunity to enjoy benefits attendant to employment.

____15. Federal law that creates the right of certain employees to take up to twelve weeks of unpaid leave in certain situations.

____16. Doctrine that prohibits discharging an employee for a reason that is unlawful.

REVIEW OF CONCEPTS

TRUE-FALSE QUESTIONS

Circle **T** (true) or **F** (false)

T F 1. Under the common law, the basic rule of employment allowed only for-cause termination.

T F 2. The Family Medical and Leave Act allows employees to take up to six months of paid leave from work if they have a medical emergency in their family.

T F 3. All states have some form of statute, which protect whistleblowers from retaliation by their employers.

T F 4. Oral promises made during the hiring process sometimes are legally binding.

T F 5. Under the Fair Labor Standards Act, employees other than professional staff cannot work more than 55 hours per week.

T F 6. The Employee Retirement Income Security Act states that employees with vested interests in pension plans may lose these benefits if they quit work after six years.

T F 7. If two computer programmers work for a company doing the same work and one is a man and the other a woman, they may never legally be paid a different wage.

T F 8. Under a Title VII claim based on disparate treatment, a plaintiff must initially prove a *prima facie* case, i.e., a showing that the employer discriminated against the plaintiff.

T F 9. Seniority systems are illegal if they tend to perpetuate the effects of past discrimination.

T F 10. A *quid pro quo* violation of Title VII occurs if any employment benefit is made contingent on an employee or job applicant engaging in any sexual activity.

T F 11. The False Claims Act permits any publicly traded company to sue an employee who commits fraud against the company.

T F 12. The Sarbanes-Oxley Act of 2002 protects an employee of a publicly traded company from being fired because the employee provides investigators with evidence of corporate fraud.

MULTIPLE CHOICE QUESTIONS

1. ____ Albert hires Veronica to work as a security guard at his office complex without stating a fixed term for the employment relationship. After working very competently for two weeks, Albert discharges Veronica. Under traditional common law rules:
   a. Albert is legally entitled to discharge Veronica because she is an employee at will.
   b. Albert is legally entitled to discharge Veronica only for a good cause.
   c. Albert is legally prohibited from firing women, such as Veronica, by Title VII.
   d. Albert is legally prohibited from firing women, such as Veronica, by the Fair Labor Standards Act.

2. ____ Millie works for Ken loading and unloading trucks that arrive at Ken's warehouse. Millie decides that Ken is not treating his workers properly and she contacts a labor union about unionizing the company's workers. Millie takes literature from the union and, after her shift is over, distributes it to her co-workers as they walk to their cars to leave. Ken finds out about this union activity and immediately fires Millie on account of it. In this case:
   a. Ken may fire Millie based on the employment-at-will doctrine.
   b. Ken may fire Millie based on the National Labor Relations Act.
   c. Ken may not fire Millie based on the National Labor Relations Act.
   d. Ken may not fire Millie based on the Lanham Act.

3. ____ Doyle works for Peter as an accountant. Peter is having financial trouble with his company. He calls Doyle into his office one day and says, "Doyle, I could really use a break with the taxes this year. How about coming up with a few imaginary deductions?" Doyle forces a weak smile and leaves Peter's office. A few days later Peter walks into Doyle's office and says, "Well, how are we doing with those deductions?" Doyle tells Peter that he can't just make up deductions because this illegal and, therefore, Peter is limited to the legitimate ones that he has. "Oh yeah?" says Peter, "You are fired. I'll find someone else who will obey my instructions." In this case:
   a. Peter is within his rights because Doyle violated his duty of obedience.
   b. Peter is within his rights because Doyle is an at-will employee.
   c. Peter is wrong because Doyle can't be discharged for refusing to break the law.
   d. a and b.

4. ____ Vivian works for a federal administrative agency. She discovers that some people in her agency are illegally smuggling arms to a small group of so-called freedom fighters in a Central Asian nation. She believes that these activities will reflect badly on the U.S. and that they are illegal, so she tells her boss about what is going on. Three weeks later, her boss fires Vivian because she spilled the beans about her agency's activities. In this case:
   a. Vivian's boss has violated the National Labor Relations Act.
   b. Vivian's boss has violated the Civil Service Reform Act and/or the Whistleblower Protection Act.
   c. Vivian's boss has done nothing wrong because this matter involves national security issues.
   d. Vivian's boss has done nothing wrong because the employer's conduct doesn't violate public policy.

5. ____ Jill is 13 years old and she wants to work as a busperson in a neighborhood restaurant. In this case:
   a. Jill may legally work but only if she works limited hours.
   b. Jill may legally work if she has her parents' permission.
   c. Jill is prohibited by law from working.
   d. a and b.

6. ____ Lyle works at a theatre as a stagehand. One evening, during a masterful performance of La Boheme, Lyle accidentally loses control of a piece of scenery and a heavy piece of hanging scenery falls on Elisabeta, the star of the opera and an employee of the opera company, which owns and operates the theatre. In this case:
   a. Elisabeta can recover nothing from the opera company because Lyle was her co-worker.
   b. Elisabeta may sue the opera company based on the tort of negligence.
   c. Elisabeta may sue the opera company based on the Fair Labor Standards Act.
   d. Elisabeta may not sue the opera company, but she may recover worker's compensation.

7. ____ Brian works for the U.S. Department of Interior as a biologist. Brian studies the habitat of fresh water crabs. One day Brian's supervisor, Elsa, randomly picks Brian to take a drug test even though she has no reason to suspect him of drug use. Elsa simply wants to make sure that none of her employees are using illegal drugs. In this case:
   a. Brian must submit to the drug test because he is an employee.
   b. Brian must submit to the drug test because he works for the government.
   c. Brian does not have to submit to the drug test because doing so would violate his privacy.
   d. a and b.

8. ____ Montgomery was an employee of Acme at the time he suffered a heart attack. When he recovered from this condition, he returned to work. However, his employer called Montgomery into her office and said, "I'm really sorry about this, but your condition may repeat itself and that would cost us too much money. You are discharged." In this case:
   a. Employer is legally entitled to discharge Montgomery.
   b. Employer violated the Americans with Disabilities Act.
   c. Employer violated Title VII of the Civil Rights Act.
   d. Employer's actions are immoral, but legal.

SHORT ESSAY

Identify three federal discrimination laws and identify what type of discrimination they respectively prohibit.

CASE PROBLEM

Kim Pak was born in Korea and she recently became a U.S. citizen. Kim speaks fluent English, but she has a mild Korean accent. Her accent does not interfere with her ability to communicate with others. Kim applied for the job of manager at the Jasper Hotel, for which she was qualified. However, Kim was not hired for this position because: (a) Kim speaks with a Korean accent; (b) Kim is fifty years old and she may not work for as many years as someone younger; and (c) Kim has a hearing disorder and the hotel would have to spend $300 to purchase a special telephone for her. Separately discuss the validity of each of these reasons for not hiring Kim.

CHAPTER TWENTY-NINE
STARTING A BUSINESS

CHAPTER OUTLINE

I. Sole Proprietorships

II. General Partnerships
   A. Taxes
   B. Formation
   C. Liability
   D. Management
   E. Terminating a Partnership

III. Limited Liability Partnerships

IV. Professional Corporations

V. Limited Partnerships And Limited Liability Limited Partnerships
   A. Structure
   B. Liability
   C. Taxes
   D. Formation
   E. Management
   F. Transfer of Ownership
   G. Duration

VI. Corporations
   A. Corporations in General
   B. Close Corporations
   C. S Corporations

VII. Limited Liability Companies
   A. Formation
   B. Limited Liability
   C. Tax Status

D. Flexibility
E. Standard Forms
F. Transferability of Interests
G. Duration
H. Going Public
I. Changing Forms

VIII. Joint Ventures

IX. Franchises

WHAT YOU SHOULD KNOW

After reading this chapter you should understand:

how a sole proprietorship is established and its key features;

how a general partnership is established and its key features;

how partnerships, corporations, and other business entities are taxed;

what a limited liability partnership means;

how a limited partnership is established and its key features;

what differentiates a limited partnership from a limited liability limited partnership;

which law governs the creation of corporations;

what a professional corporation is;

what a C corporation is and its key features;

what a close corporation is and its key features;

what an S corporation is and its key features;

what a limited liability company is and its key features;

issues that may arise when a corporation decided to change its form to a limited liability company;

how one forms a joint venture;

what franchises are; and

the obligations of franchisors to potential investors.

REVIEW OF TERMS AND PHRASES

MATCHING EXERCISE

Select the term or phrase that best matches a statement or definition stated below. Each term or phrase is the best match for only one statement or definition.

Terms and Phrases

a. Certificate of limited partnership
b. Corporation
c. Dissociation
d. Franchise
e. Franchisee
f. Franchisor
g. General partner
h. Joint venture
i. Limited liability partnership
j. Limited partner
k. Partnership
l. Partnership by estoppel
m. S corporation
n. Sole proprietorship

Statements and Definitions

____ 1. Partner in a limited partnership who controls the business of the partnership.

____ 2. Artificial legal entity whose owners are stockholders or shareholders.

____ 3. Person to whom a franchise is granted.

____ 4. Association, similar to a general partnership, whereby two or more persons combine their resources in order to accomplish a single business undertaking for profit.

____ 5. Business arrangement whereby an owner of a trademark, trade name, or copyright licenses a person or business to sell or distribute goods or services using such mark, name, or copyright.

____ 6. Association of two or more persons to carry on a business for profit as co-owners.

____ 7. Person who grants a franchise to another person.

____ 8. Business that is owned and operated by one person.

____ 9. Document that is filed with the Secretary of State in order to form a limited partnership.

____10. Partner in a limited partnership whose liability is limited to his or her contribution.

____11. Corporation, the income taxes for which are taxed to the shareholders, not to the corporation.

____12. Partnership wherein partners are generally not liable for torts of other partners or partnership agents.

____13. Doctrine that holds a person liable for a debt incurred by another because he or she misled a third party into thinking that he or she was a partner of the person who incurred the debt.

____14. Event that occurs when a partner quits.

COMPLETION EXERCISE

Fill in the blanks with the words that most accurately complete each statement. Answers may or may not include terms used in the matching exercise. A term cannot be used to complete more than one statement.

1. In many states a ______________________ corporation may lawfully engage in a number of occupations, such as the practice of law.

2. Federal law requires a franchisor to give a prospective franchisee an ______________ ____________ at least ten days prior to the sale of a franchise to the franchisee.

3. Limited liability companies must be _______________ held.

4. Identify the two types of partners in a limited partnership:

   a. ____; and

   b. ____.

5. An S Corporation can have no more than ______________-________________ shareholders.

6. A ______________ ______________ ________________ ______________ is a form of limited partnership in which the general partners are not personally liable for the partnership's debts.

REVIEW OF CONCEPTS

TRUE-FALSE QUESTIONS

Circle **T** (true) or **F** (false)

T F 1. The owner of a sole proprietorship is personally liable for all of the business' debts.

T F 2. An LLC is taxed in the same manner as a corporation if the LLC becomes a publicly traded company.

T F 3. Partners have the right to freely transfer the value of their partnership interest, but not the interest itself.

T F 4. One benefit of a partnership is that all profits of the partnership pass directly to the partners and are, therefore, reported on the partner's personal income tax returns.

T F 5. In a limited partnership, only the limited partners are personally liable for the debts of the partnership.

T F 6. The law that governs the way corporations are formed is federal statutory law.

T F 7. Some business owners may prefer the close corporation form because it allows the business to operate without a board of directors or a formal set of bylaws.

T F 8. Shareholders of S Corporations have the liability exposure of partnerships and the tax status of a corporation.

T F 9. Limited liability companies have the same liability and tax characteristics as an S Corporations, but they do not limit the number of persons who may own an interest in the business entity.

T F 10. Before a franchisor sells a franchise it must provide potential buyers with an offering circular that reveals information about the franchisor and its financial health.

T F 11. The owner (member) of an LLC is personally liable for the debts of an LLC.

T F 12. In general, a franchisor is not liable for the contracts and torts of a franchisee.

T F 13. A franchise contract cannot define a franchise's duration; statutes determine this matter.

T F 14. A franchisee is typically required to pay a franchise fee and an annual fee that is based on the net profit of the franchise.

T F 15. A partnership is typically formed to accomplish only a specific undertaking whereas a joint venture is typically formed to engage in an ongoing business.

T F 16. A shareholder is personally liable for the debts of the corporation.

T F 17. A disadvantage of a sole proprietorship is that its capital is limited to the owner's personal assets.

T F 18. The current trend is that an LLC automatically dissolves upon the withdrawal of any member and it cannot continue its business after such withdrawal.

T F 19. A partnership cannot be created unless parties specifically call their relationship a partnership.

T F 20. If a partnership does not have a definite duration or purpose, then any partner is legally entitled to withdraw at any time.

T F 21. The decision of a majority of partners controls regarding ordinary partnership matters.

T F 22. Corporations and partnerships can be members of a limited liability company but they cannot be shareholders of a Subchapter S corporation.

T F 23. A partnership and other partners are generally not liable for a tort that was committed by a partner who was acting within the scope of the partnership business.

T F 24. In general, partners in an LLP do not have personal liability for the debts of the partnership.

T F 25. A general partner has unlimited personal liability for the obligations of a limited partnership, but does not have such liability in a limited liability limited partnership.

MULTIPLE CHOICE QUESTIONS

1.____ Alex intends to start a for-profit construction business. Alex wants to control the entire business and he wants to directly receive the entire net profits from the business. These are Alex's only considerations. Under these facts, which form of business organization is most appropriate for Alex?

a. Sole proprietorship.
b. Partnership.
c. Corporation.
d. Joint venture.

2.____ Betty and Dan intend to jointly establish and operate a for-profit catering business. Betty and Dan wish to use a form of business organization that: (1) will permit them to share their profits; (2) have the income of the business taxed to them personally; and (3) will not entail any organizational fees to establish the business organization. These are the sole considerations of the parties. Under these facts, which form of business organization is most appropriate?

a. Sole proprietorship.
b. General partnership.
c. Professional corporation.
d. Franchise.

3.____ Kelly, Pinky, and Bill are planning to start a for-profit manufacturing firm. It is important to the parties that they not have personal liability for obligations of the business, and that the business will continue even if one of the parties dies. These are the sole considerations of the parties. Under these facts, which form of business organization is most appropriate?

a. Sole proprietorship.
b. Partnership.
c. Corporation.
d. Joint venture.

4.____ Nexus Co. and Tracer Inc. are competing computer manufacturers. However, Nexus and Tracer pooled their resources for the sole purpose of developing a special type of computer chip. Nexus and Tracer each have an equal right to control the business of this limited undertaking. Under these facts, the parties have formed what type of business:

a. Joint venture.
b. Limited liability company.
c. Limited liability partnership.
d. Business trust.

5.____ Rainer and some friends want to invest in the development of a shopping center. They decide to form a limited partnership for this purpose. Which of the following characteristics will this business entity have?

a. At least one general partner.
b. Limited partners who personally manage the partnership.
c. The automatic right to transfer all interests in the partnership.
d. No more than two limited partners.

6.____ Jenine wants to open a catering business. She is talented and temperamental and does not like having other people tell her what to do, so she creates a sole proprietorship. Seven months after she opens shop, Jenine caters a large party. As she is slicing off a hunk of garlic-roasted leg of lamb, her carving knife accidentally slips out of her hand. It winds up in Alfred's hand, and he sues Jenine and her business for $50,000 and wins. Whose assets are subject to being taken to pay this judgment?

a. Only the business' assets.
b. Only Jenine's personal assets.
c. Both the business' assets and Jenine's personal assets.
d. Neither the business' assets nor Jenine's personal assets.

7.____ LuLu and Beth want to open a fabric store together. After discussing their legal options as far as business organization is concerned, the women decide to create a partnership. LuLu buys the fabric and notions for the store and Beth manages the shop and does the bookkeeping. The business thrives and the women are quite happy until LuLu meets Dino who sweeps her off her feet. LuLu decides she wants to leave the partnership so she sells her partnership interest, including her right to be the fabric buyer and partner, to her good friend, Pam. In this case:

a. LuLu can transfer only the value of her interest, not the interest itself.
b. LuLu can transfer her interest to Pam so long as Pam has similar capabilities.
c. LuLu can transfer her interest to Pam so long as Pam willingly accepts personal liability for the partnership's debts.
d. LuLu can transfer neither the value of her interest nor the interest itself.

8.____ Cooper, Tex, and Chien are the partners in CTC Partnership. Cooper contributed $50,000 to the partnership, and Tex and Chien each contributed $25,000. The partnership agreement is silent regarding management rights and allocation of profits. Under these facts:

a. Cooper has the exclusive right to manage the partnership.
b. Cooper, Tex, and Chien are each entitled to an equal vote regarding partnership matters.
c. Cooper is entitled to 100 percent of the partnership profits.
d. Cooper is entitled to 50 percent of the partnership profits.

SHORT ESSAY

Explain the difference between a close corporation and an S corporation. What are the key characteristics of each?

CASE PROBLEM

Answer the following problem, briefly explaining your answer.

Sugarland granted Carlos the right to sell Sugarland's candy products and to use its trademark and trade name in connection with his business. One day, Sue bought a piece of Sugarland candy from Carlos. The candy made Sue ill because it was made with a toxic substance, giving rise to a claim for product liability. Also, the next day Tom slipped while walking in Carlos' store. Tom slipped because Carlos had negligently left a spilled drink on the floor.

1. What is the business relationship between Sugarland and Carlos?

2. Is Sugarland liable to Tom and/or Sue? Why or why not?

3. Is Carlos liable to Tom?

CHAPTER THIRTY
CORPORATIONS

CHAPTER OUTLINE

I. Incorporation Process
   A. Where to Incorporate?
   B. The Charter

II. After Incorporation
   A. Directors and Officers
   B. Bylaws
   C. Issuing Debt

III. Death Of The Corporation
   A. Piercing the Corporate Veil
   B. Termination

IV. The Role Of Corporate Management

V. The Business Judgment Rule
   A. Duty of Loyalty
   B. Duty of Care

VI. Takeovers
   A. Federal Regulation of Tender Offers: The Williams Act
   B. State Regulation of Takeovers

VII. The Role Of Shareholders

VIII. Rights Of Shareholders
   A. Right to Information
   B. Right to Vote
   C. Right to Dissent
   D. Right to Protection from Other Shareholders

IX. Enforcing Shareholder Rights
   A. Derivative Lawsuits
   B. Direct Lawsuits
   C. Class Action Lawsuits

WHAT YOU SHOULD KNOW

After reading this chapter you should understand:

how a corporation is formed;

what a corporate charter includes;

the steps that are taken after a corporation is formed;

what piercing the corporate veil means and how a corporation may be terminated;

the role that corporate management plays;

the various conflicts that managers, directors, shareholders and stakeholders face;

what the business judgment rule is and how it works;

the component duties encompassed by the business judgment rule;

what self-dealing means and how it can occur;

what the corporate opportunity doctrine involves;

how a corporate director can violate a duty of care;

how some states have revised the duty of care by statute;

the process involved in taking over a corporation;

which federal law applies to corporate takeovers;

how states regulate corporate takeovers;

how corporations can attempt to defend themselves from hostile takeovers;

the role that shareholders play in a corporation;

the rights of shareholders and how they may enforce their rights;

who has the right to manage the corporation's business;

what the shareholder right to information involves;

what a proxy is and how shareholders may make use of proxies;

what a shareholder proposal is and what kinds of proposals are valid;

how directors are elected and removed;

who decides how much money directors and officers make;

when a corporation must get shareholder approval for a proposed action;

what it means for a shareholder to have a right of dissent;

what the Sarbanes-Oxley Act of 2002 requires of public companies;

how minority shareholders are protected from other shareholders;

what a derivative lawsuit is and when it may be pursued;

what a direct lawsuit is and when it may be pursued; and

what a class action lawsuit is and when it may be pursued.

REVIEW OF TERMS AND PHRASES

MATCHING EXERCISE

Select the term or phrase that best matches a statement or definition stated below. Each term or phrase is the best match for only one statement or definition.

Terms and Phrases

a. Authorized and unissued stock
b. Bond
c. Business judgment rule
d. Bylaws
e. Common stock
f. Corporate opportunity doctrine
g. Cumulative preferred stock
h. Debentures
i. Directors
j. Duty of care
k. Hostile takeover
l. Outstanding stock
m. Preferred stock
n. State anti-takeover statutes
o. Tender offer
p. Treasury stock
q. Williams Act

Statements and Definitions

____ 1. Offer to buy stock in a corporation that is made directly to the shareholders of that corporation.

____ 2. The purchase of stock of a target corporation that is opposed by the board of directors of the target company.

____ 3. Persons who have the legal right to collectively manage the business of the corporation.

____ 4. Principle that forbids a director from personally taking a business prospect without first offering it to the corporation.

____ 5. Obligation of directors to exercise the same degree of responsibility in corporate matters that an ordinarily prudent person would exercise in his or her own affairs.

____ 6. Voting stock of a corporation.

____ 7. Federal law that regulates activities related to tender offers.

____ 8. Long-term debt issued by a corporation that is secured by corporate assets.

____ 9. Principle that directors are not liable for business decisions made while acting on an informed basis, in good faith, and with an honest belief that their acts are in the corporation's best interest.

____ 10. Long-term, unsecured debt of a corporation.

____ 11. State laws that discourage or impede the takeover of domestic corporations.

____ 12. Stock of a corporation that may be sold by the corporation.

____ 13. Preferred stock that is entitled to be paid dividends for the current year and any missed dividends for past years before common stockholders receive dividends.

____ 14. Corporate document stating rules that govern the internal affairs of a corporation.

____ 15. Stock that has been issued by a corporation and is owned by a shareholder.

____ 16. Stock that enjoys a preference to dividends and/or distributions upon dissolution of a corporation.

____ 17. Stock of a corporation that the corporation has issued and repurchased.

REVIEW OF CONCEPTS

COMPLETION EXERCISE

Fill in the blanks with the words that most accurately complete each statement. Answers may or may not include terms used in the matching exercise. A term cannot be used to complete more than one statement.

1. Identify three goals that the business judgment rule seeks to accomplish:

a. ____;

b. ____; and

c. ____.

2. Managers are forbidden from engaging in two types of self-dealing known as _______________ self-dealing and ________________________ self-dealing.

3. In a ____________________, two or more existing companies combine and only one of the companies continues to exist.

4. Courts may sometimes __________________ ______ __________________ __________________ and hold the shareholders liable for the obligations of their corporation.

5. State the three elements of the business judgment rule that is used to evaluate the conduct of managers:

   a. ____

   b. ____; and

   c. ____.

6. __________________ __________________ are various devices that may be used to defeat unwanted corporate takeovers.

7. A ________________ ____________ lawsuit is one that is brought by a group of plaintiffs who all share the same claim against the defendant.

8. A ___________ lawsuit is one that is brought by shareholders on behalf of a corporation.

9. A __________ is a writing that authorizes another person to vote one's stock.

10. List five major requirements imposed on public companies by the Sarbanes-Oxley Act of 2002:

    a. ____

    b. ____

    c. ____

    d. ____; and

    e. ____.

TRUE-FALSE QUESTIONS

Circle **T** (true) or **F** (false)

T F 1. One conflict that managers of corporations face is that they wish to protect their jobs, while shareholders may be better served having a different management team.

T F 2. Managers have a fiduciary duty to act in the best interests of the corporation's shareholders.

T F 3. A director's duty to a corporation to make sound business decisions will be partially fulfilled if he or she is not financially interested in the subject of the decision.

T F 4. If a manager violates the business judgment rule and a court determines that the manager's decision was unfair to shareholders, then the manager may be personally liable for the resultant loss to the corporation.

T F 5. Managers, but not directors, have a duty of loyalty to a corporation.

T F 6. Self-dealing might include making a decision that will benefit another company to which a director has financial ties.

T F 7. Even if a manager engages in self-dealing, the manager may not be liable for his or her actions if the shareholders approve the transaction after being informed of the manager's personal interest.

T F 8. Managers are required to use the highest possible degree of care when dealing with their corporate employer - this is the duty of care.

T F 9. Managers are personally liable for harm that they cause to the corporation as a result of a violation of their duty of care.

T F 10. To some extent the Williams Act regulates the behavior of firms that may be preparing to make a takeover bid of another firm.

T F 11. Owners of common stock have a preference to both dividends and liquidation.

T F 12. Shares of stock cannot be issued without a par value.

T F 13. A shareholder can authorize another person to vote his or her shares.

T F 14. Shareholders have the right to manage the corporate business.

T F 15. A new trend in the United States is the rise of institutional investors in the stock market.

T F 16. Proposals may be submitted for consideration at annual meetings by any shareholder who wishes to bring a complaint against the corporation.

T F 17. System Corp. fired Janna for incompetence. Janna owns several thousand dollars worth of System Corp. stock. She submits a proposal requiring the corporation to fire the man who fired her. System is required to put the proposition up for a vote.

T F 18. Assume that the chairman of the board of Acme Corporation votes himself and his other board members a $5,000 annual salary increase. Under these facts, this is legal.

T F 19. Amendments to corporate charters will not be valid unless the amendments are voted on and approved by the shareholders.

T F 20. Shareholders cannot bring a derivative lawsuit unless the board of directors first authorizes them to do so.

T F 21. Shareholder approval is required for any sale of corporate assets that is not done in the regular course of business.

T F 22. A foreign corporation is a corporation formed under the laws of another country.

MULTIPLE CHOICE QUESTIONS

1.____ Terra Inc. is considering buying land from Piedmont Co. Piedmont is partly owned by Roger, a director of Terra. The Terra board approves the sale of land to Piedmont. In which situation is the transaction void because Roger violated his duty of loyalty to Terra?

a. Roger disclosed his interest in the transaction and a disinterested majority of the Terra board approved the transaction.
b. Roger disclosed his interest in the transaction and a disinterested majority of the shareholders approved the transaction.
c. Roger did not disclose his interest in the transaction but the transaction is fair and reasonable to Terra.
d. None of the above.

2.____ The fiduciary duty of managers in corporations is primarily owed to the:

a. Stakeholders.
b. Shareholders.
c. Directors.
d. Employees.

3.____ Phil is on the board of directors of a major seed and gardening company, Excelsior Seed. Phil also owns a computer company, Acme Computer. At a meeting of the Excelsior board, Phil suggests that Excelsior should upgrade its computer system and he suggests that Acme should be awarded the contract. The cost of the contract is unreasonably high. Phil does not disclose to the other board members that he owns Acme Computer. The board of directors awards the contract to Acme. Under these facts, did Phil violate any duty to the corporation?

a. No, so long as he isn't caught.
b. No, so long as Phil did not intend to defraud Excelsior.
c. Yes, Phil's actions are business self-dealing that constitute a violation of his duty of loyalty to Excelsior.
d. Yes, Phil's actions are personal self-dealing that constitute a violation of his duty of loyalty to Excelsior.

4.____ Tyler is president of Acme Corporation, a fertilizer company. Tyler works extremely efficiently and has lots of free time. He decides to use some of his free time to start a new business. Indeed, Tyler comes across a supplier of "heirloom" fertilizer, an ancient fertilizer concoction that ancient Egyptians used. Tyler starts selling this product. In this case:

a. Tyler has violated his duty not to engage in competition with the corporation.
b. Tyler has violated his duty under the corporate opportunity doctrine.
c. Tyler has not violated any duty to Acme because he may start and engage in any business he wants as long as he does it on his own time.
d. a and b.

5.____ A corporate manager has which of the following duties under the business judgment rule:

a. Duty to act without a conflict of interest.
b. Duty to exercise extraordinary care when conducting business on behalf of the corporation.
c. Duty to make only those decisions that the manager believes is rationally related to furthering his or her best interests.
d. a and b.

6.____ Phyllis and Rod are the sole shareholders of Food Inc., which is incorporated in Iowa. Food Inc. sells produce to wholesalers and the general public in Arizona. Food Inc. is a:

a. Domestic corporation when doing business in Iowa.
b. Domestic corporation when doing business in Arizona.
c. Foreign corporation when doing business in Iowa.
d. b and c.

7.____ Jim and Todd are the shareholders of J&T Inc. In which situation would a court be justified in piercing the corporate veil and imposing liability on Jim and Todd for obligations of J&T Inc.?

a. Jim and Todd form J&T Inc. in order to obtain substantial tax benefits.
b. Jim and Todd form J&T Inc. in order to avoid personal liability for future corporate debts.
c. Jim and Todd form J&T Inc. in order to engage in illegal, fraudulent stock sales that would otherwise cause them significant personal liability.
d. All of the above situations would justify piercing the corporate veil of J&T Inc.

8.____ Many businesses incorporate in the state of Delaware because they will realize all of the following advantages EXCEPT:

a. Bylaws that favor shareholders.
b. An efficient state court system that is designed to resolve business disputes.
c. A substantial body of corporate law that serves as precedents in the event of corporate disputes.
d. State laws that favor management.

9.____ Sandra successfully forms a new printing corporation. After several years of operation, the board of directors of Sandra's corporation decides that the corporation should raise additional operating capital. The board of directors decides to borrow money from investors and use the equipment the company already owns as collateral. What kind of financing tool is the board planning to use?

a. Debentures.
b. Drafts.
c. Bonds.
d. Common stock.

10.___ Roger is a minority shareholder in Neco Inc. Roger has demanded to inspect the records of the corporation. Is Roger entitled to inspect the corporation's records?

a. No. Shareholders have no right to inspect corporate records.
b. Yes, if Roger in good faith intends to inspect financial records in order to compute the value of his stock.
c. Yes, if Roger intends to obtain confidential corporate data in order to aid a competitor.
d. Yes. Roger is entitled to inspect the records for any purpose; shareholders have an absolute right to inspect corporate records.

11.___ The Farrago Pension Fund owns 15 percent of the stock of Fuller Corporation, a publicly traded corporation. Several of the Fuller directors recently made public statements that were highly critical of pension funds. The Farrago Pension Fund is disturbed by these statements and wants to remove these directors. Under these facts, what can the Farrago Pension Fund do to remove these offensive directors?

a. As a major shareholder, the Farrago may unilaterally require that the directors be removed.
b. As a shareholder, Farrago cannot do anything because directors can be appointed and removed only the corporate managers.
c. As a major shareholder, Farrago may unilaterally require the corporation's managers to fire the directors.
d. As a shareholder, Farrago may lead a proxy fight in order to remove the directors.

12.____ Earth Corporation wants to combine with another corporation, EcoLine, Inc. The two companies will form a new corporation XYZ Corporation. Who must authorize this transaction?

a. Only the shareholders of Earth Corporation.
b. Only the shareholders of EcoLine, Inc.
c. Only the shareholders of both Earth Corporation and EcoLine, Inc.
d. The shareholders and board of directors of both Earth Corporation and EcoLine, Inc.

13.___ Gail is a member of the board of directors of VitalSigns, Inc. VitalSigns has experienced tremendous growth and the board feels that current management is responsible for this good news. The board therefore votes to increase the salary of the president, vice president, and sales manager by 50 percent. In this case:

a. The directors have exceeded their authority.
b. The directors may vote for the increase only if the shareholders first approve of this increase.
c. The directors may vote for the increase only after providing shareholders with a 70-day notification period, during which time shareholders may object to the proposed increase.
d. The directors have the authority to increase the salaries.

14.___ Gordon owns 300 shares of the common stock of S&S Corporation, a privately held corporation. S&S has validly agreed to be sold to Avalanche Corporation. Gordon, however, objects to the sale. Under these facts, Gordon has the right to:

a. Demand that the corporation buy his stock for its fair value.
b. Stop the sale based on his common shareholder rights.
c. Sue S&S Corporation for violating his rights as one of its common shareholders.
d. Sue Avalanche Corporation for violating his rights as a shareholder of S&S Corporation.

SHORT ESSAYS

1. Explain the inherent conflicts faced by managers with regard to shareholders and stakeholders. How does the business judgment rule attempt to resolve this conflict?

2. In some situations a corporation must seek shareholder approval before it acts. What types of action require shareholder approval?

CASE PROBLEMS

Answer the following case problems, explaining your answers.

1. The board of directors of Ameri Finance Inc. approved a $1 million loan to L&K. The loan was secured by collateral. Prior to approving the loan, the Ameri board reviewed (1) a credit report that showed L&K was solvent and (2) an appraisal valuing the collateral at $2 million. Later, L&K defaulted on the loan and the collateral was sold for $600,000, causing a $400,000 loss. Ameri shareholders filed a lawsuit, suing the Ameri directors for making this loan.
   a. What test is used to determine the directors' liability?
   b. Are the directors personally liable for the loss?

2. ABC Inc. issued common and preferred stock. Earl owns 60,000 shares of ABC common stock and Antonio owns the remaining 40,000 shares of common stock. Trisha owns 200,000 shares of ABC preferred stock, which has typical rights and preferences. At the annual meeting, the shareholders are to vote on a proposed pay raise for corporate officers.
   a. Who can vote on this matter?
   b. As a practical matter, who has the power to determine whether the pay-raise proposal is approved?

CHAPTER THIRTY-ONE
PROPERTY

CHAPTER OUTLINE

I. Nature Of Real Property

II. Estates In Real Property
   - A. Freehold Estates
   - B. Concurrent Estates

III. Nonpossessory Interests
   - A. Easements
   - B. Profit
   - C. License
   - D. Mortgage

IV. Sale Of Real Property
   - A. Seller's Obligations Concerning the Property
   - B. Sales Contract and Title Examination
   - C. Closing and Deeds
   - D. Recording

V. Land Use Regulation
   - A. Zoning
   - B. Eminent Domain
   - C. Three Legal Areas Combined
   - D. Lease

VI. Types Of Tenancy
   - A. Tenancy for Years
   - B. Periodic Tenancy
   - C. Tenancy at Will
   - D. Tenancy at Sufferance

VII. Landlord's Duties
   - A. Duty to Deliver Possession
   - B. Quiet Enjoyment

C. Duty to Maintain Premises

D. Duty to Return Security Deposit

VIII. Tenant's Duties

A. Duty to Pay Rent

B. Duty to Use Premises Properly

IX. Injuries

A. Tenant's Liability

B. Landlord's Liability

C. Crime

X. Gifts

A. Intention to Transfer Ownership

B. Delivery

C. Inter Vivos Gifts and Gifts Causa Mortis

D. Acceptance

XI. Bailment

A. Control

B. Rights of the Bailee

C. Duties of the Bailee

D. Rights and Duties of the Bailor

E. Liability for Defects

WHAT YOU SHOULD KNOW

After reading this chapter you should understand:

what real property consists of;

the different kinds of freehold estates;

the different types of concurrent estates;

the difference between a condominium and a cooperative;

what an easement is and how easements are created;

the other kinds of interests in real property, such as profits, licenses, and mortgages;

the legal obligations a seller of real property owes to a potential buyer of that property;

the process involved in selling and recording the sale of real property;

how zoning laws affect the use of real property;

how the government uses its power of eminent domain to acquire real property;

what a lease is and what the statute of frauds requires concerning leases;

the different types of tenancies that a landlord and tenant may create;

the legal duties that a landlord owes to his or her tenants;

the landlord's duty to maintain the premises;

the legal duties that a tenant owes the landlord;

when a tenant is liable for injuries occurring in the rented space;

when a landlord is liable for injuries occurring in the leased space;

who is responsible when a crime is committed in rented space;

what a gift is, in legal terms;

the requirements for a valid gift;

the difference between inter vivos and causa mortis gifts;

what a bailment is and who the bailor and bailee are;

what a bailee must do in order to create a valid bailment;

the rights of a bailee;

the duties the bailee owes the bailor; and

the right of the bailor and the duties of the bailor.

REVIEW OF TERMS AND PHRASES

MATCHING EXERCISE

Select the term or phrase that best matches a statement or definition stated below. Each term or phrase is the best match for only one statement or definition.

Terms and Phrases

a. Bailment
b. Concurrent estates
c. Constructive eviction
d. Deed
e. Easement
f. Fee simple estate
g. Fixture
h. Gift causa mortis
i. Inter vivos gift
j. Landlord
k. Lease
l. License
m. Mortgage
n. Profit
o. Quiet enjoyment
p. Tenant
q. Warranty of habitability

Statements and Definitions

____ 1. Property that is affixed to land or buildings and is legally considered part of real property.

____ 2. Writing or instrument used to convey real property.

____ 3. Temporary, revocable privilege to do something on land belonging to another.

____ 4. Party who owns real property and permits occupation of the property by another.

____ 5. Irrevocable right to use land belonging to another.

____ 6. Gift that is made in contemplation of death and that is conditioned upon the death of the donor.

____ 7. Lien that is voluntarily given by a property owner to secure performance of an obligation.

____ 8. Two or more people own real property at the same time.

____ 9. Present gift of property.

____10. Rightful possession of personal property by someone other than the owner.

____11. Complete and absolute real property ownership interest that lasts forever.

____12. Right to take a part of the soil or produce from land belonging to another.

____13. Eviction that results from an act or omission by a landlord that substantially deprives a tenant of the enjoyment and use of leased premises.

____14. Implied warranty that premises leased for residential use are fit to be lived in.

____15. Agreement by which one party lawfully occupies the property of another.

____16. Party who lawfully occupies (leases) real property that is owned by another.

____17. Tenant's right to enjoy and use leased premises.

COMPLETION EXERCISE

Fill in the blanks with the words that most accurately complete each statement. Answers may or may not include terms used in the matching exercise. A term cannot be used to complete more than one statement.

1. _______________ _______________ includes land, buildings, fixtures, and rights in land.

2. Equipment that is permanently attached to a rented building by a tenant is called a _______________.

3. Martin transferred title to a ranch to Tami for the duration of Tami's life and, upon Tami's death, title was to pass to Beth. Tami's interest in the ranch is a _______________ _______________.

4. _______________ _______________ is the power of a government body to take title to the property of a private person for a public purpose.

5. _______________ is the procedure by which a mortgagee enforces its rights under a mortgage.

6. In most states, a builder who sells a new home is held to make an ___________ _______________ ____ _____________________.

7. _______________________ is the act of filing a deed with the appropriate government office.

8. Identify the three requirements for a valid transfer of a gift:

a. ____;

b. ____; and

c. ____.

9. In a bailment for the sole benefit of the bailee, the bailee is required to exercise _______________ _______________.

10. In a mutual benefit bailment, the bailee is required to exercise _______________ _______________.

11. In a bailment for the sole benefit of the bailor, the bailee is required to exercise only _______________ _______________.

REVIEW OF CONCEPTS

TRUE-FALSE QUESTIONS

Circle **T** for true or **F** for false.

T F 1. If you own 5 acres of land, in most states you also own any silver located below the surface of those five acres.

T F 2. A portable dishwasher is best described as a fixture to land.

T F 3. Graham gives his sister Becka 50 acres of orchards and land with a house. The agreement provides that Becka loses the land if she marries and the land then reverts back to Graham. This is arrangement is best described as a fee simple absolute.

T F 4. Sandra lends a bicycle to her friend Don so he can go for a sightseeing bike ride. Unknown to Sandra, the bicycle has a wobbly wheel. While riding the bike, Don is injured as a result of the bad wheel. Under these facts, Sandra is liable to Don for his damages.

T F 5. If you rent a small sailboat, you are the bailor and the rental company is the bailee.

T F 6. In cooperative apartment buildings, each individual owns his or her housing unit and has an entailed fee in that unit.

T F 7. Larry gives Ken the right to use a certain piece of land so long as Ken lives. While Ken is still alive, Larry sells the right to own the land after Ken's death to Annie. This is perfectly legal.

T F 8. If Bailey gives her sister Maitlin a pearl necklace at a birthday celebration dinner, then this is a causa mortis gift.

T F 9. Bill wants to sell his house. Bill knows that the roof is substantially defective, posing safety risks to whoever lives in the house. This condition cannot be easily discovered. In most states, Bill does not have a legal duty to tell prospective purchasers about this condition unless they ask about the roof.

T F 10. If the federal government wants to take 10 acres of your land in order to create a wildlife habitat, it need only notify you of its intentions before it seizes your property.

T F 11. In general, a license can be revoked by the person granting the license.

T F 12. A condominium and a cooperative are the same thing.

T F 13. A person who owns property with others as tenants in common generally has the right to sell his or her interest in the property at any time.

T F 14. Easements are typically created by grant or reservation.

T F 15. Covenants are promises by either a landlord or tenant to do or not do something.

T F 16. If you have a tenancy for years, this means you must stay in your apartment for at least two years.

T F 17. Misha, a landlord, locked Caren, a tenant, out of her apartment because she failed to pay the rent for the past three months. Misha has constructively evicted Caren.

T F 18. In many states, a landlord who rents an apartment that does not meet the requirements of the local building code has violated the implied warranty of habitability.

T F 19. If you invite someone to your apartment and they slip in a puddle of dish detergent that you forgot to clean up, you are liable for their harm.

T F 20. A gift is completed as soon as the donor intends to transfer ownership to a donee.

T F 21. A constructive delivery occurs when a donor makes delivery of a gift by transferring ownership of the property without delivering the gift, such as by giving the donee the keys to a car being gifted.

MULTIPLE CHOICE QUESTIONS

1.____ Joseph owns a farm. In a signed writing, Joseph granted Fran the irrevocable right to use a road on his farm so that Fran could more easily reach her own property. What kind of interest in land did Joseph grant to Fran?
   a. License.
   b. Easement.
   c. Lien.
   d. Profit.

2.____ Shanti leased a building. She installed a stove and boiler in the building. When the lease expires, she intends to remove the stove, but not the boiler. The stove can be removed easily without causing harm. Removal of the boiler will seriously damage the building and boiler. Are the stove and/or boiler fixtures?
   a. The stove and boiler are both fixtures.
   b. The stove is not a fixture, but the boiler is a fixture.
   c. The stove is a fixture, but the boiler is not a fixture.
   d. Neither the stove nor the boiler is a fixture.

3.____ Alexis wants to sell her house and the meadow that adjoins her lawn. All along the meadow Alexis has planted beautiful cherry trees. What type of property are these lovely trees?
   a. Personal property.
   b. Intangible property.
   c. Temporary property.
   d. Real property.

4.____ Daneele wants to provide for her mother, Selma. Daneele buys a beautiful piece of lakefront property with a small house. After the purchase is complete Daneele gives her mother the property and the house to use for as long as she lives. What kind of interest has Daneele given her mother?
   a. A fee simple absolute.
   b. A fee simple defeasible.
   c. A life estate.
   d. A nonalienable entailment.

5.____ Eldridge lives in a fabulous three-bedroom townhouse on East 9th Street in New York City. Eldridge pays the townhouse owner $3,000 per month rent as consideration for the exclusive right to occupy this property. What kind of interest does Eldridge have in the townhouse?
   a. A tenancy in common.
   b. A leasehold interest.
   c. A concurrent estate.
   d. A nondefeasible fee simple.

6.____ Zandra lives in an apartment complex. The owner of the complex decides that she has had it with the apartment business and offers each of the apartments for sale as individual units. Each person who buys their apartment will have a fee-simple interest in the unit. Zandra decides to buy her apartment. Zandra is purchasing a:

a. Tenancy in the entirety.
b. Cooperative.
c. Condominium.
d. Reverter.

7.____ Marissa rents an apartment from Ben. Ben thinks that Marissa is just about the best tenant a landlord could possibly have. After renting from Ben for eighteen months, Ben says to Marissa, "You can stay here as long as you like. Leave when you want, but I hope it won't be for quite a while." Ben has created a:

a. Tenancy in the entirety.
b. Tenancy at sufferance.
c. Periodic tenancy
d. Tenancy at will.

8.____ Lou leased an apartment in his house to Katie for one year. After three months, Lou he wants to throw Katie out (it seems that she is very interested in tap dancing and practices her steps for hours at a time, much to his dismay). Lou mentioned nothing in his lease about making noise. He asked Katie not to tap dance at home, but she insists that she has to dance when the spirit moves her. Desperate to get rid of her, Lou starts blasting hard metal music at a very high volume continuously, both day and night. He also releases sulfuric acid into the air vents going into Katie's apartment. Ultimately, Katie is forced to leave her premises in order to save her health. What does it appear that Lou is doing?

a. Constructively evicting Katie.
b. Actively evicting Katie.
c. Creating a tenancy at will.
d. Creating a tenancy for years.

9.____ Jeff rents an apartment from Ellen. Although the place looks pretty bad when he sees it, Jeff decides to take it, thinking that it will be fine once it is cleaned. He is wrong. Once the floors, walls, bathroom, and kitchen are cleaned, other problems set in. When the temperature dropped to 30 degrees Fahrenheit the pipes froze and burst, flooding the entire apartment. Jeff called Ellen, but it took her almost four weeks to send someone over to fix the pipes. During that time Jeff had no water. He couldn't wash the dishes or floors and cockroaches invaded the place. Does Ellen probably have any liability to Jeff?

a. No, Jeff should have fixed the pipes as soon as they burst.
b. No, Jeff should have moved out after one week.
c. Yes, she breached the warranty of habitability.
d. Yes, she breached a warranty of fitness.

10.____ Evan wants to give a gift of a painting to his good friend Mark. All of the following conditions must be met in order for the gift to be legally valid except:

a. Evan must deliver the painting to Mark.
b. Mark must inform Evan before delivery of the painting that he is willing to accept it.
c. Mark must accept the gift.
d. Evan must intend to transfer ownership of the painting from himself to Mark.

11.____ Same basic facts as question No. 10 above. When Evan gives the painting to Mark, Evan says: "This gorgeous oil painting is yours so long as you don't move out of town," Evan creates:

a. A causa mortis gift.
b. An irrevocable gift.
c. A trust.
d. A revocable gift, which is really no gift at all.

12.____ Lying on his deathbed, Paul calls his old friend Ethel to his side. With his children in the room, Paul tells Ethel that he has always secretly been in love with her. As a token of his deep, abiding, and eternal love, Paul wants Ethel to have his small Pennsylvania farmhouse. He tells her that he knows he is dying and that he will die a happy man only if he knows that Ethel will take his house once he's gone. Ethel is distraught at Paul's condition, but quite pleased that she stands to get the lovely farmhouse in Bucks County. This transfer from Paul to Ethel is a:

a. Trust.
b. Gift causa mortis.
c. Inter vivos gift.
d. Irrevocable gift.

13.____ Same basic facts as question No. 12 above. Paul quite unexpectedly recovers. Once he's feeling better he decides that, while Ethel is a remarkable woman, she is not remarkable enough to get his 1789 farmhouse with the boxwood gardens out back. In this case:

a. Paul may revoke his gift of the farmhouse.
b. Paul may revoke his gift, but only if Ethel agrees to the change.
c. Paul may not revoke this gift unless a court approves of the change.
d. Paul's out of luck, Ethel gets the farmhouse.

14.____ Edna takes her 1969 Mercedes to Fred who agrees to store and maintain the car for her while she is in South America for nine months. Fred charges Edna $200 per month for this service. While Edna is in Argentina, Fred fails to pay attention to Edna's chocolate-brown Mercedes. He doesn't notice that a family of field mice has taken up residence in the back seat of the car. When Edna returns from her trip, she finds that the leather interior of the car is destroyed. In this case, who's liable for the damage to Edna's car?

a. Edna, for she is sole beneficiary of this arrangement.
b. Edna, for this is a bailment for the sole benefit of the bailor.
c. Fred, for this is a mutual benefit bailment and he failed to exercise proper care.
d. Fred, for this is a bailment for the sole benefit of the bailee and he failed to exercise due care.

SHORT ESSAY

Legally, a number of different kinds of tenancies may be created. Explain the different types of tenancies and provide a brief example of each. How is a tenancy different from a freehold estate?

CASE PROBLEM

Answer the following problem, briefly explaining your answer.

Lucy has too much furniture for her modest home. To give herself some extra room, Lucy rents a storage unit at a local storage facility. Lucy takes the furniture to the facility and signs a one-year lease for the unit. The facility's owner agrees to pack away Lucy's furniture. When the lease is up, Lucy returns to the unit to get some of her furniture. She is heartbroken when she sees that the furniture has suffered extensive water damage. It seems that the storage unit in which her furniture was stored leaked during unusually heavy summer storms, causing the damage.

1. Explain what kind of legal arrangement Lucy entered into.
2. Who is responsible for the damage to her furniture and why?

CHAPTER THIRTY-TWO
CYBERLAW

CHAPTER OUTLINE

I. Privacy

A. Internet Tracking

1. Of Cookies and Caches

2. The State of Privacy on the Internet

B. Self-Regulation of Online Privacy

1. Voluntary Principles

2. Technology: P3P

C. Government Regulation of Online Privacy

1. The FTC

2. Children's Online Privacy Protection Act of 1998

3. Gramm-Leach-Bliley Privacy Act of 1999

4. State Regulation

5. The European Directive

D. Your Hard Drive as Witness (Against You)

1. Criminal Law

2. Civil Litigation

E. E-Mail

1. Electronic Communications Privacy Act of 1986

2. Common Law Regulation of E-Mail Privacy

II. Crime on the Internet

A. Hacking

B. Fraud

1. Auctions

2. Identity Theft

C. Fighting Internet Crime

III. Internet Service Providers and Web Hosts

A. Spam

B. Communications Decency Act of 1996

WHAT YOU SHOULD KNOW

After reading this chapter you should understand:

what cookies are and how they may affect the privacy of persons using the Internet;

what actions the Network Advertising Initiative suggests regarding personal data that Web sites collect about individuals;

what actions does the Children's Online Privacy Protection Act of 1998 prohibit;

what privacy protections does the Gramm-Leach-Bliley Privacy Act of 1999 afford;

what protections the Fourth Amendment of the Constitution may provide in connection with computers;

what actions are prohibited by the Electronic Communications Privacy Act of 1986 and when this Act may allow parties to disclose, monitor, or access others' e-mail;

when intrusion into another person's private life may constitute a tort under the common law;

what hacking is;

what conduct is barred by the Computer Fraud and Abuse Act of 1986;

what fraud is;

what conduct is prohibited by the Identity Theft and Assumption Deterrence Act of 1998;

what spam is and when spam may violate the law; and

what the Communications Decency Act of 1996 provides regarding the liability of ISPs and Web hosts for actions of others.

REVIEW OF TERMS AND PHRASES

MATCHING EXERCISE

Select the term or phrase that best matches a statement or definition stated below. Each term or phrase is the best match for only one statement or definition.

Terms and Phrases

a. Computer Fraud and Abuse Act

b. Electronic communication

c. EU

d. Federal Trademark and Dilution Act of 1995

e. Fraud

f. Hacking

g. ISP

h. Lanham Act

i. P3P

j. Shilling

k. Spam

l. Trespass to chattels

Statements and Definitions

____ 1. Seller either bids on his or her own goods or agrees to cross-bid with other sellers.

____ 2. Group of countries that have adopted strict privacy regulations for collection and disclosure of personal data.

____ 3. Law that prohibits anyone from accessing a computer without authorization.

____ 4. Federal law that forbids the false use of a trademark.

____ 5. Common law tort that is committed when one deceives a second party for the purpose of wrongfully obtaining money or something of value from the second party.

____ 6. Tort committed under the common law of at least one state when a party intentionally uses someone else's property without authorization.

____ 7. Unauthorized access to another's computer system.

____ 8. E-mail and transmissions from pagers and cellular phones.

____ 9. Internet service provider, such as AOL.

____10. Web browser technology that is intended to allow a person to designate the degree of privacy that he or she wants when using the Internet.

____11. Federal law that forbids the use of another's trademark in a way that reduces the mark's value.

____12. Unsolicited commercial e-mail or unsolicited bulk e-mail.

REVIEW OF CONCEPTS

TRUE-FALSE QUESTIONS

Circle **T** for true or **F** for false.

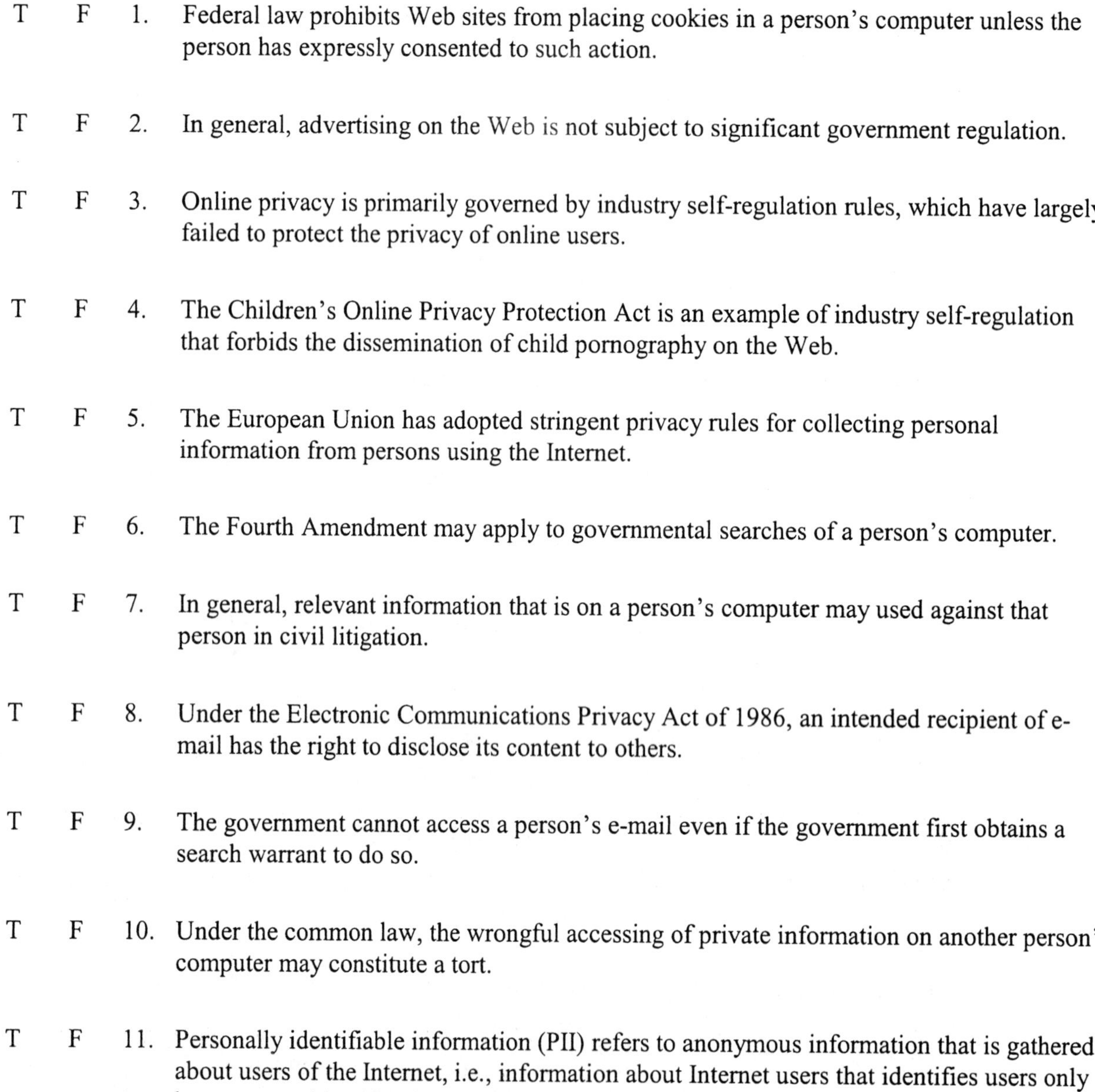

T F 1. Federal law prohibits Web sites from placing cookies in a person's computer unless the person has expressly consented to such action.

T F 2. In general, advertising on the Web is not subject to significant government regulation.

T F 3. Online privacy is primarily governed by industry self-regulation rules, which have largely failed to protect the privacy of online users.

T F 4. The Children's Online Privacy Protection Act is an example of industry self-regulation that forbids the dissemination of child pornography on the Web.

T F 5. The European Union has adopted stringent privacy rules for collecting personal information from persons using the Internet.

T F 6. The Fourth Amendment may apply to governmental searches of a person's computer.

T F 7. In general, relevant information that is on a person's computer may used against that person in civil litigation.

T F 8. Under the Electronic Communications Privacy Act of 1986, an intended recipient of e-mail has the right to disclose its content to others.

T F 9. The government cannot access a person's e-mail even if the government first obtains a search warrant to do so.

T F 10. Under the common law, the wrongful accessing of private information on another person's computer may constitute a tort.

T F 11. Personally identifiable information (PII) refers to anonymous information that is gathered about users of the Internet, i.e., information about Internet users that identifies users only by computer identification numbers.

T F 12. The Gramm-Leach-Bliley Privacy Act of 1999 forbids banks and other financial institutions from ever disclosing any non-public information about their clients to third parties.

MULTIPLE CHOICE QUESTIONS

1. ____ RetireRich, an American company, acquires detailed personal and financial information about Europeans who live in the European Union (EU). RetireRich buys this data from companies in the EU and uses this data to market retirement insurance policies to the persons from whom the information is collected. These EU companies and RetireRich agree to comply with relevant Safe Harbor Principles. Under these facts:
   a. RetireRich has done nothing wrong.
   b. RetireRich is subject to FTC sanctions.
   c. RetireRich is subject to EU sanctions because it has acquired personal information about EU citizens.
   d. b and c.

2. ____ Which of the following actions would violate the federal Computer Fraud and Abuse Act of 1986?
   a. Diane used her computer and the Internet to hack into the computers of Last National Bank and to transfer $100,000 to her personal bank account.
   b. Diane used her computer and the Internet to place cookies in the computers of persons who visited her Web site that she used to advertise and sell cosmetics.
   c. Diane used her computer and the Internet to plant destructive viruses on the Web sites of competitors.
   d. a and c.

3. ____ The federal Drug Enforcement Agency (DEA) suspected that Stanley was unlawfully selling and distributing cocaine. Moreover, the DEA had reason to believe that Stanley was using his Web site to make drug sales to people in all parts of the country. Under these facts:
   a. The DEA has the unlimited right to place "dragnet" software programs on the ISP that Stanley uses in order to intercept e-mails coming or going from Stanley's Web site.
   b. The DEA has the right to place "dragnet" software programs on the ISP that Stanley uses in order to intercept e-mails coming or going from Stanley's Web site only if the DEA first obtains a warrant or court order allowing it to do so.
   c. The DEA has the unlimited right to search Stanley's computer for evidence of wrongdoing so long as it does not require Stanley's help in searching his computer.
   d. b and c.

4. ____ Misty sent spam e-mails from South Dakota to 1,000 persons in other states telling them that they had each won $5,000 worth of her new line of clothing, but each winner had to send her $200 to cover the cost of shipping the clothing. This spam was false and Misty simply kept all of the money that was sent to her. Katie received this e-mail in Virginia and was duped out of $200. Assume that Virginia has an anti-spam statute that forbids fraudulent spam. Under these facts:
   a. Misty is subject to FTC action.
   b. Misty is subject state action in Virginia.
   c. Misty is not subject to state action in Virginia since the spam was sent from South Dakota, not Virginia.
   d. a and b.

5. ____ Sam operates an Internet business that specializes in the sale of electronic games to young children and teenagers. Sam decided to entice visitors to his Web site by letting them play one of his games for free. Sam required all visitors, however, to first provide certain personal information, which he intended to use internally and/or to disclose publicly. Which of the following actions by Sam would violate the Children's Online Privacy Protection Act of 1998?
   a. Sam collected personal information from Amy, age 18, without first obtaining her parent's permission. Sam is using this information internally and he also plans to publicly disclose it.
   b. Sam collected personal information from William, age 12, after obtaining his parent's consent by e-mail. Sam is using this information internally.
   c. Sam collected personal information from Rachel, age 11, after obtaining her parent's consent by e-mail. Sam is publicly disclosing this information.
   d. Sam collected personal information from Johnny, age 10, after obtaining his parent's written consent. Sam is publicly disclosing this information.

6. ____ Which of the following statements is correct regarding the federal Identity Theft and Assumption Deterrence Act of 1998?
   a. This Act forbids people from electronically disclosing their social security identification over the Internet.
   b. This Act forbids people from using the identification of others to commit fraud or other crimes.
   c. This Act authorizes victims to obtain restitution from persons who fraudulently used their identification.
   d. b and c.

SHORT ESSAY

Discuss industry self-regulation of online privacy and analyze how effective this type of regulation has been.

CASE PROBLEM

Answer the following case problem, explaining your answer.

Autumn is an e-mail junkie – she communicates with everyone via e-mail. In particular, Autumn sent the following e-mails: (a) Autumn sent an e-mail from her personal computer to John, her cousin, disclosing that Autumn had stolen money from her church; (b) Autumn sent an e-mail from her personal computer to Oman, an e-mail pal in a country that is hostile to the U.S.; and (c) Autumn used her employer's computer and e-mail system to send an e-mail to Sherry, a co-worker, stating that the boss was a creep. Under these facts:

a. Can John lawfully disclose the content of Autumn's e-mail without her consent?
b. Can the ISP that Autumn uses lawfully disclose any information regarding her e-mail to Oman?
c. Can Autumn's employer lawfully monitor her e-mail to Sherry?

CHAPTER THIRTY-THREE
INTELLECTUAL PROPERTY

CHAPTER OUTLINE

I. Patents

A. Types of Patents

B. Requirements for a Patent

C. Patent Application and Issuance

II. Copyrights

A. Infringement

B. Fair Use

C. Linking

D. Digital Music and Movies

E. International Copyright Treaties

III. Trademarks

A. Types of Marks

B. Ownership and Registration

C. Valid Trademarks

D. Infringement

E. Federal Trademark Dilution Act of 1995

F. Domain Names

G. International Trademark Treaties

IV. Trade Secrets

WHAT YOU SHOULD KNOW

After reading this chapter you should understand:

what makes intellectual property different from other kinds of property;

what a patent is, and the different kinds of patents available;

the requirements for obtaining a patent;

what a copyright is and how long one lasts;

what copyright infringement involves;

what the fair-use doctrine specifies;

how parodies are treated under copyright law;

problems associated with copyrights and computers;

what a trademark is and the different kinds of legally recognized marks;

what someone has to do in order to create a trademark;

what kinds of trademarks are valid and invalid;

what international treaties govern intellectual property; and

what a trade secret is and the law that applies to trade secrets.

REVIEW OF TERMS AND PHRASES

MATCHING EXERCISE

Select the term or phrase that best matches a statement or definition below. Each term or phrase is the best match for only one statement or definition.

Terms and Phrases

a. Copyright

b. Digital Millennium Copyright Act

c. Fair use

d. Federal Trademark Dilution Act of 1995

e. Patent

f. Service mark

g. Trademark

h. Trade secret

Statements and Definitions

____ 1. Private information that gives its owner a business advantage and which state law protects.

____ 2. Federal law that forbids using another party's trademark in a way that harms the value of the trademark.

____ 3. Exclusive right to use a mark that identifies a service.

____ 4. Exclusive right to use or reproduce a literary, artistic, musical, or audiovisual work.

____ 5. Federal law that provides protection of copyrights in connection with the Internet and prohibits circumventing certain electronic protections of copyrighted works.

____ 6. Limited, permissible use of copyrighted and trademarked material.

____ 7. Exclusive right to make, use, and sell a device, process, or invention.

____ 8. Exclusive right to use a mark that identifies a product.

REVIEW OF CONCEPTS

COMPLETION EXERCISE

Fill in the blanks with the words that most accurately complete each statement. Answers may or may not include terms used in the matching exercise. A term cannot be used to complete more than one statement.

1. International protection of copyrighted material is assured in approximately 120 countries by the

   ____________________ ____________________.

2. Utility patents last ____________ years and design patents last for ____________ years.

3. List the three essential requirements in order to obtain a patent for an invention:

   a. ____.

   b. ____.

   c. ____.

4. List the four major types of marks:

   a. ____.

   b. ____.

   c. ____.

   d. ____.

5. The ____________ ____________ ____ ____ ____________ ____ ____________ ____________ is an international treaty that requires member countries to accord citizens of other member countries the same rights under patent law that their citizens have.

6. The ____________ ____________ ____________ requires that member countries use the same form and content for patent applications.

7. List five ways that a mark may be distinctive:

   a. ____.

   b. ____.

   c. ____.

   d. ____.

   e. ____.

TRUE-FALSE QUESTIONS

Circle **T** for true or **F** for false.

T F 1. Trade dress is the distinctive packaging or overall appearance of a product and federal trademark law protects it.

T F 2. A patent gives the owner the exclusive right to use, reproduce, and sell his or her invention for a certain period of time.

T F 3. In order to obtain a patent, an inventor must prove that his or her invention is useful - useless products may not receive a government patent.

T F 4. The Patent and Copyright Office of each state issues patents.

T F 5. A copyright lasts for 20 years plus the life of the author.

T F 6. If your chemistry professor wanted to photocopy a one-page article and hand it out to your class, the professor would probably violate the fair-use doctrine of copyright law.

T F 7. Parodies of well-know songs illegally infringe on copyrights and may not be released without permission of the original author.

T F 8. McDonald's golden arches are an example of a collective mark.

T F 9. The little elf that you sometimes see on bags of Keebler's cookies would be an example of a valid trademark.

T F 10. In order to be protected under copyright law, a work must be original.

T F 11. The U.S. Supreme Court recently held that linking by a web site to a second web site was copyright infringement unless the owner of the second web site consented to such linkage.

MULTIPLE CHOICE QUESTIONS

1.____ Which of the following is not a requirement for obtaining a patent on a device?
   a. The device must be useful.
   b. The device must be new.
   c. The device must be nonobvious.
   d. The device must be capable of commercial exploitation.

2.____ Which of the following items cannot be copyrighted?
   a. A new book.
   b. A new idea for a movie.
   c. A new photograph.
   d. A new musical arrangement.

3.____ Ken invented a new type of mathematical calculator that he called "Wiser Guyser." Under these facts, the name "Wiser Guyser":
   a. Can be protected by registration for a patent.
   b. Can be protected by registration for a copyright.
   c. Can be protected by registration for a trademark.
   d. Cannot be protected.

4.____ Carl invented a new eating instrument for people who like to eat fast: a five-pronged fork. (Normal forks have only four prongs). Under these facts, can Carl patent his new fork?
   a. Yes, it is novel.
   b. Yes, it is useful.
   c. Yes, it is both novel and useful.
   d. No, it is an obvious derivative of an existing product, the four-pronged fork.

5.____ Which of the following names can be registered for trademark protection?
   a. "Motor oil," the name of a product that is used to lubricate engines.
   b. "Hot sauce," the name for a spicy food additive.
   c. "DuraBond," the name for a new type of glue.
   d. "Southern food," the name for food from the southern part of the United States.

6.____ Selma wrote a computer program and copyrighted it under U.S. copyright law. Selma allowed a German firm to review the program, but the German firm stated that they were not interested in the program. Unknown to Selma, the German firm duplicated the program and is selling it in Germany. Germany has signed the Berne Convention. Under these facts:
   a. Selma cannot enforce her copyright against the German firm.
   b. Selma can enforce her copyright against the German firm only if it agrees to be sued.
   c. Selma can enforce her copyright against the German firm under the Berne Convention.
   d. a and b.

7.____ For many years, Wowee Corp. manufactured and sold high-quality toy slot cars known as "Wowee Toys." Wowee registered this trademark ten years ago. One year ago, Waui Enterprises, a travel agency, commenced business and started marketing cruise packages called "Waui Cruises." Has Waui Enterprises violated Wowee Corp.'s trademark?

a. No, because the mark "Wowee Toys" was not properly registrable.
b. No, because Waui Enterprises can challenge the validity of the registration of this mark.
c. No, because the mark "Waui Cruises" is not the same or deceptively similar to "Wowee Toys."
d. Yes, because the word sounds the same.

8.____ Over a five-year period, Jackson Corp. spent considerable time and money to develop a private list of 200,000 area homeowners. This list tracks home values, year of construction, and last home-repair project. This list has proven invaluable for marketing its home-improvement services. Under these facts, Jackson Corp. should protect this information as a:

a. Patent
b. Trade secret
c. Trademark
d. Service mark

SHORT ESSAY

Contrast the different kinds of property that may be protected by federal trademark law.

CASE PROBLEM

Answer the following problem, briefly explaining your answer.

Baxco Corp. makes and sells several products, and it wants to register the products' names on the Principal Register in order to obtain federal trademark protection. Baxco wants to register: (1) "Xeri-fun," the name of a new candy; (2) "Appalachian Whiskey," the name of an alcoholic product that Baxco has sold for many years and a name that the public associates only with Baxco's product; and (3) "soft-serve ice cream," the name of Baxco's machine-dispensed ice cream. (Soft-serve ice cream is a type of ice cream that includes any ice cream that is dispensed from a machine. Numerous companies throughout the U.S. sell their own "soft-serve ice cream.")

a. Is Baxco entitled to register the foregoing marks?
b. If Baxco properly registers a mark, what can Baxco do if another party intentionally uses or infringes upon the registered mark?

CHAPTER ONE
INTRODUCTION TO LAW

MATCHING EXERCISE

1. g
2. a
3. j
4. d
5. i
6. f
7. c
8. h
9. b
10. e

TRUE/FALSE

1. F
2. T
3. F
4. F
5. T
6. T
7. F
8. F
9. F
10. T

MULTIPLE CHOICE

1. c
2. b
3. b
4. b
5. d
6. d
7. c
8. b
9. c
10. d
11. a
12. b
13. d
14. c
15. c

SHORT ESSAYS

1. Jurisprudence is the study of law. In order to study law you need to determine what law is. There is no consensus answer to this question. Therefore, you want to consider what makes law different from morality. How are legal rules different from rules of morality and behavior? In many cases these rules will overlap.

   Some people argue that law is what the sovereign power of the nation state declares it to be. These people are legal positivists. Other people believe law arises from the spontaneous interaction of individuals. That is, law is the customary behavior of people. Finally, some people believe that certain basic rules of law exist that no sovereign can take away. In other words, these people believe humans have a group of inalienable rights that should always be respected. These jurists, who believe in natural law, may debate whether these basis rights come from God or whether they exist because it is rational for them to exist.

   Think about which system is most open to abuse when you consider the strengths and weaknesses of each system. What is good about writing down the law? What is bad about it? What is good about relying on "natural" rights? What is bad?

2. The U.S. Constitution is the supreme law of the land. All statutes must comply with the Constitution. So too must state constitutions. The common law is the legal system that existed in the eastern part of the United States before the Revolutionary War. This system remains and has spread across the country so that in each state, a body of common law exists to govern many different kinds of legal disputes. If you think of the U.S. Constitution as a kind of umbrella, all other law in the United States must fit under this umbrella. The Constitution shields and protects citizens, state constitutions protect citizens, and the common law provides rules for settling disputes among citizens. Another source of law in the U.S. that is becoming increasingly important is administrative regulations.

CASE PROBLEM

1. Madeline did not violate either the civil or criminal law. The American legal system establishes a web of duties that we owe to one another, i.e., the civil law, and/or to society as a whole, i.e., criminal law. If the law does not establish a legal duty for a person to act in a particular way, then a person may choose how to act. In this case, Madeline chose not to give in order to help the needy family.

2. Under the facts stated, Madeline did act immorally based on the dominant social values stated in this case, i.e., that wealthy persons should help those in need.

3. As illustrated in this case, a person may act legally while at the same time acting immorally. As illustrated by the Martin Luther King discussion in the textbook, the reverse can also be true. While there is oftentimes a close relationship between law and morality, they are not always the same.

CHAPTER TWO
BUSINESS ETHICS AND SOCIAL RESPONSIBILITY

MATCHING EXERCISE

1. b
2. f
3. c
4. d
5. e
6. a

COMPLETION EXERCISE

1. Jeremy Bentham
   John Stuart Mill
2. Immanuel Kant
3. Consideration
   courage
   integrity
   self-control

TRUE-FALSE QUESTIONS

1. T
2. F
3. F
4. T
5. T
6. T
7. F
8. T
9. T
10. F

MULTIPLE CHOICE QUESTIONS

1. c
2. c
3. d
4. a
5. d
6. a
7. d
8. d
9. c
10. a
11. d

SHORT ESSAYS

1. Reasons why a business might choose to promote ethical behavior include the fact that society overall benefits when its members behave ethically. Society spends fewer resources "discovering" the truth, there is less litigation if people treat other people properly, and there are fewer costs associated with avoiding being defrauded by unethical businesses. Also, individuals may feel better about themselves when they behave ethically. If they feel better they may perform better and treat customers and suppliers better, thus reducing the costs of doing business and better ensuring repeat clients. Finally, the costs of unethical behavior can be quite high. Producing shoddy products may lead to costly lawsuits. Workers who lie may subject companies to legal liability as well as loss of valuable reputation. Also, unethical behavior by workers may negatively impact the behavior of ethical workers and lead to reduced productivity. Reduced costs, a better image, and improved productivity are all reasons why a company might actively promote ethical behavior among its workers.

2. This question is an opinion question. Consider whether manufacturers of high-fat products should bear the cost of the health problems and attendant costs that they contribute to or whether the consumers should accept responsibility for their choices in eating. If the high-fat food manufacturers should be allowed to produce their goods, are they under an obligation to explain to customers the possible side effects of eating such food? Also, consider individuals' freedom of choice to decide what to do or not to do in their lives.

CASE PROBLEMS

1. (a) Gordon is subject to a number of legal restraints including tort law (cannot fraudulently misrepresent the potential harm of smoking); and federal state administrative and statutory law (limits on advertising tobacco products and sales to minors).

   (b) While Gordon may think that he is acting morally by zealously trying to further his company's interests, he should consider whether this moral obligation is not out-weighed by a duty not to harm young individuals and society as a whole.

2. (a) Margaret may actually be under a legal obligation (attorney-client privilege) not to disclose to authorities the past illegal conduct of the client. On the other hand, she has a legal obligation not to facilitate or participate in any future illegal conduct by the client.

   (b) In contrast, Margaret may have ethical responsibilities to her employer and to her community in this case. Because of the harm caused by the client, she should consider encouraging the client to take steps to voluntarily clean up their illegal dumping.

3. The general manager is choosing to be loyal to his employer, which is generally considered to be moral conduct in our society. However, it is doubtful that this loyalty accomplishes a morally right consequence in this situation. Deciding what is moral conduct in a given situation often entails balancing conflicting values and rules.

4. Pal's Publishing may be using utilitarianism to decide what to do in this situation. Assuming that the universe is comprised of the employees and the value of good that Pal's seeks to promote is their health, then the drug-testing program is the morally right thing to do. Observe that the motivation for a particular action and whether or not it is moral may change depending on who comprises the universe and the values sought to be achieved.

CHAPTER THREE
DISPUTE RESOLUTION

MATCHING EXERCISE

1. b
2. h
3. d
4. j
5. e
6. a
7. c
8. g
9. i
10. f

COMPLETION EXERCISE

1. preponderance of the evidence
2. beyond a reasonable doubt
3. deposition
4. directed verdict

TRUE/FALSE QUESTIONS

1. F
2. F
3. T
4. T
5. T
6. T
7. F
8. T
9. F
10. T

MULTIPLE CHOICE QUESTIONS

1. b
2. a
3. c
4. a
5. a
6. a
7. d
8. d
9. a
10. c
11. a

SHORT ESSAYS

1. For this question briefly describe what negotiation, mediation, arbitration, mini-trials, and summary jury trials are. These processes are not litigation; that is, they are not lawsuits conducted in a formal trial setting by lawyers. Some of the strengths of alternative dispute resolution mechanisms are that they are generally quicker and cheaper than litigation. Also, because these dispute resolutions techniques are not as adversarial as litigation they may help maintain valuable relationships more effectively than litigation. Weaknesses of these dispute resolution mechanisms may be that they are less formal than courts and therefore are less threatening to opponents. Also, it may be easier to enforce a judgment from a court than an award issued by an arbitrator.

2. Three of the more important discovery tools that may be used are depositions, interrogatories, and requests for physical and mental examination. A deposition is an out-of-court questioning of a party or witness by the attorney for one of the parties. This questioning is done under oath and statements may, in certain situations, be used at trial. Interrogatories are written questions that are prepared by one party and served on the other party. They must be answered under oath. If a party to a lawsuit is seeking damages or other remedies for physical or mental harm allegedly caused by the other party, then the accused may request that the injured party submit to an appropriate professional physical or mental examination.

CASE PROBLEM

1. Yes, the parties must arbitrate their dispute because they have agreed in advance to mandatory arbitration. A contractual agreement between two parties to arbitrate a dispute is legally binding.

2. Yes, the arbitrator's award is binding on the parties. If one of the parties fails to perform in accordance with the award, the other party may request a court to issue a judgment based on the award. This judgment may then be legally enforced the same as any other judgment.

3. An agreement to arbitrate precludes the joining of other parties in a class action. The arbitration is between only the parties who agreed to arbitrate. In addition, the arbitrator decides questions of both fact and law and there is no jury involved.

CHAPTER FOUR
COMMON LAW, STATUTORY LAW, AND ADMINISTRATIVE LAW

MATCHING EXERCISE

1. c
2. e
3. a
4. g
5. h
6. d
7. f
8. b

COMPLETION EXERCISE

1. enabling legislation
2. administrative law judges
3. bill
4. promulgate
5. judge-made
6. precedent
7. Interpretive rules
8. Legislative rules

TRUE/FALSE QUESTIONS

1. F
2. F
3. T
4. F
5. T
6. T
7. F
8. F
9. F
10. T

MULTIPLE CHOICE QUESTIONS

1. a
2. d
3. a
4. a
5. d
6. c
7. b
8. d
9. b
10. b
11. c

SHORT ESSAYS

1. For this question be sure you understand the steps that are involved in creating a statute. Bills are drafted in Congress. These bills are sent to specialized committees for discussion and possible amendment. Next Congress debates the virtues and shortcomings of the bills. After the debate, the House of Representatives and the Senate vote on the bills. Once approved by a majority vote, bills are sent to a conference committee, where hopefully the Senate version of the bill and the House version of the bill are melded together to make a single version that is then sent to the President to be either signed into law or vetoed.

2. Citizens exercise control over administrative agencies primarily through the actions of their elected representatives. Federal agencies may be controlled by imposing statutory limitations on their powers, and by exerting political control over agency employees (pressure from Congressmen and women or from the Executive branch to do or not to do something). Also, agency actions may, in many cases, be subject to review by the courts. Thus, if an agency engages in an unconstitutional action, a citizen or another government official will be able to file a lawsuit against the agency. Finally, agencies have to disclose certain information if citizens request the information. This makes it more difficult for agencies to engage in secretive behavior. The Freedom of Information Act and the Privacy Act place statutory limitations on agency powers.

CASE PROBLEMS

1. a. The FAA may adopt the new regulation for emergency landings by commercial airlines. Because Congress gave the FAA broad authority in the enabling legislation, the FAA may engage in many activities that are necessary to carry out the federal statutes and the intent of Congress. Within the purview of its jurisdiction, this would include the power to enact appropriate legislative regulations.

   b. Federal administrative agencies that are given broad authority typically enjoy the power to investigate whether given regulations are necessary and also whether individuals or companies have violated the agency's regulations.

2. a. Under the modern view, an administrative agency possesses all of the powers necessary to carry out its duties. Under this view, the FDA would have the authority to conduct a hearing to determine whether Medco violated its regulations.

   b. There is no right to a jury trial in administrative proceedings.

CHAPTER FIVE
CONSTITUTIONAL LAW

MATCHING EXERCISE

1. f
2. c
3. b
4. e
5. i
6. a
7. g
8. j
9. h
10. d

TRUE-FALSE QUESTIONS

1. T
2. T
3. F
4. F
5. T
6. F
7. F
8. T
9. T
10. F

MULTIPLE CHOICE QUESTIONS

1. a
2. d
3. a
4. d
5. d
6. c
7. b
8. b
9. c
10. c
11. d
12. a
13. c

SHORT ESSAY

1. While the Equal Protection Clause generally guarantees individuals and businesses the same treatment under the law, the Constitution has been interpreted to allow different treatment in appropriate situations. Whether different treatment of classes is constitutional or not depends on two factors: the basis for the distinction and the government's need or justification for treating classes in a different manner.

   One category of classifications involves economic and social issues and the government only needs to establish that the distinction is rationally related to a legitimate goal. A second category involves gender and treatment of men and women differently. To sustain gender distinctions, the government must prove that its law substantially relate to important government objectives. For distinctions based on race, ethnicity, and fundamental rights, the government must prove that its conduct is necessary to promote a compelling state interest.

CASE PROBLEMS

1. Yes, Amax Corp. is engaging in interstate commerce. Interstate commerce is interpreted very broadly. As interpreted, interstate commerce includes any commerce going between states, and it also includes most business and labor activities.

2. Yes, the Constitution authorizes the federal government to regulate interstate commerce. Consequently, the federal government may regulate the business that Amax Corp. conducts in interstate commerce.

3. In general, Colorado may constitutionally regulate the business that Amax Corp. conducts within Colorado. Subject to certain limitations, states have the police power to regulate activities within their boundaries in order to protect the health, safety, welfare, and morals of people.

4. In regulating Amax Corp.'s business activities, Colorado cannot: (a) regulate matters that have been preempted by the federal government; (b) adopt laws that conflict with federal laws; (c) discriminate against Amax Corp.'s interstate activities; or (d) impose an unreasonable burden on Amax Corp.'s interstate activities.

CHAPTER SIX
TORTS

MATCHING EXERCISE

1.	b	8.	f
2.	l	9.	e
3.	d	10.	c
4.	g	11.	m
5.	h	12.	i
6.	a	13.	j
7.	k		

COMPLETION EXERCISE

1. public official
2. Punitive damages
3. defamation
4. reasonable person
5. contributory negligence
6. actual
7. comparative negligence
8. externalities

TRUE-FALSE QUESTIONS

1.	F	9.	T
2.	T	10.	F
3.	F	11.	T
4.	T	12.	T
5.	F	13.	F
6.	T	14.	T
7.	F	15.	F
8.	F	16.	T

MULTIPLE CHOICE QUESTIONS

1.	b	11.	d
2.	d	12.	c
3.	d	13.	a
4.	d	14.	d
5.	c	15.	a
6.	c	16.	c
7.	c	17.	a
8.	b	18.	d
9.	d	19.	c
10.	d		

SHORT ESSAYS

1. Courts may award different kinds of monetary damages. Monetary damages include compensatory damages and punitive damages. Thus, victims may recover money for: past and future medical expenses, costs of rehabilitation; lost earnings; lost future earnings; discomfort and pain the victim has suffered and will continue to suffer; emotional pain the victim has suffered and will continue to suffer; and the loss the victim has suffered in not being able to interact as freely with friends and family. These items are not part of a punitive damage award, which is additional money given to a victim for the purpose of punishing a defendant for extreme or outrageous conduct.

2. To bring a successful negligence claim, the plaintiff must prove that the defendant owed the plaintiff a duty of care, the defendant breached this duty of care, the breach of the duty was the cause of the plaintiff's injury, and the plaintiff suffered a legally recognized harm. If the plaintiff can show that the defendant could foresee that his or her misconduct would injure a particular person, the plaintiff will be able to prove that the defendant owed the plaintiff a duty of care. If the defendant failed to act the way a reasonable person in similar circumstances would act towards the plaintiff, the plaintiff will be able to prove that the defendant breached this duty of care. If the defendant's breach of duty physically led to the plaintiff's harm, then the plaintiff is able to prove the factual cause of the plaintiff's harm. The type of harm the defendant causes must be reasonably foreseeable for the defendant to be liable. Finally, the plaintiff must suffer a genuine, recognized harm; not some hypothetical or speculative harm.

3. Contributory negligence is a defense raised by the defendant. It means that the plaintiff was also negligent and the plaintiff's negligence contributed to his or her harm. In states that allow this defense, it acts as a complete bar to recovery for the plaintiff. That is, if the defendant proves contributory negligence, the plaintiff may recover no damages. Comparative negligence is also a defense raised by the defendant. It also means that the plaintiff was negligent and his or her negligence contributed to the harm. However, rather than barring recovery completely, a comparative negligence defense reduces the defendant's liability in the exact amount of the plaintiff's negligence. So, if the defendant is 80% liable for the plaintiff's harm, and the plaintiff is 20% liable as a result of the plaintiff's own carelessness, the defendant pays only 80% of any damage award the plaintiff receives. Each system creates incentives. Does a system that bars any recovery for injuries suffered if the victim is careless make individuals more careful? Or does a system that makes you "pay" for your carelessness by reducing damages awards you may receive help make you more careful?

CASE PROBLEMS

1. Todd committed battery due to his unlawful physical contact with Mabel. He also committed the tort of assault for placing Mabel in apprehension of a battery. In addition, Todd committed false imprisonment for unlawfully detaining Mabel.

2. (a) Lily owed Paul a duty to drive in the manner that a reasonable person would drive under similar circumstances. Thus, Lily had a duty to drive 30 m.p.h. (b) Yes, Lily was negligent because she breached her duty to Paul by driving too fast, and her excessive speed caused injuries to Paul. The fact that others were driving as fast as she was driving is not a defense. (c) Under common law contributory negligence, Paul could recover nothing because his negligence was a partial cause of his damages. (d) Under comparative negligence, Paul may recover $4,000, which represents that percent of his damages that were caused by Lily's negligence.

CHAPTER SEVEN
CRIME

MATCHING EXERCISE

1. i
2. l
3. j
4. d
5. g
6. e
7. a
8. h
9. k
10. c
11. f
12. b

COMPLETION EXERCISE

1. Reckless disregard
2. mens rea
   actus reus
3. RICO
4. probable cause
5. insanity
   entrapment
   duress
6. three strikes

TRUE-FALSE QUESTIONS

1. T
2. F
3. F
4. T
5. T
6. F
7. F
8. T
9. T
10. F

MULTIPLE CHOICE QUESTIONS

1. d
2. d
3. d
4. b
5. d
6. d
7. c
8. d
9. c
10. b
11. b
12. a

SHORT ESSAYS

1. (a) Typically, the prosecutor must show that the defendant intended to do what he or she did. In some cases the prosecutor will also have to prove that the defendant intended to do something more than the physical act of which she stands accused. This means the prosecutor must prove the specific intent of the defendant. In cases where the prosecutor charges criminal recklessness or criminal negligence, she is concerned with proving that the defendant acted irresponsibly. There are a few situations in which the prosecutor need not prove mens rea, only the actus reus. These are strict liability crimes and are easier to prove. Environmental crimes may be strict liability crimes.

   (b) The prosecutor must be able to prove, beyond a reasonable doubt, that the defendant voluntarily committed an act that is prohibited by law and also that the defendant had the necessary "mens rea," or guilty state of mind, at the time the act was committed.

2. The Fourth Amendment protects citizens from illegal searches and seizures by the government. Evidence that government officials gather without a valid search warrant may not be used at a trial based on the Fourth Amendment's Exclusionary Rule. There are, however, cases in which police officers may conduct searches without search warrants. The Fifth Amendment provides criminal defendants rights to due process of the law, which means that all legal action should be conducted in a fair and impartial manner. This amendment prohibits double jeopardy, which means a defendant may only be tried one time for a given crime. Finally, the Fifth Amendment also gives defendants the right not to testify against themselves. This is the right to avoid self-incrimination. The self-incrimination right does not apply to corporations, only to persons. These rights are designed to keep the government from interfering in people's private lives and to protect the liberty and freedom of the citizens of the country.

CASE PROBLEMS

1. (a) Drake has committed: (1) the federal crime of mail fraud as a result of his transmission of fraudulent information in interstate commerce; (2) *racketeering* in violation of Federal Racketeering Influenced Corrupt Organizations Act (RICO) as a result of his repeated fraudulent and criminal activities; and (3) *bribery* due to his payments to government officials in order to wrongfully obtain their approval of these land sales.

   (b) Drake may be subject to the following criminal penalties: criminal fines; order of restitution to return money paid by the land purchasers; forfeiture of property that was used to commit these crimes or property that was obtained as a result of these crimes; and imprisonment.

2. (a) Roland committed criminal fraud.

   (b) The prosecution must prove that he made a false statement of a material fact, knowing that it was false and with the intent that Roland rely upon it, and Roland did reasonably rely on the statement resulting in a financial loss.

CHAPTER EIGHT
INTERNATIONAL LAW

MATCHING EXERCISE

1. k
2. j
3. h
4. c
5. f
6. a
7. e
8. d
9. l
10. m
11. o
12. g
13. b
14. i
15. n

COMPLETION EXERCISE

1. Foreign Corrupt Practices Act
2. ASEAN
3. Exporting
4. Importing
5. Export Administration Act of 1985
   Arms Export Control Act
6. tariff
7. international comity
8. sovereign immunity
9. Act of State
10. ad valorem
11. import ban
12. direct sales
    indirect sales through distributors
    licensing a foreign manufacturer

TRUE-FALSE QUESTIONS

1. F
2. T
3. T
4. T
5. F
6. T
7. F
8. F
9. F
10. T
11. F
12. T
13. F
14. T

MULTIPLE CHOICE QUESTIONS

1. b
2. c
3. a
4. a
5. b
6. c
7. d
8. c
9. d

SHORT ESSAY

One approach for minimizing risk in international purchases is the use of a confirmed, irrevocable letter of credit as payment.

A letter of credit is a promise by a bank to pay a stated amount to the seller upon presentation of proper documents showing that the buyer is actually going to receive the goods being paid for. Such a letter is a guarantee to seller that the bank itself will pay the bill for the goods being sold so long as the seller presents certain conforming documents.

You will want to be very clear to specify just what those documents are. The bank should not pay the seller unless and until documents that exactly match your description are presented to the bank. You would probably require the seller to present a negotiable bill of lading - a document issued by a carrier (trucking, shipping company) that details what items the carrier is shipping from the seller.

A local bank (confirming bank) in the seller's country will probably advise the seller that a letter of credit is issued in its favor. The seller then checks the terms of letter of credit to ensure that they match the contract terms. If the seller presents and the bank accepts the documents, it then pays the seller. You endorse the bill of lading and the documents are forwarded to whatever bank issued the letter of credit (probably your local bank). The issuing bank then examines the documents. If they conform to the letter of credit the issuing bank then pays the confirming bank. You are responsible for paying your bank the sum it paid out to the confirming bank plus its fees for handling this transaction.

The buyer achieves greater security because the buyer is assured that payment will not be made unless the goods are being delivered. The seller achieves greater security because the seller knows that payment will be made for the goods.

CASE PROBLEM

Three approaches that Whisper Ride may use to market its products in foreign countries are direct sales, indirect sales through distributors, and licensing a foreign manufacturer.

Direct sales are good because they eliminate the need to deal with any foreign companies and dilution of profits. This approach is often hampered by a lack of necessary service for customers and the fact that some countries require foreign companies to do business with or through companies located within the country.

Indirect sales through distributors can be advantageous for a number of reasons. For instance, the local distributor is familiar with local laws and customs, can service the product, and can oftentimes more effectively market the product. Disadvantages include less control over foreign operations, dilution of profits, and the possibility of theft of inventory or sales receipts. Also antitrust concerns must be addressed.

Licensing a foreign manufacturer can be advantageous because Whisper Ride would avoid all of the difficulties attendant to foreign trade, such as shipping, payment, and service of goods. Major disadvantages include dilution of profits and the risk that the licensee may misappropriate your design and intellectual property and manufacture the product on their own. Again, antitrust concerns must also be addressed.

CHAPTER NINE
INTRODUCTION TO CONTRACTS

MATCHING EXERCISE

1. a
2. d
3. i
4. f
5. b
6. e
7. j
8. c
9. h
10. g

COMPLETION EXERCISE

1. predictable
2. noncompetition agreement (contract)
3. mixed contract
4. legal

TRUE-FALSE QUESTIONS

1. T
2. T
3. F
4. T
5. F
6. F
7. T
8. F
9. T
10. F

MULTIPLE CHOICE QUESTIONS

1. d
2. b
3. d
4. b
5. b
6. a
7. b
8. d
9. c
10. c
11. d

SHORT ESSAYS

1. Rules of contracting are important because they allow people to trade and conduct business in a cheaper, more cost-effective manner than they otherwise could do. Rules of contracting, if consistently enforced by impartial courts of law, allow businesses to plan for the future and to rely on those plans. If businesses can make plans for future behavior, they can more efficiently allocate resources than if they are only able to trade on a day-to-day basis. Disadvantages of contracting rules might be that if the rules become too rigid or become out-of-date, the rules themselves become costly to businesses and to individuals because they fail to meet the needs of a changing society.

2. Contracts may be express or implied, unilateral or bilateral, executory or executed, and valid, voidable, or void. In an express contract all material terms are clearly expressed. In an implied contract all material terms are not clearly expressed, but rather are implied from the words and behavior of the parties. A unilateral contract involves a promise by one party only to do something if the other party does something else. A bilateral contract is an exchange of promises between both parties to a contract. An executory contract is one where all the terms of the contract have not been fully performed (something remains to be done). An executed contracted is a fully performed, discharged contract. The law recognizes a valid contract. One party because of certain deficiencies in the contract formation process may disavow a voidable contract. The law does not recognize void contracts.

CASE PROBLEMS

1. (a) First consider whether Betima and Julene have a valid contract. Are the terms of the contract clear? Has there been a valid offer and acceptance. Is there valid consideration or has Julene made a friendly offer more akin to a gift? In final analysis, you should conclude that there is no contract because the facts do not show that Betima promised or did anything in exchange for Julene's promise of training. Thus, there is no consideration and no contract.

   (b) However, the facts do establish a strong case for promissory estoppel. Betima relied on Julene's promises, Julene knew that Betima was relying on these promises, and, as a result of her reliance, Betima sustained significant losses. The only way to avoid an injustice to Betima is to hold Julene liable for the harms associated with Betima's sale of her home.

2. (a) The parties did not enter into a contract. There was never a valid agreement (offer and acceptance) for painting the car.

   (b) Ken is legally obligated under quasi contract to pay for the reasonable value of the painting. He received a benefit and, under the facts of the case, he would be unjustly enriched if he did not pay for the work rendered.

CHAPTER TEN
AGREEMENT

MATCHING EXERCISE

1. c
2. b
3. e
4. g
5. f
6. i
7. d
8. a
9. h

COMPLETION EXERCISE

1. mailbox rule
2. without reserve
3. output contract
4. requirements contract
5. offer
   agreement
6. counteroffer
7. revocation
8. reasonable time
9. gap-filler provisions

TRUE-FALSE QUESTIONS

1. F
2. T
3. T
4. T
5. F
6. F
7. F
8. F
9. T
10. F

MULTIPLE CHOICE QUESTIONS

1. b
2. a
3. c
4. b
5. d
6. c
7. b
8. d
9. c
10. a
11. d
12. d

SHORT ESSAY

Offers may be terminated by rejection ("I don't want to buy your computer"); by expiration (The offeror says "This offer will expire after Tuesday" and it is now Wednesday); by operation of law (An offeror says "I offer to sell my house to you" and before acceptance the offeror or offeree dies); by destruction of the subject matter ("I offer to sell my car to you" and before acceptance the car is destroyed in an accident.)

CASE PROBLEM

Consider whether there has been a valid offer and a valid acceptance. Is there an intent to contract or merely an offer to negotiate? Are all the terms of the offer clear? It appears not for there is no price term and Estelle specifically mentions another document that will serve as the sales contract. Until that document is presented is there a valid offer?

Under the UCC we know that open terms are allowed if the parties intend to contract and if a reasonable basis for giving a remedy exists. Here the question is whether or not the parties intended to contract or merely to bargain. The equivocal nature of Estelle's statements and the intent to draw up a written contract between the parties that would spell out the terms of any contract lead to a likely conclusion that there was no intent to contract and, therefore, no contract.

CHAPTER ELEVEN
CONSIDERATION

MATCHING EXERCISE

1. e
2. f
3. b
4. g
5. a
6. i
7. d
8. c
9. h

COMPLETION EXERCISE

1. bilateral
2. unilateral
3. preexisting duty
4. mutual rescission

TRUE-FALSE QUESTIONS

1. T
2. F
3. T
4. F
5. F
6. T
7. T
8. T
9. F
10. T

MULTIPLE CHOICE QUESTIONS

1. c
2. a
3. b
4. d
5. b
6. c
7. a
8. d
9. a
10. a
11. c
12. d

SHORT ESSAYS

1. A liquidated debt exists if there is no dispute about the amount of money owed to the creditor. An unliquidated debt exists if there is some dispute whether a debt is owed or the amount of the debt.

   The distinction between a liquidated and unliquidated debt is important. If a creditor accepts from a debtor less than the full sum of money owed as a liquidated debt, then the agreement is not binding and the creditor may sue the debtor for the rest of the debt. On the other hand, if a creditor accepts from a debtor less than the full sum of money claimed as an unliquidated debt, the agreement is binding as an accord and satisfaction. In this situation, the creditor cannot sue for the balance of the alleged debt.

   An example of a liquidated debt would be a $5,000 debt for $5,000 that you borrowed from a local bank to pay your tuition. An example of an unliquidated debt would be the amount of damages that you claim for future pain and suffering resulting from an automobile accident negligently caused by another person. Because no one knows exactly how much these damages are, the amount of the debt is uncertain, i.e., unliquidated. If you and the other person agree to settle your case out of court for $10,000, this is a valid accord and satisfaction and you cannot sue the other person for more money.

2. An output contract is an agreement whereby a buyer agrees to purchase and a seller agrees to sell all of the seller's production of a particular good. On the other hand, a requirements contract is an agreement whereby a buyer agrees to purchase and a seller agrees to supply all of the buyer's needs for a particular good. An example of an output contract would be a farmer agreeing to sell his or her entire cabbage crop to a local chain of grocery stores. An example of a requirements contract would be a chain of lube shops agreeing to buy all of their motor oil from a particular supplier.

CASE PROBLEMS

1. (a) Sally's agreement not to compete is not supported by consideration. Her promise not to compete against Acme would be consideration because she is promising to forbear from doing something that she would otherwise be entitled to do. However, Acme did not give any consideration. (b) The agreement is not a contract. Each party to an agreement must give consideration in order for an agreement to be a contract. (c) Acme should have given new consideration in exchange for Sally's promise not to compete, such as promising a raise or additional benefits.

2. (a) No, the agreement with Randy is not legally binding because Randy's services are past consideration. Randy's services are not valid consideration because when the services were rendered, they were not done as the price demanded for the bonus. (b) No, the agreement with Fred is not legally binding because Fred did not give consideration. Fred's promise not to breach his contract is a promise to perform a preexisting duty. (c) No, Aries cannot refuse to perform the contract with Hill for the reason that Hill's consideration was inadequate. Courts will not examine the adequacy of the considerations exchanged.

CHAPTER TWELVE
LEGALITY

MATCHING EXERCISE

1. h
2. g
3. c
4. b
5. f
6. d
7. e
8. i
9. a

COMPLETION EXERCISE

1. bailment
2. bailee
   bailor
3. usury

TRUE-FALSE QUESTIONS

1. F
2. F
3. T
4. F
5. T
6. T
7. F
8. F
9. T
10. F

MULTIPLE CHOICE QUESTIONS

1. a
2. a
3. b
4. b
5. c
6. c
7. d
8. a
9. d
10. d
11. b

SHORT ESSAY

Courts will not enforce contracts that are in violation of "public policy." Such contracts are otherwise valid (entered into by consenting adults who have capacity to contract), but judges determine that enforcing them would have a deleterious effect on society as a whole. These contracts include agreements among businesses that restrict trade. If businesses agreed to set their prices at exactly the same level for a period of time in order to drive competitors out of the market, this would be a contract in restraint of trade and would not be enforced.

Some noncompetition clauses are not enforced because they restrain trade too much. Also, courts will occasionally not enforce otherwise valid contracts because the judge finds the contract exculpatory, meaning the contract releases one party from legal liability in the event of injury to the other contracting party. If a doctor agrees to charge you less money for an operation if you agree to release him or her from all future tort liability, this contract would be void based on the exculpatory clause.

Some courts will not enforce otherwise valid contracts based on unconscionability. In these cases courts find that one party to the contract has much more power than the other, that the parties did not bargain at arm's length, so the contract should not be enforced because to do so would be unfair. Think about whether judges, or parties to contracts, are in a better position to determine what is and what is not unfair. This is an opinion question and should be defended by using logical arguments.

CASE PROBLEMS

1. Courts will not enforce illegal gambling contracts. These contracts are illegal because they either violate statutes or because they are in violation of public policy. In this case, the agreement between Marjorie and Beth was clearly a matter of chance - they gambled on who would win the next gubernatorial election. Although elections are legal, this kind of betting on the outcome of an election is not. An illegal and void agreement is unenforceable, meaning that the court will not order the parties to perform the agreement and it will not award any remedies of any sort. In this case, Beth is out of luck.

2. (a) The required license intended to assure the competency of architects to engage in this profession and to protect the public from improperly performed work. This purpose is indicated by the experience and examination requirements. (b) The agreement is void. An agreement that requires violation of a licensing statute that is intended to protect is generally unenforceable. (c) No, Luis cannot enforce the agreement, and he cannot recover the agreed price. These remedies are not available because the contract is void.

CHAPTER THIRTEEN
CAPACITY AND CONSENT

MATCHING EXERCISE

1. h
2. e
3. j
4. d
5. i
6. g
7. a
8. f
9. c
10. b

COMPLETION EXERCISE

1. innocent misrepresentation
2. 18
3. Undue influence
4. voidable
5. Economic duress
6. necessaries
7. fact
8. Unilateral
9. Bilateral
10. Puffing

TRUE-FALSE QUESTIONS

1. T
2. F
3. T
4. F
5. F
6. F
7. F
8. T
9. T
10. T

MULTIPLE CHOICE QUESTIONS

1. a
2. c
3. d
4. b
5. c
6. d
7. d
8. b
9. b
10. b
11. d

SHORT ESSAYS

1. Misrepresentation occurs "when a party to a contract says something that is factually wrong." An innocent misrepresentation is made when the speaker does not lie intentionally or with an intent to deceive the other party. Fraud, on the other hand, occurs when the speaker says something that he or she knows is untrue or have no basis to believe that it is true. If a misrepresentation is innocent, that means there was no intent to deceive; if a misrepresentation is fraudulent, there is an intent to deceive or a reckless disregard of the truth. Puffery may look like fraud, but is instead the inflated language used to sell products. Puffery is a subjective statement of opinion, not a statement of fact. If a party suffers a fraud in a contract the party may rescind the contract or sue for damages, or in some states do both. In the case of an innocent misrepresentation, the injured party may rescind the contract.

2. Ratification is the clear and definite expression of intent by a party to be bound by the terms of a contract even though the contract was otherwise voidable. An example of express ratification would be a fully informed party stating or writing "I affirm this contract." An implied ratification often occurs when a contracting party continues to accept significant new benefits under a contract or seeks to enforce the contract even though the party knows that the contract is voidable.

CASE PROBLEMS

1. (a) Traditionally, a party does not have a duty to affirmatively disclose obvious conditions regarding the subject of the contract. The other party should inspect the property and discover that which is obvious. Thus, Lon would not have a duty to volunteer information regarding the foundation.

   (b) On the other hand, a party cannot undertake actions that hide the true nature of the contract subject matter. Doing so is fraud. Thus, if Lon plastered over the damaged foundation in order to hide the damage, this conduct would be fraud and it would render the contract voidable.

   (c) Under modern rules, Lon must disclose the asbestos because it is an important, latent defect that buyers would not be able to discover upon a reasonable inspection.

2. Yes, Dynamic can rescind the contract. There was a mutual (bilateral) mistake of a material fact (the acreage of the parcel of land). Thus, the contract is voidable.

3. (a) Seller committed fraud. Seller intentionally misrepresented a material fact, with the intent that Buyer rely on the misrepresentation, and Buyer was induced into contracting due to Buyer's reliance on this misrepresentation.

   (b) The contract is voidable at the option of Buyer.

   (c) Under the UCC, Buyer can rescind the contract and Buyer can also sue Seller for damages.

CHAPTER FOURTEEN
WRITTEN CONTRACTS

MATCHING EXERCISE

1. g
2. f
3. c
4. b
5. e
6. a
7. d

REVIEW OF CONCEPTS

1. Agreement for an interest in land
2. Agreements that cannot be performed within one year
3. Promise to pay the debt of another
4. Promise made by an executor of an estate
5. Promise made in consideration of marriage
6. Contract for the sale of goods for $500 or more

TRUE-FALSE QUESTIONS

1. T
2. F
3. F
4. T
5. T
6. T
7. F
8. F
9. F
10. F
11. T
12. T

MULTIPLE CHOICE QUESTIONS

1. a
2. d
3. b
4. d
5. d
6. a
7. c
8. a
9. c
10. b
11. c
12. a

SHORT ESSAYS

1. A written contract must contain the signature of the defendant (assuming a lawsuit exists concerning the contract). In addition, it must state "with reasonable certainty" the name of each party to the contract, the subject matter of the contract (what it is about), and all of the essential terms and promises. Incomplete or vague contracts will not be enforced. These requirements assure that the court is truly enforcing the intended agreement of the parties and not imposing what the court feels is appropriate. These requirements also reduce the chance that a party may successfully claim that a contract was made when in fact it wasn't.

2. The basic UCC rule concerning written contracts is Section 2-201, which states that contracts for the sale of goods worth for $500 or more must be in writing to be enforceable. The writing may be a sales memorandum, it does not need to be a formal contract, but the writing must contain the signature of the defendant and the quantity of goods purchased. Open price and delivery terms are permissible. This rule allows merchants to sell more cheaply and have greater flexibility in their sales because sales contracts can be less formal (and therefore less expensive).

   The exception to Section 2-201 is Section 2-201(2), which creates an exception for merchants. Merchants may enforce oral sales contracts if, within a reasonable time of making the oral contract, one merchant sends written confirmation of the agreement to the other merchant. The confirmation must be definite enough that the sender is bound by the terms. The recipient of the confirmation will be bound by the same written terms unless he or she objects in writing within ten days. This provision allows for great flexibility and for quick, inexpensive contracting among merchants.

   Also, in some special circumstances an oral contract without a subsequent written memo will be enforceable. Section 2-201(3) says that if a seller manufacturers special goods for a buyer, or a defendant admits in court that a contract existed, or goods were delivered or paid for, an oral contract may be enforced.

CASE PROBLEMS

1. (a) Yes. This is a contract for the sale of land.

   (b) Yes. The paper states the material terms of the contract and it is initialed by Jim, who is refusing to perform. Jim's initial was made with the intent of evidencing his agreement to the contract and, therefore, his initial is a sufficient signature.

   (c) Since the paper satisfies the writing requirement under the statute of frauds, the oral agreement is legally enforceable.

2. No. It is possible that Steve may fully perform within one year because he may die during this time. Therefore, the oral contract is enforceable.

CHAPTER FIFTEEN
THIRD PARTIES

MATCHING EXERCISE

1. a
2. e
3. b
4. d
5. i
6. f
7. j
8. h
9. c
10. g

COMPLETION EXERCISE

1. intent
2. novation
3. donee beneficiary
4. warranties
5. a. when an assignment would substantially change the obligor's contractual rights or duties.
   b. when an assignment is forbidden by law or public policy.
   c. when an assignment is validly forbidden by the contract.

TRUE-FALSE QUESTIONS

1. F
2. T
3. F
4. T
5. T
6. F
7. F
8. T
9. T
10. F

MULTIPLE CHOICE QUESTIONS

1. a
2. c
3. c
4. d
5. c
6. a
7. d
8. b
9. d
10. a
11. b
12. d

SHORT ESSAY

A donee beneficiary is someone to whom a gift is promised. When someone fulfills a duty, the person for whom the duty is performed is known as a creditor beneficiary. An incidental beneficiary is someone who the parties to a contract do not intend to benefit, but who would nonetheless benefit if a contract were performed.

Donee and creditor beneficiaries may enforce contracts because the parties to the underlying contract intended to benefit them. However, incidental beneficiaries may not enforce contracts because the contracting parties do not intend to benefit them.

CASE PROBLEMS

1. a. Yes, Erecto was legally entitled to delegate the excavation work to Gopher Inc. without first obtaining Owner's consent. In general, a party can delegate a duty to perform standardized, nonpersonal services that do not involve a special skill.

   b. Yes, Erecto is liable to Owner for the improperly performed work. A delegating party remains responsible for the proper performance of delegated work.

2. a. Yes, the assignment was valid. Most contractual rights may be assigned, especially ones such as this where the right to be paid money.

   b. Yes. While waiver clauses are generally valid in commercial contracts, they are generally not valid in consumer transactions. Thus, Laurie may assert her defense against Third Bank.

CHAPTER SIXTEEN
PERFORMANCE AND DISCHARGE

MATCHING EXERCISE

1. i
2. c
3. d
4. g
5. b
6. a
7. f
8. e
9. h

COMPLETION EXERCISE

1. Concurrent conditions
2. condition precedent
3. condition subsequent
4. Strict performance
   substantial performance

TRUE-FALSE QUESTIONS

1. F
2. T
3. F
4. T
5. T
6. T
7. F
8. T
9. F
10. F

MULTIPLE CHOICE QUESTIONS

1. c
2. c
3. a
4. b
5. b
6. c
7. b
8. d
9. d
10. a
11. a

SHORT ESSAY

A condition is an event that must occur before a party to a contract is obligated under the contract. Conditions may be express or implied. Conditions may be precedent, subsequent, or concurrent.

A condition precedent states that something must happen before a duty arises. A condition subsequent states that if a duty exists and a particular event occurs thereafter, an obligation is created. Concurrent conditions exist when both parties have a duty to perform simultaneously.

Conditions are created by parties who either include conditions expressly in contracts, or who create the conditions by implication -- as a result of their behavior. If Sam agrees to give Wanda $100 if she makes bakes him five dinners, the duty to pay arises only if Wanda makes the grade, so it is a condition precedent.

CASE PROBLEMS

1. No. It is not impossible to do the work, only Theo cannot do it. This type of personal inability does not establish the defense of impossibility. Theo must hire someone else to do the work.

2. No. This contract is a personal-satisfaction contract. Moreover, it involves Albert's personal taste and, therefore, he has the right to personally determine whether the work is satisfactory or not.

3. A contract may be discharged if an unforeseeable event makes it impossible for anyone to perform the contract. Also, a contract may be discharged when an unforeseeable event frustrates the essential purpose for the contract. In this case, however, the fluctuation in prices for natural gas was foreseeable. This is a risk that Mark implicitly took on and he cannot now escape from his contractual duties.

CHAPTER SEVENTEEN
REMEDIES

MATCHING EXERCISE

1. a
2. h
3. g
4. e
5. f
6. I
7. b
8. c
9. d
10. j

COMPLETION EXERCISE

1. breach of contract
2. mitigate
3. interest
4. expectation interest
5. reliance interest

TRUE-FALSE QUESTIONS

1. T
2. F
3. T
4. F
5. F
6. T
7. F
8. F
9. F
10. F

MULTIPLE CHOICE QUESTIONS

1. c
2. d
3. b
4. b
5. a
6. d
7. a
8. d
9. d
10. c

SHORT ESSAY

Expectation interests are designed to place someone who has been injured in the position they would have been in had both parties to the contract fully performed their contractual obligations. If an expectation interest has been injured, the injured party may seek compensatory, consequential and/or incidental damages.

A reliance interest, on the other hand, is designed to place someone in the position they would have been in had the parties never entered the contract at all. Courts seek to compensate injured parties for the time and money they spend performing their part of a contract.

CASE PROBLEMS

1. (a). The liquidated damage amount is valid because it was difficult to foresee the precise damage that might be caused if Mica Co. failed to complete the building on time and the liquidated amount was a reasonable estimate of the probable damages.

   (b). Pack Rat Storage can recover $2,000 liquidated damages. A party who is entitled to damages recovers the amount of liquidated damages even if the actual loss is larger or smaller than the liquidated amount.

2. (a). Kendra has fully complied with her part of the contract. The supply store, however, has materially breached the contract by failing to accept conforming goods. In this case Kendra's expectation interest are those damages that flow directly from the breach.

   (b). Under the UCC, Kendra has the option of selling the blinds to another buyer and collecting the difference between the original contract price and the price she obtains from the substitute buyer. Alternatively, Kendra may keep the goods and sue for the difference between the contract price and the market value of the blinds. Kendra may also recover any incidental damages incurred, but she probably cannot recover any consequential damages.

CHAPTER EIGHTEEN
INTRODUCTION TO SALES

MATCHING EXERCISE

1. a
2. e
3. i
4. f
5. b
6. c
7. g
8. d
9. h
10. j

COMPLETION EXERCISE

1. good faith
2. Article 2
3. Article 2A
4. statute of frauds
5. predominant purpose
6. trade usage

TRUE-FALSE QUESTIONS

1. T
2. F
3. F
4. T
5. T
6. F
7. T
8. F
9. F
10. T

MULTIPLE CHOICE QUESTIONS

1. d
2. b
3. c
4. c
5. c
6. d
7. a
8. b
9. c
10. d
11. d
12. c

SHORT ESSAY

The UCC requires both merchants and non-merchants to deal in good faith. For non-merchants this means they must exercise honesty in fact. Merchants are held to a higher standard requiring honesty in fact plus the exercise of reasonable commercial standards of fair dealing. Parties who violate these obligations face liability for damages they cause to the other contracting parties as a result of their bad faith.

Unconscionability means treatment that is shockingly one-sided and fundamentally unfair. While bad faith involves a lack of honesty, unconscionability does not. People may act unconscionably without lying. Further, the good-faith requirement is concerned with the way in which parties carry out contract obligations, while unconscionability is concerned with the substance of a contract itself. In cases of bad faith or unconscionability, courts will oftentimes not enforce contracts.

CASE PROBLEMS

1. No. As a general rule, Article 2 allows an offeror to revoke an offer at anytime and for any reason prior to acceptance. As an exception to the foregoing general rule, a merchant who makes a firm offer cannot revoke it for the time stated, and consideration is not required to make this promise legally binding. Centrex's offer is a firm offer and, therefore, it was not legally entitled to revoke it.

2. Yes. Although a sales contract for $500 or more is generally required to be evidenced by a writing to be enforceable, this rule does not apply if the goods are to be specially made, they cannot be readily resold, and the seller has substantially begun to make or acquire the goods.

3. Yes. Shawna sent Kim a written confirmation of their agreement and Kim did not object to the confirmation, in writing, within ten days.

CHAPTER NINETEEN
OWNERSHIP AND RISK

MATCHING EXERCISE

1. c
2. h
3. f
4. e
5. g
6. b
7. i
8. d
9. a

COMPLETION EXERCISE

1. bulk sale
2. entrustment
3. destination contract
4. shipment contract
5. Title

TRUE-FALSE QUESTIONS

1. T
2. F
3. F
4. T
5. F
6. T
7. T
8. F
9. T
10. T

MULTIPLE CHOICE QUESTIONS

1. b
2. c
3. d
4. c
5. b
6. d
7. a
8. a
9. c
10. c

SHORT ESSAY

Under the UCC, title to a good will pass only when the goods exist and are identified to the contract. For goods that do not exist, but might exist in the future (such as a future orange crop), title does not pass until the goods come into being. Once goods exist, they must be identified to a contract before title can pass. This means the parties either described the goods to be purchased, or the seller marks, ships, or otherwise indicates the exact goods that are being sold to the buyer. In the case of animals once they're conceived they are identified to a contract; in the case of crops, once planted they are identified to a contract.

Under the UCC, title passes in any manner the parties specify. If they fail to specify a way title may pass when the seller completes whatever transportation the seller agreed to provide, or if the goods are not being moved, title will pass when the seller delivers ownership documents to the buyer. A person has good title when they have the legal right to posses the good. A person has voidable title when they purchase a good from someone with the intent to deceive or defraud the seller. Persons with voidable title may transfer good title to a good-faith purchaser for value. However, if persons with voidable title give the goods to another person, the third party does not obtain good title.

CASE PROBLEMS

1. Yes. This was an entrustment and Ted received good title.

2. Cindy. This was a shipment contract and, therefore, the risk of loss during transportation fell on Cindy.

3. No. This is a sale on approval transaction. The risk of loss never passed to Kathy because she never accepted the bike.

CHAPTER TWENTY
WARRANTIES AND PRODUCT LIABILITY

MATCHING EXERCISE

1. d
2. a
3. c
4. b
5. e
6. j
7. i
8. f
9. h
10. g

COMPLETION EXERCISE

1. basis of the bargain
2. sample
3. model
4. warranty of merchantability
   warranty of title
5. strict liability
6. AS IS
7. shrinkwrap agreement
   clickwrap agreement
8. Value of the product
   Gravity of the danger
   Likelihood that such danger will occur
   Mechanical feasibility of a safer alternative design
   Adverse consequences of an alternative design

TRUE-FALSE QUESTIONS

1. T
2. F
3. T
4. F
5. T
6. F
7. T
8. F
9. T
10. F

MULTIPLE CHOICE QUESTIONS

1. d
2. d
3. d
4. a
5. c
6. b
7. c
8. d
9. d
10. d

SHORT ESSAY

An express warranty is created by some action or words of the seller. Thus, express warranties may be created by an affirmation of a fact or by a promise. Descriptions of goods may create express warranties. If a seller sends a buyer a sample or a model, these items also may create express warranties. However, keep in mind that the seller's conduct must have been a part of the basis of the bargain for a court to find that an express warranty existed. Express warranties are especially difficult to disclaim if they are written.

A warranty of merchantability applies automatically to goods sold by a merchant who regularly sells similar goods. These warranties may, however, be modified or disclaimed.

An implied warranty of fitness for a particular purpose automatically applies to goods sold by a party who knows at the time of the sale that the buyer wants the goods for a particular purpose and that the buyer is relying on the seller's skill or judgment that the goods will be suitable for the particular purpose. These warranties may also be modified or disclaimed.

Sellers who create express warranties or who sell goods with implied warranties are guaranteeing that the goods will do what they claim or that the goods will be fit for their ordinary purpose or a special purpose, respectively. Failure to live up to these guarantees may subject the seller to a claim of breach of warranty.

CASE PROBLEM

a. Gary can sue Aqua Boats for strict liability. Aqua designed, manufactured, and sold the boat, which was defective and unreasonably dangerous. Gary cannot sue Aqua for negligence because it exercised due care and he cannot sue for breach of warranty because Aqua disclaimed all warranties.

b. Gary can sue Crest for strict liability because the seller of a product is liable the same as the manufacturer. Gary can also sue Crest for breach of the warranty of merchantability. Crest is a merchant that regularly sells goods of this kind and Crest did not disclaim this warranty. As with Aqua, Gary cannot sue for negligence because Crest exercised due care.

CHAPTER TWENTY-ONE
PERFORMANCE AND REMEDIES

MATCHING EXERCISE

1. a
2. k
3. e
4. l
5. g
6. f
7. c
8. i
9. h
10. j
11. b
12. d

COMPLETION EXERCISE

1. Liquidated damages
2. installment contract
3. ten days
4. Cure
5. substantially impairs

TRUE-FALSE QUESTIONS

1. T
2. T
3. F
4. T
5. T
6. T
7. F
8. T
9. T
10. F

MULTIPLE CHOICE QUESTIONS

1. c
2. c
3. d
4. c
5. c
6. d
7. d
8. d
9. d
10. c

SHORT ESSAY

If a seller breaches a contract a buyer may choose to cover by purchasing substitute goods in a commercially reasonable manner. After covering, the buyer may sue for damages associated with the breach, including the difference between the cover price and the contract price, plus incidental and consequential damages. However, a buyer may elect not to cover, in which case the buyer may still sue for damages for the difference between the market price and contract price plus incidental damages, but the buyer cannot recover consequential damages that could have been avoided had the buyer attempted to cover. If the buyer accepts and keeps the goods, the buyer can recover damages equal to the difference between the value of the goods as warranted and their actual value, plus incidental and consequential damages.

Other options open to the buyer include recovering the exact goods contracted for by obtaining a court order for specific performance if the goods are unique or cannot be readily obtained elsewhere, or recovering liquidated damages if the sales contract contained a liquidated damages clause and the clause is reasonable.

CASE PROBLEM

a. Yes, Alicia must give Seller notice of the breach within a reasonable time after learning of the defective transmission.

b. If Alicia fails to give notice of the breach, she cannot sue Seller for the breach.

c. If Seller refuses to cure the nonconformity, Alicia can recover $2,200 damages. For breach of warranty, a buyer can recover damages equal to the value that goods would have had if they were as warranted ($11,000), minus their actual value ($9,000), plus incidental damages ($200).

CHAPTER TWENTY-TWO
CREATING A NEGOTIABLE INSTRUMENT

MATCHING EXERCISE

1. e
2. d
3. k
4. b
5. m
6. g
7. l
8. n
9. h
10. a
11. c
12. i
13. o
14. j
15. f

COMPLETION EXERCISE

1. non-negotiable
2. maker
   drawer
3. money
4. special indorsement
5. typed
6. restrictive indorsement
7. Negotiation

TRUE-FALSE QUESTIONS

1. T
2. F
3. T
4. F
5. T
6. F
7. T
8. F
9. F
10. T
11. T

MULTIPLE CHOICE QUESTIONS

1. c
2. a
3. a
4. d
5. c
6. d
7. d
8. a
9. d

SHORT ESSAY

Real defenses are legal defenses that may be used by issuers of negotiable instruments and other parties who may otherwise have liability to pay an instrument to avoid having to pay an instrument. Real defenses may be used against ordinary holders and holders in due course. Real defenses include: forgery, bankruptcy, minority, alteration, fraud in the execution, and other defenses that under state law render a contract void, not merely voidable.

Personal defenses are legal defenses that may be used against ordinary holders but not against holders in due course. These defenses include breach of contract, lack of consideration, prior payment, unauthorized completion, fraud in the inducement and non-delivery. The rest of the question is an opinion question, in which you should set forth a logical argument defending your position.

CASE PROBLEM

a. To be negotiable, an instrument must be: 1) written; 2) signed by the drawer or maker; 3) state an unconditional promise to or order to pay; 4) a fixed sum of money; 5) payable on demand or at a definite time; and 6) payable to bearer or to the order of a party. This instrument fails some of these requirements and, therefore, it is non-negotiable. For instance, the sum to be paid is not for a certain amount, and the obligation to pay is conditioned upon completion of the project.

b. Even though the note is non-negotiable, it still establishes a contractual obligation to pay.

c. Yes. Since it is a non-negotiable instrument, subsequent transferees who take the note cannot be a holder in due course and, therefore, they would take the note subject to all defenses, both personal and real.

CHAPTER TWENTY-THREE
LIABILITY FOR NEGOTIABLE INSTRUMENTS

MATCHING EXERCISE

1. f
2. c
3. e
4. j
5. a
6. g
7. b
8. h
9. i
10. d

COMPLETION EXERCISE

1. maker
2. accepts
3. Conversion
4. warranty liability
5. transferee is a holder of the instrument;
   all signatures are authentic and authorized;
   the instrument has not been altered;
   no defense can be asserted against the transferee; and
   the transferee believes that the issuer is solvent.

TRUE-FALSE QUESTIONS

1. F
2. F
3. T
4. F
5. F
6. T
7. F
8. T
9. F
10. T
11. T

MULTIPLE CHOICE QUESTIONS

1. a
2. b
3. c
4. d
5. c
6. d
7. d

SHORT ESSAY

Negotiable instruments may be discharged by payment that is made by a party who is obligated to pay the instrument to someone who validly holds the instrument. Discharge may also result by agreement of the parties, even if the instrument is not paid; by cancellation through the involuntary surrender, destruction or disfigurement of an instrument; by certification; and, by alteration, which discharges the issuer from responsibility.

CASE PROBLEMS

1. Yes. Peoria Bank accepted the check, thus incurring primary liability to pay whether or not Wally has sufficient money in his account to cover the check.

2. James must pay the amount of the checks to Check-Rite. Under the "imposter rule," when a person is deceived into issuing an instrument to an imposter who pretends to be an intended payee and the imposter forges the payee's indorsement, then the issuer must pay anyone who, in good faith, subsequently pays or takes the instrument, in this case Check-Rite. Michelle still has a contractual right under its lease to demand James to pay her the rent for the two months in question.

CHAPTER TWENTY-FOUR
NEGOTIABLE INSTRUMENTS: BANKS AND THEIR CUSTOMERS

MATCHING EXERCISE

1. l
2. j
3. i
4. d
5. h
6. e
7. f
8. g
9. c
10. b
11. a
12. k

COMPLETION EXERCISE

1. drawee bank
2. fourteen days
   six months
3. Certification
4. one year
5. ordinary care
6. consumers
7. automated teller machines
   point of sale terminals

TRUE-FALSE QUESTIONS

1. T
2. F
3. T
4. F
5. F
6. T
7. T
8. F
9. F
10. T
11. T
12. F
13. T
14. F
15. F

MULTIPLE CHOICE QUESTIONS

1. c
2. c
3. d
4. c
5. c
6. b
7. c

SHORT ESSAY

Businesses make large transfers of money using electronic transfers, which are subject to UCC Article 4A. One business, called the originator, issues a payment order directing the originator's bank to transfer funds from the originator's account and to pay these funds to the beneficiary. The originator's bank withdraws the money from the originator's account and wires it with instructions to the Federal Reserve Bank, which informs the beneficiary's bank that it has money for the benefit of the beneficiary. The beneficiary's bank then credits this amount to the beneficiary's account.

CASE PROBLEM

a. The Electronic Fund Transfer Act (EFTA) governs this case because it is a consumer electronic fund transfer.

b. A consumer's liability is: a maximum of $50 if notice is given to the issuer within two days after the consumer learns of a loss or theft; a maximum of $500 if notice is not given within this two-day period. A consumer bears a loss caused by a failure to report an unauthorized transfer within sixty days after receiving a statement of the account.

c. Greg is liable for $50 since he reported the theft of his card within two days.

CHAPTER TWENTY-FIVE
SECURED TRANSACTIONS

MATCHING EXERCISE

1. h
2. f
3. c
4. b
5. g
6. d
7. e
8. o
9. i
10. n
11. m
12. j
13. a
14. k
15. l

TRUE-FALSE QUESTIONS

1. T
2. T
3. T
4. F
5. T
6. F
7. T
8. F
9. F
10. T
11. F
12. F
13. T
14. F
15. F
16. T
17. F
18. T
19. T
20. F
21. T
22. F
23. T
24. F
25. T

MULTIPLE CHOICE QUESTIONS

1. b
2. c
3. d
4. c
5. a
6. d
7. c
8. d

SHORT ESSAY

Security interests may be perfected by filing with the proper authorities, by taking possession of the collateral, by purchasing consumer goods, or by following the complex rules for perfecting rights to fixtures. Perfection by filing involves completing a financing statement and filing with (typically) the state Secretary of State. In the case of consumer goods, a security interest perfects automatically, with no filing requirements, although filing a financing statement with the appropriate government office also can perfect a security interest in consumer goods. In the case of boats and automobiles, a security interest perfects by having the security interest stated on the title documents to the boat or car.

Examples of three approaches for perfection are: (1) Saul borrows $50,000 from Minda. Saul pledges stock he owns as collateral. Minda must take possession of the stock to perfect her interest in the stock. (2) Ken's Gun Shop borrows $30,000 from First National Bank, using his inventory of antique guns as collateral. The bank may perfect its interest in the guns by filing a financing statement with the Secretary of State. (3) K&T Furniture Store sells you a sofa for your home on credit. K&T's security interest in the sofa is automatically perfected.

CASE PROBLEM

1. Acme can use self-help to repossess the collateral on Debtor's default, and a court order is not required.

2. Acme cannot commit a breach of the peace in repossessing the collateral. If a breach may occur, a court order must be obtained.

3. Prior to sale, Debtor may redeem by paying the entire debt and all attorney's fees and costs incurred by Acme.

4. Proceeds from sale are applied first to the expenses incurred in connection with the repossession and sale of the collateral; secondly, to Acme's secured debt; any excess is paid to other secured parties with interests in the collateral; and any remaining surplus is paid to Debtor.

5. Debtor is liable for any deficiency.

CHAPTER TWENTY-SIX
BANKRUPTCY

MATCHING EXERCISE

1. k
2. h
3. f
4. d
5. l
6. b
7. a
8. e
9. j
10. g
11. c
12. i

COMPLETION EXERCISE

1. federal
2. trustee
3. Chapter 11
4. Chapter 13
5. three
   $11,625
6. fraudulent transfer
7. six

TRUE-FALSE QUESTIONS

1. F
2. T
3. F
4. T
5. T
6. T
7. T
8. T
9. F
10. F
11. T
12. F
13. T
14. T
15. T
16. T
17. T
18. T
19. T
20. T

MULTIPLE CHOICE QUESTIONS

1. c
2. d
3. d
4. b
5. a
6. b
7. c
8. c

SHORT ESSAY

The debtor typically files with the U.S. Bankruptcy Court a petition for Chapter 11 Bankruptcy. As debtor in possession, the debtor then sets out to develop a reorganization plan, which is submitted to the court and creditors for approval.

The plan designates the classes of creditors and others with an interest in the debtor and sets forth how much and how the creditors will be paid. In a typical plan, some of the debtor's current assets are paid to the creditors with a promise to pay some or all of them an additional amount from the debtor's future earnings.

The creditors have a right to approve or disapprove of a proposed plan. Nonetheless, the court has the right to use the "cramdown" procedure to confirm a plan if it is feasible and fair, even if some of the creditor's classes disapproved of the plan.

CASE PROBLEM

First Bank is a secured creditor and, therefore, has priority to enforce its security interest in the building. After secured creditors have enforced their rights, certain unsecured creditors enjoy a priority. In this case, creditors have priority in the following order: Mr. Atkins will be paid his $6,000 trustee fee as a cost of administration; then Tina will be paid her $1,000 in wages because they were earned within 90 days of the filing; then Bud will be repaid his $500 deposit because it was given for consumer goods. Remaining assets are paid to unsecured creditors who have no priority. Thus, Fuller Co. gets the remaining $2,500.

CHAPTER TWENTY-SEVEN
AGENCY

MATCHING EXERCISE

1.	f	10.	a
2.	m	11.	h
3.	g	12.	p
4.	q	13.	j
5.	i	14.	e
6.	o	15.	n
7.	b	16.	d
8.	c	17.	r
9.	l	18.	k

COMPLETION EXERCISE

1. consent
   control
   fiduciary relationship
2. reasonable care
3. gratuitous agency
4. duty loyalty
5. reimburse
   cooperate
6. a. Expiration of a term agency agreement.
   b. Achieving the purpose of an agency.
   c. Mutual agreement of the agent and principal.
   d. Unilateral termination of an agency at will.
   e. Wrongful termination by either the agent or principal.
7. agency
8. fully disclosed
9. undisclosed
10. *respondeat superior*
11. authority
12. control
    intent
13. principal
    agent
14. independent contractor
15. a. The agent has express or implied authority.
    b. The agent has apparent authority.
    c. The principal ratifies the contract.

TRUE-FALSE QUESTIONS

1.	F	15.	T
2.	T	16.	T
3.	F	17.	T
4.	T	18.	F
5.	F	19.	T
6.	T	20.	F
7.	T	21.	F
8.	T	22.	F
9.	F	23.	F
10.	T	24.	T
11.	T	25.	T
12.	F	26.	F
13.	T	27.	F
14.	F	28.	T

MULTIPLE CHOICE QUESTIONS

1.	c	9.	d
2.	b	10.	a
3.	d	11.	d
4.	b	12.	c
5.	c	13.	d
6.	b	14.	b
7.	c	15.	c
8.	a	16.	a

SHORT ESSAY

Principals are liable for torts committed by their agents if the agent is a servant, not an independent contractor, and if the tort occurs within the scope of employment. This means, the agent is doing something that the agent is generally responsible for doing and the agent is doing it during normal working hours. The act must be a part of and related to the principal's business; similar to conduct that the principal has authorized the agent. Even if the agent's act is expressly forbidden by the principal, the principal will still be liable so long as the agent's conduct is of the same general nature as that authorized by or incidental to the agent's normal duties.

When agents act tortiously after they have left the principal's business, the principal is usually not liable. In cases where agents commit malicious and intentional torts, principals are liable only if the principal authorized the conduct, the agent was motivated by a desire to serve the principal, or the tortious conduct was reasonably foreseeable. Principals are also typically responsible for nonphysical harms committed by their agents, such as misrepresentation and defamation, if the agent was generally acting with authority at the time.

CASE PROBLEM

1. The partners are agents of the partnership.

2. The partners are fiduciaries of the partnership, meaning they must act with loyalty and good faith in all partnership dealings.

3. Ratou clearly violated his fiduciary duty to the partnership. He was obligated to negotiate the best price he could obtain for the partnership, he should not have taken secret profits, and he should have disclosed his conflict of interest.

CHAPTER TWENTY-EIGHT
EMPLOYMENT LAW

MATCHING EXERCISE

1. i
2. j
3. e
4. m
5. d
6. k
7. f
8. o
9. b
10. g
11. c
12. n
13. l
14. a
15. h
16. p

TRUE-FALSE QUESTIONS

1. F
2. F
3. T
4. T
5. F
6. F
7. F
8. T
9. F
10. T
11. F
12. T

MULTIPLE CHOICE QUESTIONS

1. a
2. c
3. c
4. b
5. c
6. d
7. c
8. b

SHORT ESSAY

Three federal discrimination laws and the types of employment discrimination that they generally forbid are: (a) Title VII of the Civil Rights Act of 1964 (forbids discrimination based on a person's race, religion, color, sex, or national origin); (b) the Age Discrimination in Employment Act (forbids discrimination against a person because he or she is 40 older; and (c) the Americans With Disabilities Act (forbids discrimination against a person because he or she has a disability provided the person is qualified to do the work in question either with or without reasonable accommodation.)

CASE PROBLEM

1. (a) Jasper's refusal to hire Kim because of her accent violates Title VII - it is discrimination based on her national origin.

   (b) The refusal to hire Kim because she is 50 is a clear violation of the Age Discrimination in Employment Act.

   (c) The refusal to hire Kim based on her hearing difficulty violates the Americans with Disabilities Act. Jasper has a duty to reasonably accommodate this disability.

CHAPTER TWENTY-NINE
STARTING A BUSINESS

MATCHING EXERCISE

1. g
2. b
3. e
4. h
5. d
6. k
7. f
8. n
9. a
10. j
11. m
12. I
13. l
14. c

COMPLETION EXERCISE

1. professional
2. offering circular
3. privately
4. a. general partner
   b. limited partner
5. seventy-five
6. limited liability limited partnership

TRUE-FALSE QUESTIONS

1. T
2. T
3. T
4. T
5. F
6. F
7. T
8. F
9. T
10. T
11. F
12. T
13. F
14. T
15. F
16. F
17. T
18. F
19. F
20. T
21. T
22. T
23. F
24. T
25. T

MULTIPLE CHOICE QUESTIONS

1. a
2. b
3. c
4. a
5. a
6. c
7. a
8. b

SHORT ESSAY

Close corporations are taxed like regular C corporations (unless the shareholders elect to be an S corporation), are not restricted regarding who may be shareholders, and may have more than one class of stock. Close corporations typically provide legal protections for minority shareholders, they restrict the ability of shareholders to transfer shares, and they require fewer formalities than ordinary corporations (for example, they may not need boards of directors, formal bylaws, or annual meetings).

S corporations are taxed like a partnership - profits and losses are reported directly on a shareholder's personal income tax form. S corporations may have 75 shareholders at most and there are limits on who may own the stock (nonresident aliens may not own such stock). In order to form an S corporation, shareholders must vote unanimously to adopt this corporate form.

CASE PROBLEM

1. The business relationship between Sugarland and Carlos is a franchise.

2. Sugarland is not liable to Tom because a franchisor is ordinarily is not liable for the contractual or tort liabilities of a franchisee. However, Sugarland is liable to Sue because Sugarland's own action, the manufacture of the defective candy, gives rise to product liability on the part of Sugarland.

3. Yes, a franchisee is liable for his or her contracts and torts. Therefore, Carlos is liable to Tom because Carlos was negligent.

CHAPTER THIRTY
CORPORATIONS

MATCHING EXERCISE

1. o
2. k
3. i
4. f
5. j
6. e
7. q
8. b
9. c
10. h
11. n
12. a
13. g
14. d
15. l
16. m
17. p

COMPLETION EXERCISE

1. a. It permits directors to do their job.
   b. It keeps judges out of corporate management.
   c. It encourages directors to serve.
2. personal
   business
3. merger
4. pierce the corporate veil
5. a. Managers must act without a conflict of interest;
   b. With the care of an ordinarily prudent person; and
   c. In a manner they reasonably believe to be in the best interest of the corporation.
6. Shark repellants.
7. class action
8. derivative
9. proxy
10. a. All members of the board's audit committee must be independent.
    b. A company's CEO and CFO must certify that the company's financial statements are accurate.
    c. If a company has to restate its earnings, its CEO and CFO must reimburse the company for any bonus or profits they have received from selling company stock within a year of the release of the flawed financials.
    d. A company cannot make personal loans to its directors or officers.
    e. Each company must develop a code of ethics for its senior financial officers.

TRUE-FALSE QUESTIONS

1.	T	12.	F
2.	T	13.	T
3.	T	14.	F
4.	T	15.	T
5.	F	16.	F
6.	T	17.	F
7.	T	18.	T
8.	F	19.	T
9.	T	20.	F
10.	T	21.	T
11.	F	22.	F

MULTIPLE CHOICE QUESTIONS

1.	d	8.	a
2.	b	9.	a
3.	c	10.	b
4.	d	11.	d
5.	a	12.	d
6.	a	13.	d
7.	c	14.	a

SHORT ESSAYS

1. The primary conflict between managers and stakeholders and shareholders is that managers, quite understandably, want to keep their jobs and protect their positions within the corporation. Sometimes, however, shareholders would be better off (their investment would be more valuable) if other people were managing the corporation. Managers have few incentives to give up their jobs to make shareholders happy. Managers and stakeholders may form alliances that favor the continuation of the managers - suppliers develop relationships with people, not corporations, and so they may prefer to work with one person rather than another. However, this person might not run the corporation as efficiently as someone the shareholders might prefer. Additionally, stakeholders have incentives to see a corporation stay in business (otherwise they have one fewer business with whom to trade), while it might be better for shareholders to terminate the corporation and liquidate its assets.

   The business judgment rule imposes a fiduciary responsibility on managers that helps to protect the shareholder's interests in the financial well being of the corporation. However, this rule also gives these managers some leeway in making difficult business decisions. By requiring a duty of care and a duty of loyalty from managers, the business judgment rule cuts a middle path between shareholder's interests and managers' self-interest.

2. Corporations must seek shareholder approval before they merge or consolidate with another company, sell corporate assets not in the ordinary course of business, dissolve, or amend the corporate charter, among other things.

CASE PROBLEMS

1. a. The business judgment rule determines whether directors are personally liable for losses that a corporation suffers due to their decision.

   b. Under this rule, directors are not liable for losses caused by their decision if the decision was made on an informed basis, in good faith, and in the honest belief that it was in the corporation's best interest. Also, this rule creates a presumption that directors acted in accordance with these requirements. In this case, this presumption shields the Ameri directors from liability because they acted on an informed basis and they met the other requirements of this rule.

2. a. Only Earl and Antonio are entitled to vote. In general, preferred stockholders are not entitled to vote.

   b. As a practical matter Earl can control the outcome of most, if not all, matters voted upon by the shareholders including the proposed pay raise for corporate officers. Regarding the pay raise, f or example, Earl is entitled to cast 60,000 votes, Antonio is entitled to case 40,000 votes, and Trisha has no voting rights since she is a preferred stockholder.

CHAPTER THIRTY-ONE
PROPERTY

MATCHING EXERCISE

1. g
2. d
3. l
4. j
5. e
6. h
7. m
8. b
9. i
10. a
11. f
12. n
13. c
14. q
15. k
16. p
17. o

COMPLETION EXERCISE

1. Real property
2. fixture
3. life estate
4. Eminent domain
5. Foreclosure
6. implied warranty of habitability
7. Recording
8. a. Intention to transfer ownership
   b. Delivery
   c. Acceptance by donee
9. extraordinary care
10. ordinary care
11. slight care

TRUE-FALSE QUESTIONS

1. T
2. F
3. F
4. F
5. F
6. F
7. T
8. F
9. F
10. F
11. T
12. F
13. T
14. T
15. T
16. F
17. T
18. T
19. T
20. F
21. T

MULTIPLE CHOICE QUESTIONS

1. b
2. b
3. d
4. c
5. b
6. c
7. d
8. a
9. c
10. b
11. d
12. b
13. a
14. c

SHORT ESSAY

The following kinds of tenancies are permitted under the law: a tenancy for years; a periodic tenancy; a tenancy at will; and, a tenancy at sufferance. If you rent an apartment for six months, from January to the end of June, you have a tenancy for years. If you rent an apartment for six months with an automatic renewal of the lease for another six months unless you notify the landlord you intend to move, you have a periodic tenancy. If you have an open-ended lease, for no fixed duration, which may be terminated by either party at any time, you have a tenancy at will. Finally, if your landlord wants you to get out of his or her apartment and you refuse to go, you have a tenancy at sufferance.

CASE PROBLEM

1. Lucy has entered into a bailment. In this case Lucy is the bailor - the person who delivered goods into the possession of another person, and the storage facility is the bailee. The storage company has physical control of Lucy's furniture and so has a duty of due care towards the furniture. Because both parties in this situation receive some benefit from the bailment (Lucy has her furniture stored, the storage facility receives payments from her) the storage facility owes Lucy a duty of ordinary care.

2. The issue in this case would be whether or not the storage facility met its duty. Once Lucy is able to prove that she had a bailment agreement with the storage facility, and that her furniture was harmed while at the facility, an assumption arises that the facility acted negligently. The facility will have to prove that it did use adequate care in dealing with Lucy's furniture if it wants to avoid legal liability for the harms Lucy has suffered.

CHAPTER THIRTY-TWO
CYBERLAW

MATCHING EXERCISE

1. j
2. c
3. a
4. h
5. e
6. l
7. f
8. b
9. g
10. I
11. d
12. k

TRUE-FALSE QUESTIONS

1. F
2. T
3. T
4. F
5. T
6. T
7. T
8. T
9. F
10. T
11. F
12. F

MULTIPLE CHOICE QUESTIONS

1. a
2. d
3. b
4. d
5. c
6. d

SHORT ESSAY

At present, there is little government regulation that protects the online privacy of persons using the Internet. To date, the government has relied primarily on industry self-regulation to protect the privacy of individuals using the Internet.

The industry group, Network Advertising Initiative (NAI), has established the primary industry self-regulation of online privacy. Under NAI principles, Web sites are to adhere to NAI regulations regarding notice, consent, access, security, and sensitive data regarding information collected on persons visiting their sites. The NAI also calls for an independent third party to monitor Web sites for compliances with these principles. In particular, a Web site is supposed to: (a) provide clear and conspicuous notice of its privacy policy; (b) allow consumers to choose whether or not their data will be collected; (c) provide consumers reasonable access to their own data; (d) provide reasonable security for collected data; and (e) Web sites are prohibited from using sensitive date, such as social security numbers.

While the NAI is an important beginning, it suffers from several weaknesses. First, roughly 10 percent of advertisers do not belong to NAI, Web sites that do not advertise are not subject to NAI regulations, and enforcement remains weak.

A new form of technology may help increase privacy online. The Platform for Privacy (P3P) helps Web users to choose the degree of privacy that they want when using the Internet.

CASE PROBLEM

a. Yes. Under the Electronic Communications Privacy Act of 1986 (ECPA), the intended recipient of electronic communications, which include e-mail, can disclose the content of the communication without the sender's consent.

b. Yes. Under the ECPA, Autumn's ISP can disclose the existence of the e-mail and the parties to the communication. The ISP, however, cannot disclose the e-mail's content.

c. Yes. An employer can monitor employee's e-mail that is transmitted using the employer's e-mail system.

CHAPTER THIRTY-THREE
INTELLECTUAL PROPERTY

MATCHING EXERCISE

1. h
2. d
3. f
4. a
5. b
6. c
7. e
8. g

COMPLETION EXERCISE

1. Berne Convention
2. twenty
   fourteen
3. novel
   useful
   nonobvious
4. trademark
   service mark
   certification mark
   collective mark
5. Paris Convention for the Protection of Industrial Property
6. Patent Law Treaty
7. fanciful
   arbitrary
   suggestive
   secondary meaning
   trade dress

TRUE-FALSE QUESTION

1. T
2. T
3. T
4. F
5. F
6. F
7. F
8. F
9. T
10. T
11. F

MULTIPLE CHOICE QUESTIONS

1. d
2. b
3. c
4. d
5. c
6. c
7. c
8. b

SHORT ESSAY

Federal trademark law seeks to protect the name, symbol, or other mark that serves to distinguish one company's product or service from another's. To be protectible, however, the mark must be distinguishable from other marks.

Marks must be one of the following: fanciful (a made-up word or symbol - "uyu" for the name of a brand of towel); arbitrary (a word applied to something that is unrelated ("Dog Bones" - for the name of the name of a new beer); suggestive (it is like a mind teaser - it makes you work to figure out what the product is - "Big Gulp" for the name of a drink). Also marks are protectible if they acquire a secondary meaning or if they are distinctive trade dress, i.e., the packaging or appearance of a product.

CASE PROBLEM

a. Baxco can register the mark "Xeri-fun" for its candy product. A person is entitled to register a fanciful or arbitrary mark that distinguishes a product or service from the products or services of competitors. Baxco can also register the mark "Appalachian Whiskey." One can register a geographical mark if it has acquired a secondary meaning. Baxco cannot register the mark "soft-serve ice cream" because it is merely a generic mark.

b. If a party intentionally infringes on its registered mark, Baxco can obtain an injunction to prevent the party's wrongful use of the mark, and it can also recover any wrongful profits made by the other party.